W9-BLZ-611

*Western
Resources Papers
1961*

LAND AND WATER:
Planning for
Economic Growth

Western

Resources Papers

1961

LAND AND WATER:

Planning for

Economic Growth

Edited by
Harold L. Amoss and
Roma K. McNickle

GREENWOOD PRESS, PUBLISHERS
WESTPORT, CONNECTICUT

208605

Library of Congress Cataloging in Publication Data

Western Resources Conference, 3d, Colorado State University, 1961.
    Land and water.

    Reprint of the 1962 ed. published by University of Colorado Press, Boulder, which was issued as the 1961 v. of Western resources papers.
    "Sponsored jointly by the Colorado School of Mines, Colorado State University, and the University of Colorado."
    Bibliographical footnotes.
    Includes index.
    1. Water resources development--United States--Congresses. 2. Natural resources--United States--Congresses. I. Amoss, Harold Lindsay, 1918-
II. McNickle, Roma K. III. Colorado. School of Mines, Golden. IV. Colorado. State University, Fort Collins. V. Colorado. University. VI. Title.
VII. Series: Western resources papers ; 1961.
[HD1694.A5W38 1961a]   333.7   76-44432
ISBN 0-8371-9037-1

The Colorado School of Mines, Colorado State University, and the University of Colorado sponsor an annual conference on natural resources. Selected papers of these conferences are published in the series, Western Resources Papers, of which this is the third volume.

Originally published in 1962 by University of Colorado Press, Boulder

Reprinted with the permission of Colorado Associated University Press

Reprinted from a copy in the collections of the Brooklyn Public Library

Reprinted in 1976 by Greenwood Press, Inc.

Library of Congress catalog card number 76-44432

ISBN 0-8371-9037-1

Printed in the United States of America

CONTENTS

Editors' Preface

This is the third volume to present papers of a Western Resources Conference sponsored jointly by the Colorado School of Mines, Colorado State University, and the University of Colorado. The conferences are part of an ongoing cooperative program of study and research in the conservation and development of the natural resources of western United States.

The program had its beginning in the spring of 1959, when a committee made up of social and physical scientists from the three institutions made plans for research and study which would identify the special resource problems of the West and solutions which could be developed through an interdisciplinary approach to these problems. A further objective was to contribute to the solution of such problems in any setting—regional, national, even international. One method of advancing solution was to be a series of annual conferences, rotating among the three campuses and focused upon resource areas where problems were of special urgency at the moment.

The first conference, held in the summer of 1959, was centered on five areas—water, land, recreation, minerals, energy—and the research needed for assessing and solving problems in these areas. The 1960 conference had as its theme "Water: Measuring and Meeting Future Requirements." In 1961 the conference reported in this volume focused on land and water—planning for economic growth.

It is perhaps instructive to look briefly at several things that took place between the summers of 1960 and 1961, for these events among others gave particular point to the third conference. The concept of economic growth was a central theme of the 1960 presidential campaign. In the same election, the people of California voted for a bond issue of $1.75 billion to finance the development of water supplies which would ensure continuous growth of the largest state in the contiguous West.

In the following spring the United States Supreme Court received the report of a special master appointed to investigate and recommend a decision in the suit of Arizona vs. California, regarding rights to the waters of the Colorado River. The Court's decision will have bearing not only upon the future economic growth of the litigant states but on all the other five states of the Colorado basin, and perhaps upon law and other institutional arrangements developed over the past century for the management of water.

Early in 1961 the Select Committee of the U.S. Senate on National Water Resources produced a report which showed that five regions, all of them in the West, will require full development of all available water resources by 1980 or earlier, if projected increases in population and economic activity are to be achieved. Indeed, said the report in a footnote, "It might be said that the South Pacific region [Southern California] has already run out of water. Present deficiencies are being met by importation of water from other regions and plans are being made for additional importation."

The Committee report was based on projections of data which had been revealed by the 1960 census. As these data were analyzed and released during 1960-61, they revealed that the spectacular growth of the West's population had brought increasing urbanization even to states which had always been predominantly rural. The oasis pattern of population typical in much of the West was being preserved, but the oases were enlarging to the point where some of them were about to meet if they had not done so already.

Rapid urbanization always means competition for the use of land. In the West it means also competition for water. Urbanization, mobility, leisure, and other factors have resulted in greatly increased demand for the use of land and water for recreation, which is important to the economies of all the western states.

Thus the stage in the West was well set in 1961 for a conference which would assess the importance of adequate planning for the use of land and water to ensure economic growth and orderly development. On the larger stage, American foreign aid, designed to assist the emerging nations of the world, had at several points run into institutional barriers which effectively blocked development of natural resources.

The papers in this volume reflect all of these concerns and more. Public officials charged with the management of resources repeatedly state the need for more adequate analysis not only of physical resources but of agencies and other institutional arrangements which must be developed to ensure wise use of resources. Scientists reflect upon the philosophy of resource development and the contributions which their own disciplines can make to the solution of resource problems.

Some of the most stimulating moments of the conference do not appear in this volume because it proved impossible to include the discussions which followed each session. There was, for example, after the panel on pure science and research in natural resources, some discussion of the possible effect on global wind flow (and thus on weather) of abrupt increases in solar activity. It is thus not without interest that, as this volume goes to press, there has just been orbited a solar observatory, developed by several American universities and the National Aeronautics and Space Administration, which is expected to provide spectacular advances in knowledge about solar flares and their effects. If these effects do prove to include changes in weather, man may have learned something which will help him to develop the resources he has on this planet as well as to explore outer space.

Harold L. Amoss

Roma K. McNickle

A State's Interest
in Water Research

A MESSAGE FROM STEPHEN L. R. McNICHOLS,
GOVERNOR OF COLORADO, DELIVERED BY
FELIX L. SPARKS, DIRECTOR, COLORADO
WATER CONSERVATION BOARD

Governor McNichols, who is out of the state today, has asked me to bring you his greetings and to welcome you to this conference. The fact that many of you have traveled a long distance is welcome assurance of the growing awareness of responsible people in this country that there must be increased emphasis on our national water problems.

It is highly appropriate that a conference on land and water resources should take place on this campus. Colorado State University and the University of Colorado are engaged in filling many gaps in our knowledge of water and its management. Scientists and engineers at the two institutions are carrying on basic research in hydrology, in engineering, in atmospheric sciences, and in other areas concerned with water.

The Colorado Water Conservation Board is an independent agency of the state. The board makes its own analyses of problems connected with water development in Colorado. It is dedicated to the utmost development of the state's water resources, including use for recreation and power.

In discharging these duties, the Colorado Water Conservation Board for some time past has been acutely aware of the lack of knowl-

Stephen McNichols was elected governor of Colorado in 1956, after serving six years as state senator and two years as lieutenant governor. Throughout his career in office, he has been actively interested in planning for resource development. One of his first acts as governor was to commission a series of research studies in the problems of developing the state's natural resources and organizing a state agency with responsibility to coordinate planning and administration in the resource field.

Felix L. Sparks, an attorney with long experience in the fields of water and irrigation law, was appointed attorney for the Colorado Water Conservation Board in 1957 and became director the following year.

edge on many important aspects of water-resources planning. For instance, in the development of any water-resource project we must predict streamflow conditions anticipated for a considerable period in advance.

It is simply not possible, in the light of present knowledge, to make streamflow predictions with even a remote degree of certainty. About two years ago our board turned to the University of Colorado and Colorado State University for some basic research in the field of streamflow forecasting within the Colorado River basin. The two institutions, along with the High Altitude Observatory at Boulder, are now engaged on this complex research problem under the sponsorship of the Colorado Water Conservation Board and the Upper Colorado River Commission.

Some of the work is basic research into the possible effects of sun on our weather, specifically on precipitation. Sitting on the ridgepole of the continent as we do, our state has no "upstream" except the atmosphere. So any discoveries about the fundamentals of weather will have real meaning to us.

Another part of the research is an effort to construct a synthetic hydrology for the Colorado River, to see what the possibilities are for streamflow in the years ahead. Since the Colorado River is the major source of water supplied to this state, we are leaving no stone unturned to determine availability of the waters of that river and its tributaries for use in Colorado. The Colorado River poses a particular problem to us because of interstate compact commitments. No one at this time can predict with any degree of certainty the amount of water which will be left in the river for use within our state.

Support of basic research is a new thing for the Colorado Water Conservation Board. Because research often leads to dead ends, there is always a reluctance on the part of laymen to spend money for such projects.

In fact, a few years ago we were approached with a proposition to assist in an evaluation of the hail-suppression program which is carried on annually in northeastern Colorado. Northeastern Colorado and southwestern Nebraska are chronically plagued with heavy hail damage. Our board at that time felt that weather-modification programs had no effect whatsoever upon subsequent hail fallout. As a rather amusing contrast, however, the Cattlemen's Association in northeastern Colorado felt that the hail-suppression program was depriving them of moisture on their cattle ranges.

The point I wish to emphasize is that no one can be certain as to the results of basic research. We know, however, that without question basic research is the foundation of every scientific development. Without research we progress little, if at all.

We are looking forward with great anticipation to the establishment of the National Center for Atmospheric Research near Boulder, a project of the National Science Foundation. The research that will be conducted by that institution, along with our state universities, will of course have local importance. It will also be of national and international concern.

Water-resource development almost always involves controversial issues. At the present time, there is the matter of the transmission of power to be generated at Glen Canyon Dam. Every water development project which is to be built in the future by the Bureau of Reclamation in the upper basin of the Colorado River is heavily dependent on power revenues to be generated from the main-stem projects. Our board is firmly dedicated to the proposition that power to be generated from reclamation projects should be carried to load centers over lines to be constructed by the Bureau of Reclamation. It is our belief that only in this manner can the maximum power revenues be achieved for the construction of our many participating projects.

The distribution of power by public agencies is nothing new or spectacular. By 1930, most cities in the United States had taken over the distribution of water for their citizens. An increasing number are taking over the distribution of power. This is true right here in Fort Collins, and it is true quite generally throughout the state of Colorado.

I must not go further into this controversy now, for you have many problems to discuss. It is gratifying to see the experts in the field of water-resource development who have traveled a long way to be here today. With your dedicated assistance, this country will be able to approach with more confidence one of its most difficult problems: the optimum use of water.

Some Major Problems for Research in Resource Management

MESSAGE FROM STEWART L. UDALL, SECRETARY OF THE
INTERIOR, DELIVERED BY HENRY P. CAULFIELD, JR.

It is with sincere regret that a conflict of meetings has made it impossible for me to be with you here today. During its brief history, the annual Western Resources Conference has become an enduring focal point of ideas about the management of our natural resources. Too seldom do busy administrators have the opportunity to gain perspective on consequences of actions taken and, more particularly, to gain new knowledge for future decision-making. I hope that sponsors of this conference will make available the proceedings, so that they can be widely disseminated for use by large numbers of people in the field of natural-resource management.

In reviewing your program, I am impressed by both the wide range and the depth of the subject matter included in your deliberations. Because those of us in positions of responsibility for natural-resource conservation and development are in need of new knowledge and ideas which can be brought to bear on proposed solutions for

---

Stewart L. Udall was elected to the House of Representatives from the Second Arizona District in 1954 and served in that body until he was named Secretary of the Interior by President John F. Kennedy in 1961. As a native of Arizona and a lawyer, Udall has had long acquaintance with problems of resource development, particularly in the field of water. He was a member of the House Committee on Interior and Insular Affairs, which handles reclamation matters. The department which he now heads includes several agencies with wide responsibilities for resource management, among them the bureaus of Reclamation, Mines, Fish and Wildlife, and Land Management, the Geological Survey, the National Park Service, and the Bonneville Power Administration.

Henry P. Caulfield, Jr. is assistant director of the Resources Program Staff, U. S. Department of the Interior. Caulfield delivered a major paper of the conference, to which is attached information about his activities in the field of resource management. [See page 171.]

problems facing this country today, I would like to take this opportunity to pose some of the major questions which are looming on the
horizon, and which I hope you will probe in more detail than any
of us have been able to do up to now.

For example, on the relationship between natural resources and
economic growth, we need to know a great deal more than we do
about two aspects in particular: What influence do investment expenditures in resource conservation, such as reforestation and range re-
vegetation, have on the growth rate of the economy, both in the short
run and in the long run? Put another way, what contributions will an
expanded capital-investment program in natural-resource conservation
make toward achieving an annual growth goal of 3.5 per cent or more?
How much would the resulting increases in productivity add to our
Gross National Product in the next few decades?

Many other aspects of natural-resource investment require extensive investigation. For instance, we need better techniques for
selecting resource conservation and development projects. Despite
the notable advances in this field in recent years, we need still more
aids in evaluating the competing demands on capital funds for recreation, pollution control, water development, land improvement, and
all other investment possibilities.

Close study also needs to be made of the local and regional impacts of investment programs. Resource investment is more than
a western problem. Recreation facilities, water development, forest
improvement, and many other resource programs are needed in every
region of the United States. The financing of resource developments
also has important local impacts. We know remarkably little about
the effects of our resource development and conservation program on
the various geographic areas and on different groups in our society.

I am pleased to see that you are giving hard thought to problems
of natural-resources planning. Underlying any plan must be a generally agreed upon set of goals to meet our future needs, both in material
goods and in recreational opportunities where resources are strategic.
Since planning is a process and not a discipline, I hope you will give
serious attention to the problem of relating plans to future national
requirements and how they may be translated into local and regional
action programs.

Economists' fascination with econometric model building in recent years has been both praised and criticized, but other social
scientists, particularly those concerned with the science of government, have not followed with similar attempts in the field of structural
arrangements in our political institutions. Few people feel that we

have reached the ultimate in systematic organization of our natural-resource functions in our state and federal governments. What new thinking has taken place in the years since the first Hoover Commission's proposals? I hope that your conference will stimulate renewed discussion in this long-dormant area.

These, then, are some of the major intellectual roadblocks to more effective resource management. Again, let me express my best wishes for a successful conference and my regrets that I cannot be with you.

National Sources of Economic Growth: The Qualitative Problem

CHANDLER MORSE

The topic on which I have been asked to talk is capable of broad interpretation, and I am going to interpret it broadly. It is also capable of treatment in empirical terms or in conceptual terms, and I am going to treat it conceptually.

National sources of growth, broadly conceived, are the natural resources, labor, supply of capital, stock of socio-technical knowledge, and level of productive organization available to a national economy. As these are capable of supplementation through international trade, the national sources include, in a certain sense, those of the world at large. How effectively the nations of the world can take advantage of trading opportunities, and how the realized advantages will be distributed among them, depends on economic, political, and social factors affecting international trade and investment. These factors, too, must be included among the national sources of growth.

Thus, given the possibilities of trade, "national" may not be a limiting adjective. Just as the growth of cities depends on the potentialities of the environment with which they maintain an active circulatory relation, so does the growth of nations. For many purposes, a global view is therefore more appropriate than a national.

The traditional global view is that the fixed mass of the earth sets an ultimate limit to growth possibilities and that this limit ex-

---

Chandler Morse is professor of economics at Cornell University, following a long career as economist with the Federal Reserve System and other federal agencies. He was a contributor to and co-editor of National Resources and Foreign Aid, *the "Krug Report" of 1947 which preceded the Marshall Plan. In 1959 he headed a British economic survey mission to the High Commission Territories in Africa.*

The present paper is based on part of a larger study, tentatively titled The Economics of Natural Resource Scarcity, *which Morse and H. J. Barnett are making for Resources for the Future, Inc.*

tends its shadow forward in time. This is the classical doctrine of diminishing returns, which postulates an eventual retardation of growth. But it is important to emphasize that this doctrine depends on two central notions of fixity: fixity of the natural resource base and fixity of the stock of socio-technical knowledge.

If one takes a view of the natural resource base suited to the 20th century, the classical notion of fixity appears inappropriate. Many items included in the resource inventory today were not recognized as such 200 years ago: petroleum, ferro-alloys, aluminum, nitrogen, mineral fertilizers, uranium, and many others. Items not now included in the resource stock are likely to be important in the inventories of the future: sand, rock, sea water, and captive solar energy. The natural resource spectrum, if we may call it so, undergoes continual modification.

THE CHANGING RESOURCE SPECTRUM

Under the circumstances, it is the variability of the effective resource base rather than its fixity that strikes one as important. It may be accurate to postulate that the world is a fixed mass of specific materials which receives a stable flow of solar and cosmic energy, but the economic significance of the postulate proves elusive when one tries to pin it down.

Similarly, we can no longer think in terms of an unchanging mass of knowledge, of constant socio-technical conditions. Science, which continually alters the dimensions of the resource base, also keeps changing the parameters of the social production function. The sources of growth, therefore, lie less in nature and more in ourselves than is suggested by traditional thinking on the problem. The early 19th century view of the world is too simple, its implications too categorical, for a modern analyst. A different sort of perspective is needed.

This perspective is one that rejects absolutes. Growth and depletion, to say nothing of socio-technical change, continually alter our perceptions and measurements of the resource stock. By so doing they confront us with a never-ending stream of new problems, an ever-present need for adjustment. When the problems are solved imperfectly, as they often are, unit costs increase, and we have classical diminishing returns. When they are solved well, as they are to an increasing degree in the modern world, we avert diminishing returns and often bring within our horizon new goals, once too far beyond our reach even to be imagined.

In short, *the* growth problem is one of continual accommodation, adjustment, to an ever-changing economic resource spectrum. The required adjustments are of two kinds, quantitative and qualitative. In the quantitative sphere, the physical properties of the natural resource base impose a series of initial constraints on the growth and progress of mankind, but the resource spectrum undergoes kaleidoscopic change through time. Continual enlargement of the scope of substitutionality—the result of man's ingenuity and technological wisdom—offers a multitude of opportunities for escape from nature's bonds. The fact of constraint does not disappear, however. It merely changes form. New constraints replace the old; new scarcities generate new offsets.

Quantitatively, then, resources impose a far less rigid and certain physical obstacle to a continual increase in the return to effort than economists have been wont to believe. Man's growing mastery over nature promises to free him from the inevitable prospect of diminishing returns in the quantitative, classical economic sense. At the same time, man's lack of mastery over his own affairs confronts him with an increasing prospect of diminishing returns in a qualitative sense.

Thus the measures man must take to avoid an increasing labor-capital cost of output often entail increasing social cost. Provision of low-cost energy and transport usually requires huge installations that often despoil natural beauty and sometimes pollute the atmosphere. Increased automation, so saving of labor and capital (per unit of output), tends to increase the remoteness and insignificance of the individual, to aggravate the alienation of the workman from the meaning of his work. Mass production, with its impressive economies of scale, places a premium on conformity in matters of taste and diminishes the satisfactions that derive from the achievement of a self-assured individuality. The science that has endowed man with the means to overcome the limitations of nature has thus provided instruments which, in careless hands, will undermine the quality of life. The unanswered question is whether man can develop the wit and the will to forestall this threat to his future social welfare—whether he can continue his successful battle against quantitative diminishing returns and, at the same time, avoid qualitative diminishing returns.

Who is to deal with this threat? Natural scientists and engineers can presumably be entrusted to handle the quantitative problem, but they cannot be expected to devise solutions for the qualitative problem as well. Economists and other social scientists have this responsibility. Unfortunately, the conceptual and analytical apparatus that we bring to the task is inadequate. A good part of what follows is designed to show the respects in which this is so.

WELFARE ECONOMICS AND SOCIAL WELFARE

Economists (and other social scientists as well) are but poorly prepared to contribute to a solution of the problems posed by the prospect of qualitative diminishing returns. Economists are not merely ill-prepared for thinking along these lines; they have often been schooled to deny their relevance. Traditional value theory's exclusive concern with market prices has prevented it from taking adequate account of non-economic values; its unshakable adherence to the individualistic value premise[1] has rendered it incapable of recognizing the possible existence of a social value premise. It is able to reach rigorous (and limited) conclusions concerning economic welfare only for highly restrictive conditions of parametric invariance; that is, for a given "state of the arts," given resources, given wants, given institutions, and so on.

Critics of traditional value theory, from 19th century socialists to economists like Pigou and J. M. Clark, have endeavored to loosen these bonds; but the strength of adherence to traditional value premises and the difficulty of handling parametric change in a rigorous manner have left the orthodox position represented by welfare economics more or less intact. Yet the content has progressively shrunk. The newer welfare theorists, such as Hicks, Kaldor, Scitovsky, Samuelson, and Little, have accepted the constraints of traditional theory but have pursued its logical implications to the point where it is now generally recognized that, given these constraints, the theory can provide only modest and uncertain criteria for the choice of welfare-oriented policies.[2]

Three Levels of Analysis

But economic welfare involves other dimensions than the subjective value dimension which is the concern of traditional value theory. Dr. Hla Myint has suggested that the measurement and evaluation of welfare involve three levels of analysis: the physical, the subjective, and the ethical.[3] The first focuses on changes in the physical dimensions of the goods and services (including productive services)

---

[1]E. J. Mishan formulates this premise as follows: "(a) that the individual—and no one else—is the best judge of his own welfare; (b) that the welfare of the community depends on the welfare of the individuals comprising it, and on nothing else; (c) that if at least one person is better off, no one being worse off, the community as a whole is better off." See "A Survey of Welfare Economics," *Economic Journal*, LXX (1960), 199.

[2]See I. D. M. Little, *A Critique of Welfare Economics* (2d ed., Oxford, 1958), Ch. XV; also Mishan, *op. cit.*

[3]Hla Myint, *Theories of Welfare Economics* (Harvard, 1948).

that provide the objective core of human well-being, the value dimensions being constant. The second undertakes to deal with the problem posed by simultaneous and interdependent changes in the physical and value dimensions of input and output, that is, in quantity and price, under conditions of socio-technical invariance. The third must be invoked whenever the socio-technical parameters undergo change. A physical conception of welfare, Myint argues, is implicit in classical theory; the subjective view is that of the neo-classical marginal utility school; and pleas for an ethical view, rather imperfectly developed, are found in the writings of German historical, Fabian socialist, and American institutional critics of neo-classical economics.

Myint describes classical economics as "welfare analysis at the physical level" because "it implicitly assumes that quantities of satisfaction of given wants are roughly proportional to quantities of physical products."[4]

Subjective analysis endeavors to take account of the value dimension of output. Relative prices are deemed to reflect relative degrees of utility or satisfaction, but absolute prices have no meaning. This is the basis of the familiar index-number problem. Indexes of value at constant prices eliminate the meaningless effects of absolute price change, but they freeze relative values at a base level. Thus they are, in effect, "physical" indexes which implicitly assume proportionality of welfare changes to quantity changes.

This assumption is untenable in the long run. With changes in wants, products, and methods of production, the index-number problem becomes so formidable that, strictly speaking, no provable case can be made for any purely deductive assertion about the direction of change in the quantity of value, that is, welfare. It would be quite possible for output per capita to increase steadily in real terms over a long period while welfare, by general consensus, was declining. Some people would contend that this happened during the early decades of the industrial revolution. Others would contend that it is happening today. Index numbers may serve tolerably well to show whether or not we are solving the quantitative problem of growth, but they cannot be relied on to inform us whether we are solving the qualitative problem.

The difficulty is partly attributable to the inherent ambiguity of money prices as absolute indicators of economic value. This we can do nothing about. It is also attributable to the failure of market forces to take effective account of non-economic values of all kinds and of non-private—that is, social—values. To correct this, it is necessary

---

[4]*Ibid.*, p. xxi.

to make value judgments that are based on something more than price and quantity data, and that are arrived at by procedures different from those of the market place. This approach to value, which extends beyond prices, quantities, and market processes, is what Myint means by the ethical level of analysis.

Conservationists' Position

The leaders of the first conservation movement recognized the need to make direct value judgments and to take direct action to implement them. These convictions appear in their evaluative statements about the importance of resource conservation, in their implicit and explicit criticisms of laissez-faire policies, in their own policy recommendations, and in their many expressions of doubt concerning the effectiveness of the market as a mediator of non-economic and social values. These attitudes have continued to find expression down to the present day. Ordway inveighs against the wasteful and senseless excesses of an affluent society that gluttonously eats its way through a limited resource pie; Leopold and Sears decry the disregard and destruction of the beauties of nature. The implication of both positions is that we are producing too much, rather than too little. The solution is to reduce consumption and, apparently, investment in order to "conserve" resources for future use. If the present generation cannot use resources well, it should not use them at all.

Conservationists have correctly emphasized the ethical and qualitative aspects of the resource problem. They correctly view the problem as one of maintaining (or increasing) social welfare over time, of meeting our moral obligation to future generations. What that obligation is and how it should be met are the crucial issues.

The customary approach to this issue is largely influenced by the classical doctrine of diminishing returns. If the stock of natural resources and the state of the arts are predetermined, the total amount of output that can, so to speak, be extracted from these resources is also predetermined. Different rates of growth of labor-capital and different rates of resource depletion will lead to different time shapes of output, and so will spread it over longer or shorter periods, but they will not materially affect its total.[5] Under the circumstances, it would not seem to make much ethical difference whether resources were conserved for the use of future generations or not. However, a moral case can be made for avoiding the wasteful, senseless, and destructive use

---

[5]Conceivably, a greater rate of growth of capital than of labor or a slower rate of depletion might raise total extractable output, but the possibilities are limited in the absence of socio-technical change.

of such resources, because it deprives future generations without conferring defensible benefits upon the present generation. If some resources are renewable, conservationists presume that the allocation of labor and capital to maintaining them will increase the stock of effectively permanent resources and therefore raise the level of permanently sustainable output. On this presumption a moral case can also be made for full maintenance of renewable resources in the interest of future generations.

Conservation Economics Approach

There is a "physical bias" in these views, reflecting that of classical economics. Modern economists, by contrast, have attempted, implicitly or explicitly, to apply the *subjective* criteria of welfare economics to the resource problem. They view the problem mainly or wholly as a matter of arriving at a correct estimate of the economic value of resource use at different points in time, resolvable by the rational and accurate application of economizing principles. There is a further tendency to suggest that these principles can and will be applied by the market, provided only that certain (relatively minor) inadequacies in the valuation procedures or behavior patterns of the market are rectified by governmental interventions. In this they betray an "economic" bias.

Ciriacy-Wantrup epitomizes the problem thus: "Apparently there is a most economical way of accomplishing conservation and an economic limit in conservation. Somewhere, in conservation, an economically optimum distribution of rates of use over time is reached. This distribution we call the optimum state of conservation."[6]

The major problem, according to this subjective approach, is to achieve an optimal distribution of resource use over time, but this conceptualization of the problem also derives from the classical doctrine of (quantitative) diminishing returns and, like it, depends on assumption of unchanging socio-technical parameters and fixity of the natural resource base. All the grounds for doubting the relevance of the classical hypothesis of diminishing returns are grounds also for rejecting the corresponding doctrine that resources must be *quantitatively* conserved. What we need instead is a *qualitative* approach to conservation. The physical and subjective levels of analysis need to be supplemented by thorough and systematic analysis at the ethical level.

The problem is to translate this general principle into a more explicit guide to policy. To this end, we shall first present more specific

---

[6]S. V. Ciriacy-Wantrup, *Resource Conservation* (California, 1952), p. 58.

reasons for rejecting the notion that physical resources must necessarily be conserved in the sense of postponing their use.

SOCIAL WELFARE OVER TIME:
THE CASE AGAINST QUANTITATIVE CONSERVATION

The economic rate of natural resource utilization in a market economy is that rate at which the present value of the stream of net income over the life of the resource, when discounted at the effective (opportunity) rate of interest, is equal to the cost of the initial investment. In most analyses, the production function and state of the market are assumed given, and attention is focused on two determinants of the economic rate of use: the expected future price of the resource and the rate of interest.

Conservation economists, reasoning from the doctrine of quantitative diminishing returns, argue that resources actually do tend to be conserved in something approximating the optimal economic degree. In a world of increasing resource scarcity, the prices of resources can be expected to increase and thus to bring about the very increase in conservation that, on ethical grounds, has been held desirable.[7] Similarly, as the growth of income and the levels of saving and capital accumulation tend toward zero in a static economic world, the rate of interest steadily falls. Again, ethical presuppositions are supported by the operation of market forces in response to presumed empirical changes.

Increasing Conservation Unlikely

The empirical grounds for expecting an increasing degree of conservation in the modern world are exceedingly dubious. Growth, depletion, and qualitative change in the resource base have helped to stimulate the socio-technical innovations that have forestalled any increase in the trend of cost of extractive output in the United States over the past hundred years. Productivity of labor and capital has increased steadily. If these conditions continue, and it is exceedingly difficult to hypothesize the contrary, there will be little reason to ex-

---

[7]A subconscious blending of ethical and economic reasoning is not uncommon, as the following passage illustrates. "Every advance of the price that is paid for the ore at the place of consumption thus makes it possible to meet the demand better. However, the question how rapidly we *ought* to exploit the treasures of nature has another side. *We must keep an eye to the wants of the future* in regulating our present consumption." Gustav Cassel, *The Theory of Social Economy* (Harcourt Brace, 1924), p. 282, italics added. Cassel's exposition of the principles of conservation economics and of the role of price expectations and the interest rate in determining the rate of utilization of resources, is exceptionally clear and non-technical. (See pp. 279-87.)

pect either rising resource prices or falling interest rates. Thus the empirical changes ordinarily postulated as directing the utilization of resources are not likely to be those that foster physical conservation. On the contrary, it seems likely that various developments will bring about a reduced degree of conservation in the purely physical sense.

For reasons hinted in the following passage from Scott,[8] this state of affairs is socially desirable rather than otherwise. "The exploitation of resources is not necessarily destructive. It is the first step in a constructive process which produces goods and services for consumption and maintains the national capital in new and more efficient forms. Hence the exploitation of natural resources need not imply the impoverishment of posterity." And he stresses the corollary view that there is no essential difference between stock (or exhaustible) and flow (or renewable) resources. "The refutation of the importance of this distinction," he says, "is crucial," although Ciriacy-Wantrup and others make it central to their discussions.

A forest is the prime example of a resource that can be handled either as a stock or as a flow. Consider a forest that is being handled on a continuous-flow (sustained-yield) basis. In this case, part of the gross annual value of the forest's output is plowed back through re-planting, cultivating, fertilizing, spraying, pruning, so as to maintain a constant annual physical output of lumber. This constant *physical* product, of course, is consistent with a constant, increasing, or decreasing net *value* product, depending on the direction and extent of cost and price changes. Moreover, the direction and magnitude of net value change are not necessarily an index of welfare change. Prices and costs are not always good indicators of economic welfare, to say nothing of non-economic welfare.

Sustained Physical Yield and the Public Interest

Yet it is frequently assumed that it is in the public interest to manage forest preserves on a sustained-physical-yield basis. There are circumstances under which this assumption would be correct, but they are less common than might be supposed.

Consider the case in which constant physical product *is* associated with constant price and constant unit cost. This means that the net value of forest output and the stock of wealth represented by the forest are being maintained constant, and that this is achieved by investing a part of the output in creation of new trees. The forest represents a wasting asset which is being maintained by transforming

---

[8]Anthony Scott, *Natural Resources: The Economics of Conservation* (Toronto, 1955), p. 13 ff.

it into another asset of an identical kind. But this is justified only if (1) there is no other investment that would yield a higher return than forests, and (2) the yield is at least equal to the effective interest rate. According to these criteria, the clearing of forests to create agricultural land and the ruthless cutting of timber in the United States in the 19th century were not necessarily mistakes. Similarly, sustained yield is not necessarily the correct policy now. A society that wants to maintain its social wealth intact, or to increase it, is not required to replace each asset with one of the identical kind and market value.

Now consider a mine. It is not possible, literally, to operate a mine on a sustained-yield basis. As an asset it can only be used by being used up. Yet, this in a way is a misnomer. Any part of the product stream that results from depletion of this resource can, as in the case of forests, be transformed into another productive asset. Aggregate productive wealth need not be destroyed but can remain constant or be increased.

It may be objected that the difference between this case and the preceding is that the forest is an asset that can be transformed into itself, whereas the mine cannot. Yet this is only partially true. If that part of the product of the mine which is invested takes the form of research and capital formation that permit the same extractive product to be obtained at the same unit cost from mineral deposits of lower grade, no qualitative change of any kind is forced upon society, and no quantitative change either. Society has, in this case, operated as effectively on a sustained-physical-yield basis as in the forest example. And the justification for doing so or not doing so must be the same. Even if it is not possible to continue to produce the same extractive product at constant or lower cost from lower-grade resources, it may be possible to produce a close substitute. Little if any loss of value or welfare was entailed by the substitution of aluminum conductor for copper in high-tension lines. Nor does it seem likely that loss of welfare has been the consequence of substituting margarine for butter, synthetic for natural fibres, plastics for metals, and so on. On the contrary, the lower costs that have made these substitutes so popular suggest a gain of welfare.

Consequently, the sustained-yield principle is capable of indefinite extension, provided we take a wide enough view. Indeed, there is neither need nor justification for expecting each particular type of asset to be self-maintaining. Those that can be should perhaps not be; and those that cannot be maintained identically often can and should be transformed into other productive forms of wealth, so that no loss of welfare results. When Ciriacy-Wantrup says that sustained yield is "meaningless for stock resources,"[9] he is clearly referring to the impossibility of maintaining a flow of output from particular mineral deposits and has not considered the possibility of maintaining an equally valuable flow of substitute extractive or final products.

Thus there is little to be said in favor of quantitative conservation, of simply postponing use, as a general criterion of resource management. It is less important to achieve an optimal *distribution* of resource use over time than to achieve an optimal *kind* of resource use today. The latter, indeed, subsumes the former, as I now attempt to show.

SOCIAL WELFARE OVER TIME: THE CASE FOR SUSTAINED WELFARE YIELD

To reject the principle of quantitative conservation as a suitable basis for determining social policy toward natural resources is not to deny the existence of a moral obligation to future generations. It is only to maintain that the obligation must be framed and discharged in the most sensible manner available to us. Having rejected the view that our obligation to future generations requires us to conserve natural resources for later use, I propose the following alternative.

The initial premise is a fundamental value judgment: it is the moral obligation of each generation to maintain per capita productivity in terms of social welfare—that is, to maintain *social welfare output per capita*. Since wealth is the capitalized value of a stream of income, we may also speak of this as an obligation to maintain the per capita value of social wealth.

"Social welfare output" means the gross output of society valued in non-economic as well as economic terms, full provision being made for the replacement of wasting assets, for research to assure an adequate continuing flow of socio-technical innovations, for maintaining the qualitative dimensions of the consumption mix, for avoiding deterioration in the esthetic qualities of the natural and man-made environment, and for avoiding deterioration in the conditions of human work. The excess of the gross social welfare output over these provisions is available for increasing social wealth (including the stock of knowledge) or for improving current standards of consumption, work, and leisure. This might be called the *net* social welfare product, or the disposable welfare surplus.

Whether any part of the surplus should be used to increase the stock of social wealth depends on the relative strength of the current generation's desires for present and for future income. To attempt to

---

[9] *Op. cit.*, p. 49.

look further ahead than this in a rapidly changing world and to anticipate cultural variations in the wants of future generations, is in no sense possible.

On the other hand, it seems reasonable to assume that any steps taken by the present generation to remove its own grounds for dissatisfaction will be more likely to benefit (and be approved by) future generations than the contrary. Thus, we may and should act on the assumption that future generations will welcome—or at least will have no legitimate cause to complain if they receive—an unimpaired per capita stock of social wealth. No generation can anticipate in detail the conditions to be faced by future generations, or how they will think best to deal with them. But every generation is able, on the basis of accumulated human experience, to arrive at a judgment concerning what sorts of conditions and consequences are good or bad for the human animal and human society. To the extent that each generation interprets past experience intelligently and puts the lessons learned to work to the best of its ability, no more is required. That which is good for mankind has great "stability in the large" despite great "variability in the small," and we have as much of a moral obligation to assure the stability as we have to cater to the variability. We may note in passing that the per capita specification makes population one of the elements in the moral obligation.

THE OPTIMAL RATE OF RESOURCE UTILIZATION

The proposition that per capita social wealth should be maintained necessarily relates to the aggregate of social wealth and asserts nothing whatsoever about conserving particular assets. But as some assets are used up and others take their place, there is a problem of maintaining the qualities of the final product mix unimpaired in social-welfare terms.

We may call this the problem of variability of the resource base. As the result of growth, depletion, and technological progress, the qualitative dimensions of the resource base undergo change. The changes in the qualities of the resource input to the extractive sector may, but also they may not, change the character of the final product mix. And if this changes it may, but it may not, materially reduce social welfare. Regardless of what happens along the way, the aim must be to avoid a final loss of social welfare.

It may be thought that this is too ambitious an objective. Eventually, surely, the depletion of resources of particular kinds, the destruction or degradation of the beauties of nature as metropolis sprawls across the land, the exhaustion of space in which to manoeuvre, will make it impossible to maintain the qualitative dimensions of the final product stream unchanged. Synthetic fibres are one thing; a protein diet of algae is something else again. Smog and fallout are high prices to pay for high productivity. Skyscrapers are poor substitutes for green fields. Sooner or later, it seems, the variability of the resource base will force diminishing qualitative returns upon us. We cannot blithely assume the contrary.

This may be right. But if it is, what does it signify? Does it mean that we should "conserve" resources today so as to postpone (though not, by hypothesis, to avoid) qualitative diminishing returns? Does it mean that our obligation to future generations is to preserve man's natural heritage intact in physical terms?

The answers to these questions cannot be given in a categorical affirmative. To do so would imply that "conservation," in the sense of postponing physical use, is the appropriate policy. The situation is too complex to admit of so simple a solution. Criteria are needed for optimal resource use, not for non-use.

The special problem posed by variability of the resource base is that continual change in the qualitative dimensions of the resource input to the social production function imposes a necessity—indeed, a moral obligation—to work out effective, productivity-sustaining adaptations. Let us consider the following possibilities.

1. Society is able to work out socio-technical innovations and maintain a rate of investment that make it possible to produce a social output with the same qualitative dimensions as before (or an acceptable set of substitute qualitative characteristics) but only at higher average real cost—that is, higher labor-capital cost. This would not meet the postulated moral obligation.
2. Society is able to work out a set of innovations and maintain a rate of investment that make it possible to produce a social output with inferior qualitative dimensions at constant (or decreasing) real cost. This too would fail to meet the postulated obligation.
3. Rates of innovation and investment are maintained that make it possible to maintain (or improve) the qualitative dimensions of social output and to produce it at constant (or decreasing) real cost. This would meet the obligation.

The first of the above possibilities is essentially the classical case of quantitative diminishing returns (physical level of analysis). The second corresponds to the situation with which the world is now or soon will be faced. According to the traditional (subjective) level of welfare analysis, price-quantity adjustments in a free market situation will "optimize" welfare, and the only measures required are those needed to encourage and permit the free play of market forces.

The contention here is that there is a different "social welfare optimum" for each conceivable set of socio-technical conditions. The problem is to choose, from among these many conceivable sets, one that will at least maintain social welfare, that will, in other words, satisfy the third of the above conditions. Any of the many possible rates of resource utilization that is consistent with, or helps to further, achievement of this goal, is an *optimum rate of resource utilization.*

Policy should be framed in the positive terms of optimal resource use, not in the negative terms of optimal conservation. Optimal use requires that current output and resource use be at least high enough to provide the research and the gross investment needed to achieve a sustained welfare yield and that they be of the right kinds.

REQUIREMENTS OF SOCIAL POLICY

What has just been said implies that the main task confronting modern man is to achieve and maintain a sufficient flow of investment and socio-technical innovations to maintain per capita welfare in the face of rapid changes in the effective natural resource spectrum. This flow of investment and innovations, and therefore the tasks of social policy, fall into three categories, corresponding to the three dimensions of welfare analysis: the physical, the subjective, and the ethical. The physical problem is to devote enough natural resources, capital formation, and effort to assure avoidance of *quantitative* diminishing returns. The subjective problem is to provide sufficient flexibility of market structure to permit individuals to maximize welfare by attaining "chosen positions"[10] freely, subject only to the requirement that social benefits and costs be taken into account. The ethical problem is to devise procedures that will permit evaluation of the quality of life and provision of incentives designed to assure, if possible, the avoidance of *qualitative* diminishing returns.

Solution of Physico-Technical Problems

The first concern of social policy must be to make sure that the physical problems of resource use are adequately solved, that quantitative diminishing returns are avoided. For this purpose we need to solve the physical problems of production sufficiently well to make sure that real output per unit of real cost will show a constant or increasing trend through time. The aim must be to maintain the real price and income elasticities of supply of extractive products when these are favorable, to increase them when they are not. To do this it will be necessary to assure that a sufficient amount of research and investment

---

[10]See Little, *op. cit.,* p. 37 and ch. III.

is allocated *in time* to: (a) developing low-cost methods of obtaining output from resources of increasingly lower grade; (b) developing low-cost substitutes for materials for which (a) does not yield a technically promising approach; (c) assuring a continuing supply of energy at low cost and in convenient forms; (d) maintaining low-cost systems of transport; (e) adapting products and methods of production in the non-extractive sector to the unavoidable changes in the qualitative dimensions of extractive input to that sector.

Optimum resource utilization is thus a problem in the allocation over time of research and investment, not of natural resources per se. *Less* conservation of resources may be required for optimum resource utilization, not more, because *more* research, investment, and output are required. A policy of physical conservation designed to save British forests from the destructive activities of the charcoal makers and the shipbuilders would probably have delayed the industrial revolution. On the other hand, if a qualitatively crucial resource should be in danger of exhaustion before alternative low-cost methods of extraction or substitution could be developed, some measure of physical conservation might be desirable as a means of buying time.

Economic Efficiency and Economic Welfare

Solution of the physico-technical problems posed by resource variability is only one of the ends to be achieved by social policy. For, no matter how efficient society may become in a technological sense, it must also achieve a high degree of economic efficiency if anything like optimum economic welfare is to be attained. An increase of real output per unit of real cost presumably represents a physical gain but whether it also represents a subjective gain depends on the effectiveness of market procedures (either free or planned) in solving the economic problem, in permitting individuals (in whatever economic capacity) to attain their chosen positions or a close approximation thereto. The effectiveness of market structures and of all the vast interrelated activities of government is affected by changes in the conditions of production, and must, if their effectiveness is to be maintained or improved, be modified accordingly. This defines another sphere for social policy.

There is no need to discuss here the imperfections of markets and the policies suitable for their rectification. This is the familiar stuff of micro-economic theory and of a great number of quantitative, historical, and institutional studies of production and distribution. Market imperfections as they relate to resources specifically have been well analyzed by Scott.[11]

---

[11]*Loc cit.*

It is important to stress, however, that free market procedures operate only as mediators of economic values; that is, of values that are or can be brought into relation with the measuring rod of money. Non-economic values are not effectively represented, or may even be represented perversely. Moreover, free market procedures operate within a framework of tastes that has been determined largely by past history but which undergoes change as a result, mainly, of the operations of the market, including the operations of producers who wish tastes to change in a particular way. The resulting direction or rate of change may not be one that is consistent with the policy criteria we have laid down.

The fact that a market system tends to generate changes in socio-technical parameters, to modify its own conditions of operation, does not demonstrate that high efficiency of the allocative mechanism will produce a stream of socio-technical innovations which will provide escape from both quantitative and qualitative diminishing returns. Indeed, a market may function better as an "economizing" mechanism if its structure does not tend to induce socio-technical innovations. It is generally recognized, for example, that producers under perfect competition are less likely to introduce new products and production methods than oligopolists (unless assisted, as in agriculture).

If we are prepared either to forgo making judgments concerning the social-welfare value of market-generated decisions to invest and innovate, or to adopt the uninquisitive postulate that such decisions always promote the social welfare, the question of subjecting them to independent evaluation does not arise. If we are not prepared to take either of these steps, there is need to look beyond the "automatic" processes by which changes in socio-technical conditions are brought about, and to attempt to guide them aright if they seem to be leading us in the wrong direction.

The question at issue is one of social valuation, meaning valuation of what is good for mankind in general as opposed to what is good for each individual in particular. It calls for a social, as opposed to a personal, frame of reference. This brings us to the ethical or, as we prefer to call it, the social dimension of resource policy.

SOCIAL VALUE AND THE TREND OF SOCIAL WELFARE

Any action that may or will change the socio-technical boundary conditions of the production and allocation process involves a question of social value. These are the conditions that govern the functioning of society, and society alone must be the final arbiter of the value of change or non-change. It must devise procedures for granting or withholding approval of individual efforts to modify or retain the status quo, for rewarding valued changes and for penalizing disvalued changes. An improvement or deterioration of productivity, a modification of the structure of wants (or an effort to effect such modification, as through advertising), a change in the rules of the game defining access to productive resources, to income or to final products—any of these, by altering what is possible or permissible for an individual to accomplish, may augment or diminish the opportunities to violate the conditions for survival of a given quality of life, and so may call for a social value judgment, a policy decision.

In sum, one may accept the desirability of maximizing the scope for individual choice (itself a value judgment) while maintaining that a series of social value judgments is necessary to define the limits of choice in accordance with the criterion of what helps to maintain society as a cooperative enterprise, and recognizing as a corollary of this proposition the implicit involvement of social value questions whenever there is the possibility of change in the conditions that define what can or cannot be done.

Let us now return to the thesis that it is a moral obligation of each generation to maintain the social value productivity of the stock of social wealth it inherited from the past. To anticipate the future in detail is, of course, impossible, but it is not impossible to postulate that man's biological, psychical, and social characteristics have considerable stability in the large, however great may be their variability in the small. Whatever maintains or extends provision for a health-maintaining quantity and a pleasing quality of food, clothing, and shelter; for healthy and enjoyable working conditions; for a work and play environment in which order, beauty, and calm predominate over disarray, ugliness, and noise; for a suitable amount of leisure; for increase of knowledge and opportunity to learn, can hardly be said to reflect a set of ephemeral or inconsequential values. Capital formation and innovations that promote or are consistent with these (and perhaps other) values are certainly to be favored over those that produce contrary results. And if conflicts arise, as for example when maintenance of a low-cost energy supply threatens destruction of natural beauty or pollution of living space, it must be a matter of high priority to devise alternative technical solutions that resolve the conflict.

The conflict between quantitative solutions and qualitative acceptability is likely to become more, rather than less, serious as time goes on. The avoidance of quantitative diminishing returns often requires the adoption of measures with negative welfare implications, raising those questions of ethics and esthetics, of waste, ecological damage, and wise use, of population control, and the welfare of future generations, which exercised the members of the first conservation movement and have remained a central concern of many observers ever since. Conversely, by taking thought for the infinitely various value dimensions of life, man can (as he often has done) increase welfare without necessarily taking an increased bite from the physical resource base. Many, though of course not all, of the improvements in diet, health, clothing, housing, entertainment, and education are of this sort, and serve to explain why the real value of the social product has increased so much faster than its resource content, over the past century at least. In the process of learning how to avoid the negative welfare effects of his devices for circumventing physical constraints, man can and hopefully will learn how to extract greater welfare from a given quantity of resources. Thus the avoidance of quantitative diminishing returns may, but need not, imply qualitative diminishing returns. The question is whether it will.

THESIS REVIEWED

Modern science has probably brought it within man's grasp to maintain a high and perhaps increasing level of real output per capita. But even if this objective should be attained, the quality of life could nonetheless deteriorate. Only by taking more thought for the qualitative implications of (a) changes in the effective natural resource spectrum and (b) measures for escaping the constraints imposed by the natural environment, is there a reasonable prospect of avoiding an eventual constriction of social welfare.

This view of the relation of natural resources to economic growth requires revision of certain accepted habits of thought. Conservation doctrine suffers from a physical bias and conservation economics from a subjective bias. The latter, indeed, is welfare economics with a special twist and, like it, fails to take adequate account of socio-technical change or to provide useful policy guidance for a world in which such change is rapidly becoming the major determinant of social welfare. More particularly, market valuation procedures are unsuited to choosing among alternative possibilities of socio-technical change, and market-generated innovations are not necessarily best or even acceptable from a social point of view.

In short, the individualistic value premise of traditional economic theory is irrelevant when the decisions to be made affect the parameters of the social production process, thus determining the framework within which individual choices must be made. To reach decisions of this kind we need special standards of social value and special evaluation procedures, analogous to but different from those of the market place. The calculation of social benefits and costs is a step in this direction but, as J. M. Clark observed many years ago,[12] this is really only an effort to extend the scope of the individualistic value premise. A social value premise is needed. Moreover, there is a static bias in the concept of social benefits and costs. It was purely static in Pigou's original formulation and has only become pragmatically dynamic in application.

What is needed is a theoretically dynamic concept of social gains and losses, and one that does not require, as does the benefit-cost concept, that we affix a dollar sign to every index magnitude. There is need, in short, to develop an *ethical* system of analysis of social welfare that is as rigorous, complete, and solid as the classical and neo-classical systems of physical and subjective analysis. It is not a question of displacing the older methods of evaluation but of supplementing them. Otherwise our efforts to avoid qualitative diminishing returns will be wholly pragmatic and largely random, lacking a sure sense of objective and discrimination.

Looking at all this with a somewhat parochial eye, it seems to me that this nation's ability to grow in the purely quantitative sense has been and presumably will remain impressive enough. On the other hand, its ability to invent and introduce the social innovations that will be needed to avoid qualitative diminishing returns is a scarce resource, perhaps its scarcest at present.

The need is to give a greater and more rational emphasis than we now do to the qualitative aspects of resource use and, more broadly, to those of human activity in general. This is a matter of evolving evaluation procedures that will permit social values to be taken into account at least as rationally and effectively as the procedures of the market (whether planned or unplanned) take account of economic values. This conception is much closer to what the members of the first conservation movement thought conservation was about than it is to "conservation economics." But the problems to be met are more international, less purely national, than the early conservationists conceived them to be.

---

[12]*Preface to Social Economics* (Farrar and Rinehart, 1936), p. 49. Quoted in Myint, *op. cit.*

The Role of Public and Private Agencies in Planning the Use of Water Resources

VINCENT A. OSTROM

In considering the role of public and private agencies in planning the use of water resources, I shall first explore the types of "goods" in the water economy in terms of their amenability to provision by private or public agencies. The consumptive uses of water supply are considered to be most amenable to private provision, while the non-consumptive uses appear to require public provision. The second section of the paper will consider the types of organization that have been associated with consumptive uses and land-related development of water resources, as contrasted to the patterns of organization for in-the-channel management of water resources. The final section will explore some aspects of the problem of organization in relation to planning for comprehensive multi-purpose development of water resources.

TYPES OF GOODS IN THE WATER ECONOMY

Water is the source of a complex multiplicity of "goods" which have value to human beings. Water is essential to the continuity of life itself, for all living organisms require a regular supply of water for survival, growth, and development. In addition to supplying water to meet the consumptive requirement of living organisms, flowing water may also be used to provide a major source of power. The same water course may provide a habitat for valuable supplies of fish and

Vincent A. Ostrom is associate professor of political science at the University of California, Los Angeles. His acquaintance with planning for water development is the result of extensive research and of experience as member of, or consultant to, public water agencies and research groups. The present paper is based on research supported by the California Water Industry Study under a grant from Resources for the Future, Inc., and by the Water Resources Center of the University of California. This support is gratefully acknowledged.

wildlife and a place for human recreation. It may be used to transport a variety of goods and commodities. A stream may also be used to dilute and purify waste products, or it may be used for washing or processing purposes or as a cooling agent in industrial production. Finally, since water may wreak injury and havoc upon human endeavors, to control or prevent floods becomes a positive good.

The bundle of goods which can be derived from a water course includes both the uses of water as water and the uses that can be made of the flow of a stream. The various uses of water are highly interrelated. One pattern of use frequently precludes some other possibility of development. As demands for water increase, competition and conflict among the various users of a stream are apt to become accentuated. The wastes of an industrial civilization, for example, place an increasing load upon waterways at the same time that new opportunities for leisure reflect a bounding demand for water sports. When demands exceed certain minimal levels, the use of a stream for sewerage is not easily reconciled with its use for recreational purposes. The maintenance of an anadromous fishery may pose a substantial conflict for large-scale water storage facilities essential to flood control and the production of hydroelectric power.

Theoretically, the competition for the different "goods" to be derived from the uses of a water-resource system might be resolved by economic allocation in the market. Under market conditions, priorities would be determined by the preferences of users spending their earnings upon one or another water-resource product. However, market mechanisms are only partially available in allocating water-resource products or uses because a number of the goods derived from a water-resource system do not meet the criteria for allocation in the market economy.

A private good must be "packageable" in the sense that it can be differentiated as a commodity or service before it can readily be purchased or sold in the market economy. It must also be appropriable in the sense that the commodity or service is subject to the legal claim of a property right which vests control in the owner as against other possible claimants and users. A loaf of bread, for example, is both packageable and appropriable. Those who are not willing to pay for the loaf of bread can be excluded from enjoying its benefits. These are the conditions for meeting the exclusion principle, the criterion which must be met as a necessary condition for the operation of a market economy.

In considering the economic character of the different uses of water, a rather basic distinction can be made between consumptive and non-consumptive uses. A consumptive use implies that water is taken from its natural course and is used upon the land. Irrigation, domestic consumption, municipal and industrial uses are among the consumptive or "on-the-land" uses of water supply. Non-consumptive uses on the other hand are "in-the-channel" uses. These include navigation, dissipation of wastes, recreation, propagation of fish and wildlife, and flood control.

Consumptive Uses as Goods

The consumptive or on-the-land uses are generally appropriative uses, since they involve a taking of the water and placing it under control in an out-of-the-channel storage and distribution system. Both water used for consumptive purposes and electricity can be metered and sold in measurable units, such as gallons, cubic feet, or kilowatt hours. The conditions of the exclusion principle can be satisfied. Water can be sold as a commodity in relation to the demands of the various users who are willing to pay the market price to meet their various consumptive demands. As a result, the water supplies and water products which can be appropriated for on-the-land uses are generally more amenable to private organization and distribution in a market-type economy than are the non-consumptive or in-the-channel uses.

The competitive dynamics of the water economy, however, is seriously constrained by the relatively large proportion of investments required in fixed distribution facilities. These relatively large capital costs lead to two separate consequences. One is a tendency to require organizations of a larger scale than that of the individual proprietor. The other is that each water supply system tends to function as a natural monopoly in its service area. Both of these factors limit the operation of market forces in the water economy.

In the early days of the arid West, the individual proprietor could thrive only on land in close proximity to a stream or where there was an abundant ground-water supply. Beyond the limit of these opportunities, the provision of consumptive water supplies generally had to be organized through non-profit cooperatives or mutual water companies, limited-profit public utility companies, municipal utility systems, or public distribution systems created by a variety of special public districts or quasi-municipal corporations established to provide special water supplies for various groups and communities of people. Today the special public water districts, which have evolved from the irrigation districts, and the municipal water systems are the organizations which assume the dominant role in the distribution of water supplies for consumptive use.

None of these agencies operate in conformity with the rule for maximization of profits. Even the privately owned water company organized for profit is considered to be a public utility whose service arrangements and rate structure are subject to detailed control by state public utility commissions. Water is generally so priced that it functions as an intermediate product in the economy. The payoff is derived not by the water producer but by those who make use of water in the land-related economy. Hence, water simply becomes one of the factors contributing to the land promoter's development scheme in which he derives his return from land values. Or, in the case of a local community, water may be used as an instrument for controlling patterns of economic and political development. The history of the growth and development of Los Angeles, for example, reveals the conscious use of water as a tool to build the "great metropolis of the Pacific."

Non-Consumptive Uses as Goods

Most in-the-channel or non-consumptive uses do not meet the criterion of the exclusion principle. The benefits of flood control, for example, cannot be distributed solely to those individuals who are willing to pay for the benefits. When flood-control programs are undertaken, all individuals in comparable situations on the flood plain are benefited alike. If the flood-control measure is a local levee or dike, the group benefited may be relatively small and the enterprise might be organized as a public diking or flood-control district. Where the flood-control program involves the general regulation and control of a whole river system through large storage reservoirs, it becomes much more difficult to allocate flood-control benefits among the various beneficiaries even if they could be encompassed within a common political jurisdiction.

The fish resources of a river system pose a somewhat ambiguous problem for economic organization. The fish which are taken from a stream are as readily subject to the market allocation as are loaves of bread. The taking, processing, and distribution of fish *products* are thus largely conducted in the private sector of the economy. However, the operation of a *fishery* is not subject to the same type of organization and control. An entrepreneur who decided to "farm" salmon, for example, would not be in a position to assure the exclusion of others from the benefits of his crop. Hence the management of fish resources has generally been conducted as a public function.

The use of streams for the dilution and discharge of waste deals with a negative good or by-product which communities, firms, and households attempt to dispose of at minimal costs to themselves. Unregulated use of a stream for pollution abatement is apt to poison the stream and destroy its usefulness for many other purposes. As a result the use of a stream for pollution abatement has never been recognized as a "good" for which a private property right vests. Rather it has been the subject of extensive regulation by state governments under their police powers, which emphasizes the public character of the use of streams for pollution abatement.

The use of water in a water course for recreation poses another ambiguous problem for economic organization. Where access can be controlled, the conditions for the operation of the exclusion principle can be met and recreational uses can be organized by private enterprises. In this case, control of the land may afford control over the use of the adjoining stream. However, the use of the water course *per se* for recreational purposes is usually open to anyone who can gain access.

The same principle applies to the use of a stream for navigation. All who can gain access to the stream are generally free to use it as a public highway, subject to public regulation and control. However, particular works that may be constructed to circumvent natural obstructions to navigation could be amenable to private organization and use through the charge of a toll.

Other types of in-the-channel uses of a stream are usually intermediate aspects of transactions that are more clearly directed to the use of the water product for some on-the-land function. Hydroelectric power production, for example, requires the regulation of the flow of the stream, but the product is controlled and marketed on the land. Private development of hydroelectric power thus is usually associated with rather detailed public regulations which take cognizance of the public interest in the control of river flow.

Thus none of the various in-the-channel uses of a stream is easily packageable or appropriable. They are not generally amenable to control by an individual proprietor who may want to produce the good or service for sale in the market economy. As a result, we must generally turn to public agencies to take appropriate courses of action in assuring adequate provision of in-the-channel uses of water resources.

The problem is further complicated by the high degree of interdependency among the various in-the-channel uses. This interdependency requires those who plan any in-the-channel development to take account of the effect each use will have on the other possible uses. The requirement of multi-purpose planning for interdependent uses poses one of the fundamental problems in the organization for the planning and administration of water-resource programs.

Any effort to optimize output of in-the-channel uses of a river system depends upon the general regulation and control of flow characteristics. Reducing flood flows increases the benefits to be derived from flood control. Increasing minimum flows increases the benefits that can be derived from most of the in-the-channel uses as well as increasing the supply for on-the-land consumptive uses. Under these circumstances any waterworks project which modifies the flow of a stream must be evaluated in relation to the consequences which it produces. Since each project which affects the flow pattern has consequences for each other project, it becomes necessary to take account of each as it affects the total pattern of development in a river system. This condition imposes another basic requirement: that a water-resource management system be organized so as to account for water production in a river system as a whole.

The types of organization associated with the uses of water in the political economy have derived from different vantage points in the American political system and in response to different patterns of demands at different points in time. These organizations constitute quite different commitments to the relative importance of different patterns of water-resource development in relation to many different communities of interest. Since the form of organization tends to determine the capabilities for undertaking programs of water-resource development and, at the same time, to articulate demands in relation to planning for those interests, this analysis of the role of public and private agencies in planning the use of water resources will turn to a review of the different types of agencies and their function in water-resource development.

ORGANIZATIONS FOR DEVELOPING LAND-RELATED USES OF WATER

The earliest use of water resources in the United States involved simply the use of a stream in its natural state. No special form of organization was required for the individual entrepreneur to use the stream for navigation, for water power, for fishing, or for any other use of a stream in its natural state. The early waterworks which were constructed to make greater use of a stream's potential tended to be local single-purpose developments. These developments tended to emphasize consumptive or non-consumptive uses depending upon the region of the country.

In the humid eastern regions of the country, local projects involving non-consumptive uses took a higher order of importance. These uses might involve the diversion of water into a mill race where the flow could be directed over a water wheel to provide power for the individual proprietor before the water was returned to continue its course in the natural channel of the stream. In other cases, local navigation canals and locks might be provided by private entrepreneurs or by public agencies to circumvent local obstructions to navigation. In a similar way, people in a local community might construct and maintain dikes and develop drainage works in order to reduce flood damage to their property. Diking and drainage districts were among the first local improvement districts used to undertake public water-resource projects in the United States.

In the arid West, the use of water for consumptive demands took priority. The first appropriators were largely individual proprietors who diverted water from a local stream to their adjoining land. The centrifugal pump later gave many proprietors direct access to ground water. As a result, the individual proprietor who directly appropriates at least a portion of his own water supply today comprises a relatively large portion of the agricultural and industrial users in such states as California.

Proprietors in the early days of the West who could not appropriate water directly from an adjoining stream or their own wells often established mutual water companies to supply water on a non-profit basis. These companies were either organized by a group of individual farmers who pooled resources to develop a common water supply, or they were established by a land developer who organized a water company as an adjunct of his development and conveyed shares of stock in the water company in proportion to the amount of land sold in each farmstead. When the developer had completed the sale of land, he had at the same time conveyed control of the water company to the settlers, who were then responsible for operation and management of the water company. In the course of time, the organization of mutual water companies developed a rather complex structure. A new company might be organized by several established companies in order to develop large-scale supplementary water supplies, which would then be distributed on a pro-rata basis among the cooperating mutual companies.

Where private companies have been organized to provide water supplies for a profit, they have uniformly come under state laws governing public utilities. These laws require a company to secure a license of "public convenience and necessity" in order to engage in a public service enterprise, and the rates which they may charge for their services are subject to detailed approval by a public utility commission. Private companies which provide water as a public service are in effect limited-profit enterprises.

Special Public Districts

The Wright Act, adopted in California in 1887, is generally used to date the rise of the special public district as an agency for the development of public water supplies. Earlier use had been made of special assessment and improvement districts to develop water supply or drainage systems in which local beneficiaries were assessed to pay for the local improvements made under the jurisdiction of local county authorities. The Wright Act, instead, made the general principles of organization in municipal corporations applicable to neighborhoods or communities which sought to develop common water supplies.

A municipal corporation is a legal device whereby a local community of people are permitted substantial authority to organize themselves and to govern their own local affairs. The government of a municipal corporation is usually vested in a governing board or council elected by the local people. The governing body is usually vested with authority to enact ordinances, resolutions, and by-laws in relation to its purposes and functions, which are binding upon the people comprising the corporation, unless contrary to the general laws of some higher political jurisdiction. Similarly, a municipal corporation is usually vested with control over its internal administrative organization and the management of its own affairs. It may purchase, hold, and dispose of property. If necessary, it may exercise the power of eminent domain to acquire property for public purposes. A municipal corporation is usually vested with the power to incur bonded indebtedness for financing capital improvements, to levy taxes, and to manage its own fiscal affairs. A municipal corporation stands as an individual before the law; it can sue and be sued; and it has perpetual succession in its corporate name. In general, a municipal corporation has competent powers to develop, operate, and maintain a public service program subject mainly to local responsibility and control. It is primarily an instrument of local self-government whereby the people of a local community are enabled to take public action in furtherance of their common interests.

From a beginning with irrigation districts, the special public districts, organized along the model of the municipal corporation or the quasi-municipal corporation, have come to include a vast range of activities related to water-resource administration. These institutions have enabled a local community of people to use public authority to raise the necessary capital as a charge against the local community and upon the local water users, subject to local political control. In California alone, state law authorizes the organization of some 30 types of special public districts for various aspects of local water-resource administration. The function of the local public district has been primarily directed to storage and distribution of water for consumptive, on-the-land uses for both rural and urban populations. These have included irrigation districts, reclamation districts, municipal water districts, utility districts, and county water districts, as well as the cities themselves which maintain municipal water supply systems.

In more recent years, other types such as water conservancy districts, water replenishment districts, water storage districts, metropolitan water districts, county water authorities, and county water agencies have been created to develop supplemental water supplies or to realize more efficient water management by reducing the costs of pumping or of salt-water intrusion. This latter type of district often encompasses an area that may serve a variety of local water distribution systems. However, their function in the water economy is completely dominated by the consumptive demands of the various types of water distribution systems which are served by the supplemental supplies and the regulatory measures. They serve as water producers and wholesalers for the local distribution systems. The new form of organization simply allows the various units which distribute water for consumptive purposes to develop a scale of organization adequate to undertake larger-scale programs for production and transportation of water.

In southern California, where these various local government agencies have seen their fullest development, private and public agencies function as a complex interrelated system. Some are engaged in water production, including surface storage and ground-water spreading. Others regulate pumping and control ground-water extractions. The Metropolitan Water District maintains its Colorado River aqueduct to provide a supplemental supply for most of the region. Beyond this is a vast complex of private and public distribution systems, each of which may produce a portion of its own water supplies. Finally, there are thousands of individual industrial and agricultural users who maintain their own supply systems largely by pumping ground water.

Since an adequate supply of water tends to be the critical element in controlling patterns of development in the arid West, the policy pursued by many of the private and most of the local public agencies is one of securing an adequate supply of water to assure a favorable position for future development of the local community. As a result, a major investment is made in political efforts to influence decisions which will assure control over ample reserves of water and thus maintain a favorable competitive position in relation to other communities. The payoff is not measured in terms of the immediate dollar return upon the operation of the distribution system but upon the adequacy of the reserve supply to meet future contingencies of growth. In many communities, the basic capital costs for developing new sources of supply are financed as a general demand upon taxpayers, with the water utility, whether public or private, paying for its operation and maintenance costs and only a portion of the capital charges. As a result water pricing policies rarely reflect the costs of production and distribution, and values associated with the nonconsumptive uses of water are apt to be completely subordinated to demands for consumptive supplies.

Role of the States

This vast structure of local private and public agencies concerned with consumptive uses and land-related development of water resources functions largely within the framework of state law. Since agencies will articulate the demands which they are organized to represent, the overwhelming political tendency of the western states has been to reinforce the commitments of these local agencies. Western water law, for example, is built around the concept of appropriating water for beneficial consumptive use. Water flowing to the ocean is frequently looked upon as wasted water.

The role that the states have defined for themselves in relation to non-consumptive uses of water has largely been that of a policeman seeking to regulate the behavior of persons who make non-consumptive use of water systems for fishing, recreation, boating, pollution abatement, and other such purposes. The emphasis is upon the regulation of the conduct of *persons* rather than regulating the behavior of the *water course* so as to realize a greater resource potential. The states have done surprisingly little in water-resource management *per se*.

Rarely have the states developed a coherent water policy that takes cognizance of both consumptive and non-consumptive uses in a comprehensive state water plan. An exception has existed since 1955 in Oregon. There the State Water Resources Board is charged with the responsibility of formulating a comprehensive state water program which recognizes both consumptive and non-consumptive uses—including, but not limited to, domestic use, municipal water supply, fire protection, irrigation, power development, mining, industrial purposes, navigation, sanitation, flood control, protection of commercial and game fishing, public recreation, and scenic attraction—as beneficial uses of the state's water resources. However, even in Oregon, with a clear statutory mandate recognizing the beneficial character of non-consumptive uses, it has been difficult to change the perspectives of some state administrative officials who are inclined to recognize only consumptive use as having a valid claim for a commitment of the state's water resources.

ORGANIZATIONS FOR IN-THE-CHANNEL DEVELOPMENT OF WATER

Organization for in-the-channel control of large river systems has posed a complementary set of problems which is fully as complex as the creation of institutions for the distribution of water supplies for consumptive uses. In fact, the two types of organization for consumptive and non-consumptive use may not always stand in contradistinction to one another. In-the-channel management of a river system affects the total production of the water economy in both consumptive and non-consumptive uses. The stored waters captured during flood flows substantially increase the yield of a stream for both types of uses when these waters are released during the low-water season. Many of the early reservoirs built to store flood flows for subsequent use during the irrigating season also contributed to the general function of river regulation. As an agency responsible for some of the first large-scale, multi-purpose water projects, the Bureau of Reclamation was definitely committed to the priority of the consumptive use of water for irrigated agriculture. Nevertheless, its operating responsibilities also involved major commitments to in-the-channel management of water resources for non-consumptive purposes.

Few questions of organization as such have been the subject of such persistent inquiry and controversy as the organization of programs for the management of America's major rivers. On one hand there is the task of creating a pattern of organization which recognizes the functional interdependencies among the various uses that can be made of a river system. On the other hand, in-the-channel management of water resources needs to recognize the integrity of the river system so that projects will complement one another in a comprehensive system of control for the river basin as a whole.

Thus far the states have not demonstrated a capacity to negotiate a satisfactory interstate arrangement that would provide an adequate vehicle for the regional management of an interstate basin. The hope that the interstate compact might become the appropriate vehicle for realizing the principle of "a regional problem, regionally administered" has been marked with disillusionment since the first negotiation of the

Colorado River Compact. The states, oriented to the dominance of consumptive uses, have been primarily concerned with getting their "piece of pie" rather than with the development of regional programs related to regional and national communities of interest as well as to state, local, and private interests.

Federal Responsibility for Managing Interstate Rivers

As a consequence, the federal government has become the most appropriate level of organization to undertake the development of water resources of the large interstate river systems. Furthermore, the U.S. Supreme Court has recognized that the authority over the development of waterways for purposes of navigation vests exclusively in the federal government under the commerce clause of the Constitution. Federal authority over navigation constitutes an important commitment to recognize the values of non-consumptive uses of a river in planning its development. However, the proprietary interest of the federal government in large tracts of western lands has also been the source of important commitments to the development of the consumptive uses of water in that region.

With federal responsibility for in-the-channel management of the larger rivers has come the problem of formulating institutional arrangements which recognize the diversity of interests and potentialities for development among the different river basins while at the same time recognizing the extensive interdependence of interests within a particular river basin. The Columbia River with its anadromous fisheries and arid lands poses a development problem quite different from that posed by the Tennessee River. Within the Columbia basin the anadromous fisheries must be taken into account in the development of nearly every water project. This task of recognizing a diversity of interests and potentialities as between different river basins and an interdependence of interests within individual river basins has been approached with some variations in organization patterns in each major river basin in the United States. However, for purposes of analysis, specific reference will be made only to experience in the Tennessee valley and in the Columbia basin.

The Tennessee Valley Authority

The most heralded American experiment in the regional development of water resources is the Tennessee Valley Authority. The Tennessee Valley Authority Act authorized integrated multiple-purpose river development by a federal public corporation with jurisdiction over the whole Tennessee valley, a region impinging upon seven states.

The act included sweeping powers to provide flood control for the Tennessee basin, to improve navigation on the river, and to develop hydroelectric power. In addition, the TVA was authorized to encourage the conservation and development of natural resources generally in the Tennessee basin, and specific reference was made to reforestation, the production and sale of cheap fertilizers, and the proper use of marginal lands. Thus, the TVA was charged with the task of undertaking the comprehensive development of the Tennessee valley which had been a seriously depressed economic area. Since this responsibility was primarily vested with one agency functioning at the regional level, the program was characterized as an integrated approach to comprehensive resource planning.

As a water-resource management agency, the TVA is primarily concerned with in-the-channel management and control of the river system for purposes of flood control, navigation, and power production. It has voluntarily excluded power distribution from its operating responsibilities, while encouraging the organization of local electric distribution systems by municipal and cooperative organizations. The TVA has also divested itself of responsibility for providing shipping terminal facilities and is inclined to look upon the construction of levees and dikes not directly related to the management of the river as a local responsibility.

In regard to other values or uses to be derived from the management of a water-resource system, the TVA has indicated sensitivity to the problems while avoiding any primary operating responsibility. For example, the TVA operates no recreational areas or facilities of its own but has encouraged state and local government agencies to take advantage of the recreational opportunities created by its river-control projects. It has maintained a small recreational staff to advise and consult with state and local officials and with representatives of private groups regarding the development of recreation facilities and programs. A similar approach has been used in the field of pollution abatement.

TVA operations in the areas of resource management which relate to the general social and economic development of the Tennessee valley have also been conducted with primary reliance upon previously existing agencies and institutional arrangements. The TVA has defined its role as an agency to provide technical assistance, financial support, and demonstration projects, rather than to assume operating responsibility in those fields. Its operating methods have emphasized cooperative arrangements, advice, and consultation. In these areas the TVA is obviously dependent upon the decisions of others regarding the course of action to be taken cooperatively.

Thus the TVA has tended to impose upon itself functional boundaries which limit its commitments in relation to interests that diverge from what it has defined as its primary operating responsibility for controlling the main-stream system. It is much less than a fully integrated water-resource management agency for the Tennessee basin. It has avoided, or divested itself of, responsibility for values that relate primarily to local communities of interest. It has greatly limited its operating responsibility for resource-management problems that are not directly involved in flood control, navigation, and power production. What *has* been integrated are the dominant values relating to flood control and power production. Other values are realized only as other agencies are willing to coordinate their programs with the TVA.

These commitments are also reflected in choices made regarding fiscal policy. TVA's commitment to low-cost public power has led to rigid restrictions which limit the use of power revenues to finance power developments only. This fiscal inflexibility has led a sympathetic commentator to observe that, over time, the nonpower programs have suffered "both a relative and an absolute decline." These nonpower resource activities, "almost wholly dependent upon congressional grants, have seen their appropriations dwindle year after year until they are in some instances little more than shadow operations."[1]

There is evidence that TVA's initial period of enthusiastic growth and development has been replaced by a more routine administration of an in-the-channel river-control program operated as an adjunct of a power production and wholesale business. Since the early 1950's, the TVA has expanded its steam generating facilities until its hydroelectric facilities are being dwarfed by comparison. When hard decisions require choice about the employment of limited funds for resource-management activities, those decisions are apt to reflect values which conform to the central commitment of an agency while sacrificing other values with a lower order of priority. In the long-term process, the TVA's experience seems to indicate that an integrated, comprehensive approach to the regional development of water resources is apt to become something less than fully integrated and wholly comprehensive.

Organization for Columbia Basin Development

In contrast to the valley-authority approach, water management in the Columbia basin has often been referred to as a piecemeal approach which involves competing agencies with overlapping jurisdictions. The traditional water management agencies of the federal gov-

---

[1]Roscoe C. Martin, "The Tennessee Valley Authority: A Study of Federal Control," *Law and Contemporary Problems*, XXII (1957), 374.

ernment with their special-purpose orientation are all involved in the administration of water programs in the Columbia basin. The Corps of Engineers, with its commitment to functions of navigation and flood control, is probably the most significant single operating agency on the Columbia River. The Bureau of Reclamation has developed some of its largest reclamation projects and river-control structures in the Columbia basin. The Fish and Wildlife Service has substantial program obligations in the Columbia basin with its vital runs of salmon and steelhead as well as other sport and commercial fisheries. The Federal Power Commission has jurisdiction in the Columbia basin over some of the best hydroelectric power sites to be found anywhere in the United States.

Only the Bonneville Power Administration among the federal agencies has a regional jurisdiction exclusive to the Pacific Northwest. BPA is responsible for operating an integrated power transmission grid which distributes power from the various damsites to the principal load centers in the Pacific Northwest.

In addition to these functions performed by federal agencies, the states have had important responsibilities for: controlling stream pollution; regulating commercial and sport fishing; operating fish hatcheries in cooperation with the federal fisheries program; developing and operating recreational facilities; determining water rights among different types of consumptive water users; and, more recently, comprehensive planning for the multi-purpose development of local water resources. The states of Washington and Oregon, in particular, conduct major programs in their fields of responsibility for administration of water resources. Local government agencies or districts also have essential responsibilities for operation of distribution systems for power and for irrigation and municipal water; they also maintain local levees and channel improvements for flood control. Several private electric utilities maintain extensive service areas in the Columbia basin. Both private utilities and the public utility districts and municipal power systems operate large projects which produce a portion of the power load distributed to their local customers.

The growth of regional interests in the Pacific Northwest has been associated with the development of institutional arrangements for the preparation of research studies and planning reports and for fuller communication, consultation, deliberation, and negotiation on a regional, interagency basis. The first attempt to give a regional focus to resource planning was the organization of the Pacific Northwest Regional Planning Commission as a part of the effort of the National Resources Committee (later the National Resources Planning Board) to deal broadly with questions of social and economic development. The 1936 report, *Regional Planning, Part I: Pacific Northwest,* was a milestone in formulating perspectives on problems of regional development, notably the development of the Columbia River.[2]

The Regional Planning Commission's concern for the development of a public power policy which would encourage the general economic growth and development of the Pacific Northwest led to the creation of the Bonneville Power Administration and its low-cost public power policies. The commission was also instrumental in organizing the Northwest Regional Council of Education, Planning, and Public Administration to provide a common agency for the organization of research activities and a common forum for the exchange of ideas among professional personnel of the region's academic institutions, planning bodies, and public administrative agencies concerned with resource problems and economic development.

Changing conditions of war and peace and of national politics and public policy led to the demise of the Regional Planning Commission, of the Northwest Regional Council, and of other institutional arrangements. They have been replaced by rich and varied institutional arrangements for planning, consultation, and negotiation on an interagency, regional basis. Many of the primary resource agencies have regional advisory committees which have become a part of their planning and decision-making processes. Intradepartmental-interagency and interagency-interdepartmental field committees have seen extensive use. The Departments of Interior, Agriculture, and Commerce have maintained regional representatives to facilitate coordination among departmental agencies. Finally, many of these arrangements have been coordinated since 1946 by the Columbia Basin Inter-Agency Committee. The CBIAC serves in part as a forum for the exchange of ideas and a conference for the negotiation of interagency interests. It also provides an important means for professional administrative personnel to coordinate operations through the work of the vital water and power committees.

As these arrangements have led to decisions and to programs of action, basic operating commitments have been formed which require the various operating agencies to take each other into account in the conduct of a coordinated resource development program. Today, the Corps of Engineers is dependent upon the Bureau of Reclamation, which operates the larger upstream reservoirs, to provide its principal

---

[2]National Resources Committee, *Regional Planning, Part I: Pacific Northwest* (Government Printing Office, 1936).

regulation for flood control. The Bonneville Power Administration depends upon the coordinated operations of the Bureau of Reclamation, the Corps of Engineers, and a variety of publicly and privately owned electric power systems to produce the power transmitted over its regional grid. All of these electric power facilities are coordinated in a regional power pool. The financial feasibility of most of the region's reclamation projects is in turn dependent upon the pricing policies of the Bonneville Power Administration. Some of the most imaginative work in engineering of fish facilities is being done by a private electric utility and by a municipal power system. These interagency operations have made regional interagency institutional arrangements an imperative necessity in the Pacific Northwest. Independence of action without regard to other coordinated values can no longer be tolerated in the development of the Columbia River.

Differences in the Two Organization Patterns

By and large, the difference between the organizational patterns for water management in the Tennessee valley and those in the Columbia basin is one of degree rather than of kind. The TVA has a relatively more dominant position in the control of the Tennessee River than any one of the water agencies in the Pacific Northwest. Even the TVA, however, has divested itself of primary operating responsibility for such non-consumptive, in-the-channel uses as recreation, fish and wildlife, and pollution abatement. In both basins, the primary federal agencies can be viewed as the basic water-producing agencies.

Water production is more nearly monopolized by the TVA in the Tennessee valley, while a number of local government agencies and private companies maintain water-producing facilities to supplement the basic federal control system in the Columbia basin. However, the licenses for these projects usually require the utilities to meet specific standards for maintaining public values regarding recreation, fish life, and flood control. The problem of coordinating these systems in a water-production program has been the source of some of the most intense controversies over water developments in the Pacific Northwest.

The land-related developments of water resources which bear upon the local communities of interest have invariably been organized by private or by local government agencies. These include the full range of agencies concerned with the consumptive use of water and electricity as well as port districts and flood-control districts which provide local diking and drainage facilities. These private and local government agencies have come to serve more as retail agencies in meeting the water-service demands of their communities while the basic burden of water production has been assumed by the large river-management agencies of the federal government.

ORGANIZATION AND PLANNING FOR COMPREHENSIVE MULTI-PURPOSE DEVELOPMENT

In the evolution of American institutions concerned with the development of water resources, the earlier period saw a reliance upon private and local public agencies concerned mainly with consumptive uses of water or upon waterworks related to on-the-land developments. These agencies were primarily related to local communities of interest in land and land-related developments. Not until much later did there emerge a concern for comprehensive management of rivers on a multi-purpose regional basis. These tasks have been predominantly organized through agencies of the federal government. Both sets of agencies have performed roles which are vital and essentially complementary. The one set emphasizes the retail distribution function; the other set emphasizes the production function.

This specialization in function has resulted in selective commitments and biases in the development of water policies at the different levels of government. The private and local public agencies have been overwhelmingly committed to the priority of values related to the consumptive use of water. The predominant interest of these agencies in state politics has tended to reinforce a comparable commitment in state water law and water policies. The federal water-production agencies, on the other hand, have tended to emphasize the interests associated with non-consumptive uses of water, to the extent that these interests have been emphasized at all.

Pious platitudes are everywhere expressed in support of comprehensive multi-purpose planning for development of water resources, but such planning is much harder to do than to talk about. If all goods in the water economy were amenable to production and distribution in the market, the solution to the problem would be relatively simple. Contrariwise, if all goods realized in the use of water resources were subject to provision as public goods for a single community of interest, the problem of comprehensive multi-purpose development could be solved in a relatively simple way. Instead, the water economy includes a variety of goods, some of which are more or less amenable to allocation in the private market, others which might be supplied through private agencies but are involved in substantial questions of public interest, and finally those which seem to be amenable only to public provision if they are to be provided at all.

Furthermore, these goods affect many different communities of interest. The variety of local communities of interest alone is immense. In addition, regional interest in developing water resources has been one of the chief factors directing attention to the problems of regional organization within the American political economy. Finally, inter-basin transfers of water and hydroelectric power indicate that the basin is not an isolable unit for defining interests in water-resource development, and tend to point up inter-basin regional and national interests of substantial proportions.

Theoretically, the allocation of water among competing demands for consumptive uses would be relatively simple to solve by market-type arrangements except for the essentially monopolistic character of water distribution systems and the necessity for making choices concerning the relative balance between consumptive and non-consumptive uses in the water economy. Any resolution of the latter problem will require a fundamental re-evaluation of state water law and of public policies regulating the consumptive use of water supplies.

State Water Law and Public Policy

State water law requires re-evaluation since it determines the nature of the property rights by which proprietors can make enforceable claims on water supplies. The constraints applicable to the exercise of a right to the use of water, the character of the use that can be made, and the degree of transferability of a water right are all defined by water law. Unfortunately, the bramble bush which some of the states have permitted to grow under the name of water law defies comprehension even by those who are the most learned in the law. Many proprietors, unwilling to risk the security of their rights, insist upon an exclusiveness of control which denies many obvious economies of scale in interrelating distribution systems, in the interchange of water supplies, or in reallocating surplus or waste waters.

If greater reliance is to be placed upon market allocation of water for consumptive use, the law must define the property in a water right with a view to the exclusiveness of proprietary interests, in relation to some readily specifiable and measurable unit of water which can be simply transferred in whole or in part. A definition of rights by reference to various correlative doctrines simply creates unavoidable confusion for market economies.

The interest of others, and especially the public interest in non-consumptive uses, can best be recognized by an enunciation of public policies which specify the conditions for allocating water for consumptive uses as against reserving it for non-consumptive uses and also indicate the public responsibilities of the various appropriators making consumptive demands upon water supplies. Here the state of Oregon has pointed the way with its emphasis upon comprehensive multi-purpose planning for water development. The amount of water available for appropriation for consumptive use is related to the development of plans which, when adopted by the State Water Resources Board, become a part of the state's water policy indicating the order of preferences among various consumptive and non-consumptive uses and the streamflows to be maintained for non-consumptive uses in particular watershed areas.

Any resolution of the conflicting interests of the federal and state governments over the validity of state water rights should take cognizance of the necessity of defining the public interests, especially in relation to various public non-consumptive uses of water resources. A comprehensive water policy can be developed only when these interests are articulated. Federal agencies should be concerned that the federal interests regarding in-the-channel water management are formulated as a part of the federal water policies that bear upon state water law.

Role of Economic Analysis

The task of making plans regarding the relative allocation of water resources to non-consumptive uses or in making allocations among the non-consumptive uses is the most difficult area for decision-making in water-resource development. Reliance upon methods of economic analysis where a dollar value is assigned to public uses is only a partial solution. Since the non-consumptive uses do not have a directly salable market value, an approximate dollar value must be assigned and this assignment of value must be somewhat arbitrary.

It is entirely possible that the commercial potentialities of the salmon fisheries, for example, have been seriously underestimated. Anadromous fish have a built-in guidance system which takes them to the ocean to pasture and to mature unattended, and then leads them back to spawn in the stream of their birth. It is even unnecessary for people to engage in such inefficient games as salmon fishing when fish ladders could direct a run of salmon to a fish market as easily as they can pass brood stock upstream. If a reasonable portion of the effort had been devoted to salmon husbandry that our state universities and agricultural experiment stations have devoted to animal husbandry, salmon might be an extraordinarily valuable water product which would merit a much more important place in the water economy.

Organization for Complex Decisions

Since economic analysis at best provides a tool for making a gross approximation to questions of evaluation in planning for resource developments, attention should also be given to the way that organizations are constituted and related to one another as a political framework for making decisions and exercising control over events. The structure of organizational arrangements implicitly determines the basis for distinguishing the sets of events to be controlled, the order of preferences for ranking the values to be achieved by organized activities, and the standards for determining the relevancy of information to be communicated in the decision-making process. Since the patterns of organization have a fundamental influence upon the development of perspectives, values, and ideas regarding resource policies and patterns of resource development, any question of comprehensive planning must involve comparable questions about the design of organizational arrangements.

All aspects of administration and of economic development are based upon the assumption that efforts to control events will produce greater benefits than if the events were not controlled. The initial problem in organization is to determine which set of events is to be controlled in relation to some value reflected in the consequences to be realized. What these interests are and how they are ordered in relation to one another comprises the basic task in constituting any general system of organization.

In dealing with the development of water resources, the interests that are related to the various uses of water and of the flowing stream can theoretically be tied together in an integrated water agency. But such a decision necessarily means that land and water interests in recreation, energy, transportation, fish and wildlife, and rural and urban community developments cannot be organized in similarly integrated agencies. The fact that the universe is not organized in mutually exclusive sets means that any form of organization must take account of the patterns of interrelationships among the different sets of events that are being controlled.

The experience in both the Tennessee valley and the Columbia basin would seem to indicate that comprehensive planning and the comprehensive development of water resources cannot be organized within the framework of a single integrated agency. Too many values are at stake in relation to too many different communities of interest. Changing requirements and conditions of life do not permit a simple ordering of values in which one set of values can be arbitrarily rejected and subordinated to another set of values. Organization for comprehensive planning must be able to tolerate conflict, so that the various interests about controversial issues can be clarified, adequate intelligence can be organized, and decisions can be reached. Programs can then be coordinated through a variety of operational agreements and contractual arrangements.

Because of the rich interrelationships among the various values or goods which can be derived from water, administration of water resources will require a complex system of organization in order to realize the diverse values of multi-purpose development. As patterns of demand change, patterns of organization will also change. Increasing competition for the available water supplies will certainly require a much greater clarification of the place of non-consumptive uses in relation to the various consumptive uses of water. The choices among these uses will reflect the preferences which we as individuals make when we function as consumers and as citizens. If we are organized so that we can inform and articulate our interests both as consumers and as citizens, we should be able to arrive at those settlements in the use of water resources that represent the requirements for comprehensive development at any given time. A rich variety of both private and public agencies would be required in order to realize any such objective.

Institutional Limitations to Economic Development of Underdeveloped Countries

ERVEN J. LONG

This is the only occasion, I believe, in which the conference will focus upon foreign underdeveloped countries. This brief diversion is justified by the importance to all Americans of development efforts in these countries, and by the fact that development and utilization of our own resources are inevitably intertwined with similar activities in other countries.

The word "institutional" was dropped from the title on the printed program, probably because of my reaction to the implication in the title that institutions are necessarily "limiting" to economic development. This is, of course, not the case. Institutions are the means by which people work together to do things. Murder, Inc., is an institution, to be sure. But so is the Red Cross, a cooperative, a church, a family. It probably is not necessary to labor this point; yet only a few years ago it was extremely popular among agricultural economists to postulate economic ideals in terms of the unimpaired workings of free economic forces and to consider "institutions" essentially as impediments to the free and effective working of these economic forces. This view is no longer dominant in the profession, largely because of recent experience in underdeveloped countries, where economic development is impeded at least as much by the simple lack of necessary institutional structures as by the presence of the wrong ones.

Indeed, one can quite intelligently approach the problem of institutional barriers to economic development by looking first at the

Erven J. Long is a specialist in land policies and programs with the U.S. Agency for International Development. The views expressed in this paper are his own and do not necessarily reflect policy of the AID. From 1956 to 1960 Long was group leader of the agricultural program conducted at Bangalore, India, by the University of Tennessee. He had taught economics for a decade and was head of agricultural economics and rural sociology at the University of Tennessee. On leave in 1954, he served as consultant to the Belgian Congo.

institutions which are needed and must be built, and second at the institutions which must be modified or somehow accommodated to economic development objectives. If circumstances permitted a complete cataloguing of "institutional limitations to economic development," this is the approach I should take. But space limitations require a highlighting rather than a cataloguing procedure.

Underdevelopment is essentially and fundamentally an institutional phenomenon. In most economically underdeveloped countries, the social, economic, and political institutions were developed and crystallized out of the characteristics and needs of pre-modern civilization. For many reasons, these institutions did not adjust and were not developed to meet the demands of (or more accurately, to create) a modern civilization. Consequently, in such countries capital does not develop because the institutions are not designed to develop capital. Human capacities are not developed because institutions have not evolved to develop these capacities. Resources are not developed because the institutions for developing resources have not existed.

We can take a look, in these few minutes, at only a few of the types of institutional shortcomings characteristic of many underdeveloped societies.

By far the most important institutional limitations are those which result in underdevelopment of the potential capacities latent in human beings. It is on these institutional limitations that I shall center my attention.

SURVIVAL VS. PROGRESS AS A CENTRAL VALUE

Such existing basic institutions as family organization, religions, legal systems, land-tenure systems, even ethical concepts, in many countries originally were addressed to entirely different ends, different values, than obtain today. Survival, rather than progress, was more nearly the original central social value. And, as in nature, survival of the group, rather than of the individual, was the unarticulated but very real social goal. In many primitive societies—such as most American Indian tribes—stealing was a much more heinous crime than murder, and more heavily punished, because it constituted a more serious threat to the survival of the group. The "greater-family" or "joint-family" system so prevalent in Asia, and the tribal organization of African and other societies, are specific devices to protect the group, at the expense of virtually all incentive to or reward for individual development.

The extremely symbolic, non-literal way in which language is used by most African and many Asian peoples is apparently an historic device to keep knowledge in the custody of the elders who have had a lifetime to devote to learning the intricacies of oral communication. This serves to keep decision making on important matters out of the reach of the rash young individualist—i.e., of keeping the society "conservative," of protecting its survival at the expense of its progress. Peoples who are dedicated, even though subconsciously, to survival do not risk that survival in the interest of possible gain for the individual or even of progress for the group.

Progress, as a value, an ideal, is essentially a modern phenomenon, just a few centuries old. As an ideal, it swept across Western Europe and most exported European societies with amazing speed. In a manner equally amazing, however, it left almost entirely untouched the great masses of people elsewhere in the world until very recent years. Now, throughout the world, the ideal of progress is beginning to take shape, in the consciousness of the people in the huts, and even in the consciences of the people in the palaces.

In its economic dimension, the ideal of progress motivates a desire for economic development. But in a typical underdeveloped country this ideal of progress, this seed of desire for economic development, falls on predominantly hostile institutional soil. This is not because the institutions are bad, but because they have been developed for and dedicated to the achievement of different values. It is not for us to suggest what values people should hold. But if people do in fact strongly desire economic development, then their institutions must somehow be brought into position to serve this purpose.

United States effort at providing technical and economic assistance to underdeveloped countries during the last decade has brought this fact into sharp focus. Our earlier programs of assistance to Western Europe, under the Marshall Plan, provided an entirely different type of experience. European institutional structures were already essentially designed to serve the objectives of economic development. The need there was primarily for capital assistance and for merely the repair, restoration, and improvement in details of basic institutions. Therefore, the development assistance problem was basically simple.

But as our programs of assistance moved eastward and southward into the truly historically underdeveloped countries, they encountered economic, social, and political institutions essentially at odds with progress and development as basic objectives. There the economic assistance problem is primarily institutional. Reform and profound adaptation of existing institutions, and the building of new institutions of types that do not now exist, are the central burdens of attempts at assistance to such societies. In general, minor tamperings with existing institutions accomplish little in these countries. And direct transplantation of our own institutional structures is even more ineffective. These facts provide the imperative that guided the reorganization of the United States aid agency—that our efforts at assistance be built entirely upon integrated, purposive efforts within the countries themselves—efforts to bring about those institutional reforms that are prerequisite to economic development.

INSTITUTIONS TO DEVELOP INDIVIDUAL CAPACITIES

Many needed changes in institutions are implicit in such basic shifts in social objectives as are now under way in aspiring underdeveloped countries. As indicated earlier, the most important are those that define the role of the individual in society. Progress requires that each participant in society contribute as nearly as possible to the limit of his capacities, and that those capacities be fully developed. This, in turn, requires that he be given a meaningful role in determining his own destiny, that he live to some degree with the consequences of his own actions (or inactions), that he be encouraged to innovate, to take risks, to act intelligently—i.e., analytically—by being rewarded in some manner and to some degree if he succeeds.

A cluster of institutions combine in varying ways in different countries to limit the development of human capacities. Family organization of the greater-family type operates very strongly in many countries to inhibit incentives to individual action and also limit decision making on important matters to the greater-family elders. Individuals who up to age 50 or older make no important decisions of their own—not even whom to marry—but defer always to parental judgment do not develop into high-capacity economic agents. Nor do they normally work hard or effectively if they must turn over virtually all their earnings to elders, to be distributed at will to nonworking brothers, sisters, or cousins. New ideas take root slowly in such a situation.

Land ownership and tenure institutions are among those which most seriously limit the economic development of many countries. The peasant whose culture dictates that he must not smile, lest the landlord think he is unnecessarily affluent and raise his rent, is not inclined to work hard or to take risks in the interest of such precarious gain. The tenant whose tenure on his piece of land is entirely at the will of the landlord invests neither his savings nor his labor in capital improvements. These actions might serve merely as an incentive to the landlord to dispossess him in order to reap the capital gains.

In countries where there are very few opportunities off the land, those who control the uses of the land thereby control those who must make their living from it. People so controlled have little access to, or interest in, meaningful roles of citizenship. Under such circumstances, the great majority of rural people acquire neither economic nor political bargaining power. Extreme inequality of resource ownership is perpetuated. Capital formation in agriculture stagnates. And, for the country as a whole, such capital as exists is invested in land ownership, with surpluses often being exported by the wealthy for deposit in foreign countries as safety capital. With extremely low incomes among the majority of the people, mass markets have little chance to develop. So there develops neither the push of capital formation and investment nor the pull of effective markets. Thus is economic development inhibited by faulty land-tenure systems.

Even more importantly, perhaps, the development of human capacities is discouraged by tenure institutions which offer no rewards for such capacities. Basic human resources of energy and skills either remain dormant or are channeled into activities of dissension and disorganization.

Time does not permit analysis of several other land-tenure institutions which are serious inhibitors of economic development. An example is the shifting cultivation characteristic of tribal societies in much of Africa and parts of Latin America, Asia, and various island countries. Under this institutional pattern, cultivators slash, burn, cultivate a year or two, and move on. In perhaps 20 years, they or others come back over the same land. Under this system, no capital formation or permanent land improvement takes place. And institutions to support development of the capacities of the people are difficult to establish. In Taiwan, in Kenya, and elsewhere, programs of replacing such shifting agriculture with more permanent tenure forms have sharply increased investments in both land and people.

CHANGES NEEDED IN GOVERNMENTAL INSTITUTIONS

Economic development requires the enhancement of human capacities not only in individual action, but also in joint or group action. Institutions of government in societies dedicated largely to survival usually serve poorly the purposes of progress. Such governmental institutions, particularly as they touch the masses of the people, are designed primarily for maintenance of order and for collection of funds. Almost by definition, any factor of social dynamics is suspect. This has nothing to do with the degree of governmental benevolence or tyranny—only with the basic objectives of such governmental institutions. As a colonial civil servant once explained to me, the three R's of administration are Rule, Revenue, and Reprimand. Under the criteria imposed by their values, such governments can administer justice with the wisdom of Solomon and the gentleness of Joseph and still stand squarely opposed to progress, simply because the dedication is to other values, under which change is regarded as an evil, or at least as a danger. This is the real indictment of colonialism.

How different are the requirements placed upon governments by societies committed to progress as a central objective! The entire machinery—and even more difficult, the entire personnel—of government must be readdressed to the function of service. Anyone who has worked at grass-roots levels with government personnel making this transition will realize how radical is the shift in their role and how complex the process by which it is achieved. Though not superficially conspicuous, some of the most heroic undertakings by the progressive emerging nations are those concerned with bringing about this change in function of government civil services. Similarly, though not superficially obvious, this represents one of the most formidable barriers yet to be overcome by many countries desiring economic development.

At a different level, there is in many countries a great lack of institutions for effective local group action. This is true both for institutions of voluntary group action and for local government, as distinct from local administration of central government. Institutions of voluntary group action and of local government are the two types of institutional mechanisms by which individuals work together to expand most directly control of their own immediate affairs. This takes such forms as a cooperative to market their products, a school board to build their school, a local government to establish security, an organization to lobby their interests with the central government. The forms are diverse; they cannot be designed by prescription. They must be developed from the ingredients of the local situation. But the development of human capacities requires that, somehow, institutional mechanisms of effective group action on local problems be developed. The reasons are those already stressed. People work most energetically, most thoughtfully, most willingly—and hence most effectively—when the results of their efforts redound to their own benefit. As John R. Commons so frequently stated, the key to effective administration is the enlistment of the willing participation of those involved in the activity. On matters of economic development which are local in character, and yet which lie beyond the reach of individual action, the willing participation of people is most effectively enlisted by institutional devices which give an effective role to organized local group action, whether through voluntary association or through local government.

INSTITUTIONAL FACTORS IN TRANSFER OF POWER

One final comment on what I personally feel to be perhaps the most strategic issue for the future of economic development: In many underdeveloped countries, economic development aspirations are interrelated with the transfer of political power from a colonizing government to a national self government. Almost by necessity, these new national governments are comprised primarily of people most closely related by education and experience to the previous colonial government. They represent, in a very real sense, a special élite.

In our own country, this special élite was characterized by an extraordinary quality of thought and of motive. In perspective it can be seen that it performed almost a custodian function—to develop the institutions which would prepare the country for the transfer of power to the people at large beginning with what we now call the Jacksonian Revolution. This transfer of power to an ever-widening base of participation has been the process by which the integration of our society has been achieved and its democratic character secured.

India today is working with great steadfastness of purpose and at times almost breath-taking vision to bring about this kind of transfer of power from the governing élite to the people of India at large. This is an extremely difficult undertaking because the prevailing institutions of government are primarily imported, whereas the prevailing institutions of the Indian people at large are indigenous—and the two must be brought together in an effectively functioning relationship.

Some countries, on the other hand, have had independence from the colonizing government for a century or more; and yet the second transfer of power—to the people at large—has not been achieved or even seriously undertaken. The hard, rough process of institutional development still lies ahead for these countries. And, of course, many other countries have not yet had time to begin the process. Perhaps the greatest challenge and the toughest task facing democratic countries aspiring for economic development is that of achieving this transfer quickly enough for it to be accomplished in an orderly, non-violent manner.

I have indicated some of the institutional limitations to economic development of underdeveloped countries. We Americans must recognize the significance of these and other institutional barriers—and appreciate the difficulty of removing them. Especially, we must understand them, with deepest possible comprehension, so that our helping hands may be firm, uplifting, and well-guided.

Meeting Public Needs and Providing Support for Outdoor Recreation

HAROLD G. WILM

Because of rapidly mounting pressures, outdoor recreation has become one of the most crucial subjects on which the managers of natural resources are having to focus their attention. The population of the United States is increasing rapidly; it is characterized by the growth of young postwar families; and people in general have more leisure than they had a decade or two ago. Although the population of most western states is still far less dense than in our Northeast, proportionately the increases in the West are even more pronounced. Thus, all of our recreation resources are feeling pressures which most of us would not have imagined even at the close of World War II.

In the planning of natural-resource development, therefore, recreation must assume a leading role; and full allowance must be made for recreation in consideration of all the elements of multiple-use programs. The western states recognize these needs, I know, and are taking steps to meet them in varying degrees.

In New York State we have taken some rapid and dramatic steps to meet these expanding needs; so the logical thing for me to do is to use our activities as an illustration of what can be done. Thus, the purpose of this paper is to review briefly the steps that we have taken to assess our outdoor recreation problems and to tell about the financing methods we are using to build a program which will meet our present and predictable needs for outdoor recreation facilities.

RESOURCES AND NEEDS IN NEW YORK

In most ways New York State presents a rather extreme example of conditions that are characteristic of many eastern states. In addition,

Harold G. Wilm is Commissioner of Conservation, New York State Conservation Department. From 1932 to 1953, Wilm held various posts with the U.S. Forest Service; from 1951 to 1953 he headed the Division of Watershed Management Research. Appointed associate dean of the State University College of Forestry, Syracuse University, in 1953, he served in that capacity until January 1, 1959, when he was appointed to his present post.

we have a few unique problems which make our task a little more
difficult than usual. For one thing, about half of New York State's 16
million people live in New York City. The rest are concentrated in a
number of upstate cities or scattered over 30-odd million acres of land
in villages and towns and on farms. Of the total area of the state,
about 2½ million acres of largely forested land constitute the New
York State Forest Preserve which, under our Constitution, must remain
"forever wild." This preserve is now 75 years old. Its primary value
is for public recreation in the form of hunting, fishing, camping, hiking,
and mountain-climbing and other specialized pursuits of nature-lovers
of all kinds. Last year the public campsites in the forest preserve
provided 1½ million man-days of camping and over 800,000 man-days
of uses such as picnicking and bathing.

We are the beneficiaries of a unique system of state parks which
was started back in 1924. Last year these parks provided the enormous
total of 31 million man-days of public recreation.

In addition, the people of New York own a half-million acres of
reforestation lands which are also open to the public and find great
use, particularly by hunters and to some extent by fishermen. We also
own 34 specialized game-management areas totalling some 106,000
acres, and over the years we have acquired perpetual public fishing
rights on over 860 miles of some of the state's finest trout waters. Within our forest preserve we also have thousands of miles of additional
state-owned waters and innumerable lakes and ponds. Our geography
is such that we also enjoy a vast frontage on two of the Great Lakes,
on the Atlantic Ocean, and on Long Island Sound. Our large and
scenic Adirondack and Catskill Mountain regions make ideal outdoor
playgrounds within a day's travel for all of our millions of people.

However, despite these pioneering efforts of the past and our
great natural potential, we have been overwhelmed in recent years by
the tremendous upsurge in demand for outdoor recreation. In so well-
informed a group as this conference, I shall not treat at any length the
factors which have created this problem for us in New York and for
many other states and provinces.

The postwar population explosion which still continues has been
analyzed ad nauseam. The larger-sized families so characteristic of
the postwar period, their great mobility, the trend toward family outdoor activities, and other related factors are now pretty well understood. What it all adds up to is simply that we have more people and
they are taking to the outdoors as never before.

This is a healthy and fortunate trend, because it comes at a time
when help is badly needed to keep our minds clear and our bodies

strong in an era which has come to demand so much of America and its people. It is a trend which should be encouraged by prompt and vigorous action in providing the additional recreational facilities which are required right now and in the predictable future.

In New York those directly responsible for outdoor recreational developments consider themselves very fortunate to have in Governor Rockefeller a chief executive who thoroughly understands the large dimensions of the problems which we face in this field. He not only understands their importance and magnitude but he has encouraged, inspired, and directed us to think and act in equally large dimensions. In 1959-60, at his direction, the Conservation Department and the associated State Council of Parks undertook the first statewide survey of outdoor recreation needs and what it would take to meet them.

STATEWIDE RECREATION SURVEY

In carrying out this recreation survey, we had in the Conservation Department a number of professional leaders who have a broad perspective of outdoor recreation problems in New York State and throughout the country. Also, in Robert Moses, chairman of our State Council of Parks, we had the dean of America's state park planners, who was the principal architect of our park system and has been the driving force behind it since its beginning 36 years ago.

And finally, we had at our command a well-trained and experienced corps of district game and fish managers, district foresters, regional park engineers and executives, and other experts in specialized outdoor recreation problems.

Methodology of the Survey

It was largely through these field men that our recreation survey was carried out. Each one was asked to take a new, hard look at his district; to assess its recreation needs; and, looking ahead, to list every likely recreation site in his territory. This was a large and difficult assignment—the more so because much of it had to be carried out during the busiest time of the year for our field people.

In our central office we set up a special committee, recruited from each of our major divisions, to receive, summarize, and analyze the reports from the field. The committee's job was to screen recommendations, hold down any overly eager beavers, stimulate those who were too conservative, and come up with one comprehensive report representing the composite findings and recommendations of our various conservation services.

This was an exciting operation. Old hands who had been through the lean years of the depression and the belt-tightening war years suddenly saw the opportunity to translate their dreams for their districts and regions into reality. And the younger hands saw the chance to take part in a new forward surge to meet some of the unprecedented challenges of our times. Thus, under a full head of steam from the governor on down through the ranks, the first phase of the survey and a report of the major findings, together with recommendations to the legislature, were completed in less than one year. Moreover, our legislature then acted promptly to pass the necessary implementing legislation.

In order to accomplish so much in such a short time, we obviously had to use the most simple and direct methods of establishing our needs and developing our program. There was no time for profound studies or sociological research. We had to come to grips as quickly as we could with such basic questions as:

1. What kind of additional recreational facilities do we need?
2. How many do we need?
3. Where do we need them and where can we put them?
4. When will they be needed?
5. What kind of an action program will get first things done first?
6. And the $64 question—how do we pay for it?

Some Keys to Success

At this point I should like to emphasize again that the key to the success of such an operation is the trained, experienced professional conservationist who knows his district or region like the palm of his own hand. Most of the information he needs is in his files, or where he knows he can get it quickly from cooperating agencies.

Next in importance, assuming high-grade supervision, is a simple, clear-cut, and uniform method of collecting and tabulating, county by county, the essential data and recommendations which are being sought. This method must be carefully and thoroughly reviewed with all hands before the survey starts.

Once under way, it is essential to have a few veterans with proven judgment who move quickly from district to district to check, inspire, prod, or do whatever is necessary to see that a good job, and a reasonably uniform job, is done across the board. Even so, after the field data are turned in and tabulated at the central office, gaps and holes will appear which require that the veterans go back to the districts to see that these deficiencies are overcome.

And finally, as in all such operations, there comes the task of report preparation which can spell the doom or the success of the whole operation. We found that two types of reports were necessary. The first was filled with the kind of facts and figures which are needed to sell the experts in program, finance, and legislation on the merits of the final recommendations.

The second type of report, designed for the public and the non-expert, must be concise, colorful, graphic, and compelling. Most of you have already seen our report, *Now or Never*, which did this part of the job for us.

Findings and Recommendations

The recreation problems and programs presented in this report were set up with two target dates: 1965, the recreation development that is needed immediately; and 1976 to coincide with the planning date of the federal Outdoor Recreation Resources Review Commission. In both dimensions, we found that we need more of every kind of state-operated recreation facility.

For example, in the case of camping (our fastest-growing recreation activity, where we already have an annual deficiency index of about 110,000 persons) our projections showed that we would need 43 more public campsites by 1965 and 63 more by 1976. Our immediate need is for more land for suitable sites which have specialized requirements.

In the case of state parks—we will need 50 percent more capacity by 1965—and two to three times the existing capacity by 1976. Here the land requirement is obviously even more critical.

You will find our needs for state facilities spelled out for wilderness areas, multiple-purpose areas (largely upland), fishing rights, hunting areas, the preservation of salt and freshwater "wetlands," winter sports, and boating facilities (principally boat-launching sites).

Similarly, and we consider this extremely important, there is an urgent need for our municipalities—our counties, cities, villages, and towns—to do their part of the job in creating local parks and recreation facilities which do not properly come within the state's jurisdiction.

Our most important single finding, which applies to both state and local needs, is the need to save, by prompt acquisition, at least some of the fast-disappearing open lands and choice recreation sites which otherwise will be lost for all time.

Following a crash program of land acquisition to be made possible by special financing would come careful planning as to the use and development of the lands secured. And finally, development must go forward, year by year, as fast as our means will permit.

FINANCING THE PROPOSED PROGRAM

We now come to a part of our planning which I think will be of interest to a great many of you because it has to do with the method of financing such a large program.

Our survey clearly demonstrated the need for a large sum of money ($75 million), which should be made available as fast as needed and on a rather flexible basis. The idea of a series of annual appropriations was set aside because, in our state, appropriations are only good for one year, and they are apt to be inadequate and somewhat uncertain, depending upon other emergencies which arise in connection with the annual state budgeting procedure.

Instead, Mr. Moses, out of his long experience, came up with a suggestion for a special kind of bond issue. This then became the subject of intensive study by the governor and his counsel, our department and the state's various fiscal experts, both in the administration and in the legislature. The result was that the governor recommended—and the legislature passed—two pieces of legislation.

The first was a measure referring to the people of New York State a bond issue in the amount of $75 million. This bond issue was approved by the people of the state at the general election in November 1960. The bond issue is specifically for the acquisition of land for park and recreation purposes. It provides for outright acquisition by the state and also for state aid to our city, county, town, and village governments on a 75 percent state aid, 25 percent local contribution basis.

The second piece of legislation is the enabling act, which went into effect shortly after approval of the basic proposition at the election. This enabling legislation carries all the usual definitions, the way the monies shall be allocated, and various other provisions covering the use of the proceeds of the bond issue. *By passing this enabling act in advance on a contingent basis, it is possible to save several months, if not the best part of a year, in putting the program into effect.*

Allocation of Funds

The allocation of monies will, I think, be of interest to you. It is as follows:

1. For the acquisition of lands for state park purposes: $20 million.
2. For the acquisition of lands for other than state-park or municipal-park purposes, to provide additional opportunities for outdoor recreation, including public camping, fishing, hunting, boating, winter sports, and, wherever possible, to also serve multiple purposes, involving the conservation and development of natural resources, the preservation of scenic areas, watershed protection, forestry, and reforestation: $15 million.

3. For state aid in the amount of 75 percent of the cost of acquisition of land for parks by cities other than the city of New York, or by improvement districts within cities other than the city of New York: $12 million.

4. For state aid in the amount of 75 percent of the cost of acquisition of land for parks by the city of New York, or by improvement districts therein: $12 million.

5. For state aid in the amount of 75 percent of the cost of acquisition of land for parks by counties, towns, and villages, or by improvement districts therein: $16 million.

Time is lacking today to discuss all the thought and study which went into the allocation of funds. However, I should like to make a special comment on the allocation of a total of $40 million for aid to our political subdivisions. We believe that this was an extremely wise provision because our outdoor recreation problems have become intensely critical in many urban and suburban areas, in many towns which are heavily populated, and indeed in some of our counties which have become thickly populated since World War II.

For those municipalities which have already made advance recreation plans, this state aid will provide the means for them to get under way without delay. To those who, for one reason or another, have failed to do a good job of planning, this aid will provide a powerful stimulus which will have a very great and immediate effect in many cases.

After it had been decided how much money should be devoted under the bond issue to land acquisition by municipalities, of course it was necessary to acquaint these municipalities with the mechanisms which they would have to use in order to avail themselves of this state support. Accordingly, we prepared a small, simple brochure which folded out into a single large sheet. On one side were the proposition and enabling legislation in detail, with a summary of their provisions. On the other side was outlined the series of steps which any municipality (from a village on up through counties to the largest cities including New York City) should follow in order to obtain state financial assistance in the amount of 75 percent of the actual cost of land to be acquired. Aside from acquainting the municipalities with these mechanisms, of course the brochure served another useful purpose. As it was distributed in very large quantities during the late summer before the referendum came to a vote, it made every municipal officer in New York State aware of the program, so that they and the voters of their communities could use intelligent judgment in their vote on the referendum.

State Pay-As-You-Go Policy

I think one more point is worth mentioning, because of the way it ties in to Governor Rockefeller's whole financial policy of the state of New York. We work in general on a pay-as-you-go basis. One of the most courageous steps taken early in the present administration was to increase state income taxes sufficiently to put the state "in the black" and to give us a little working capital to build up the state's resources.

In the various fields of conservation, the results have already been astoundingly progressive. We have been able to bring inadequate programs up to the standards demanded by current conditions. We have stepped up work in forestry, and are embarking upon an expanded and very progressive program of water-resources administration. In the particular field of recreation, this year we not only have increased staffing of the operation of existing facilities, but we also have approximately $10 million of capital construction funds allocated to the building of new recreation facilities. All of this is pay-as-you-go, to meet current demands of an expanding population for the various resources administered by the Conservation Department. Without the governor's tax program, this kind of progressive, imaginative development could not have been possible.

You may say that a $75 million bond issue is not pay-as-you-go. Of course it is not. But everyone will recognize that it is sound business to borrow money in order to purchase land which otherwise would become prohibitive in price within a very few years, or even disappear completely through conversion to suburban or industrial sites rather than parks and recreation facilities. And, of course, the bond issue will be paid off, using the income from park and recreation facilities owned by the state. Except for slowly increasing fees, this source of money does not represent new income to the state. But it does employ the very sound socio-economic philosophy of asking those who receive a benefit to help pay for it.

CHALLENGE OF THE FUTURE

This, then, is a brief rundown on our outdoor recreation problem and steps we are taking to meet it. I should like to close by emphasizing something which I know is already understood by most of you. This is that those of us who are professional conservationists have probably never faced a challenge of such magnitude as the one which is posed by the nation's present and future outdoor recreation needs. As our governor remarked in one of his talks on this subject, "Future generations are at the mercy of those of us who carry these responsibilities today. In the interest of our state and our nation—we cannot afford to fail them."

Multiple-Use Planning in National Forest Management

EDWARD P. CLIFF

Sixty-four years ago a law was enacted. Eight years later a letter was written. From this combination, the Organic Act of 1897 and the Secretary of Agriculture's letter of instruction to Chief Forester Gifford Pinchot, national forest multiple-use management was born.

The Organic Act stated a purpose: to protect and improve the forests and to secure favorable conditions of water flow. But the door was left ajar for other values by these words: "The Secretary will make rules and regulations . . . to regulate occupancy and use." The inference was that other uses were to be considered and enjoyed. Interest at the time may have weighed heavily in favor of water and timber, but uncertainties of the future dictated a broader land-use policy.

Secretary James Wilson's letter in 1905, sent to Gifford Pinchot, chief of the newly organized Forest Service, expanded opportunity for other uses and included social as well as economic values. Concern for the future was also indicated. One sentence from the letter has been remembered above all others, and has been a guiding principle in management of national forests for the past 56 years. That sentence is, "In the management of each reserve, local questions will be decided upon local grounds; the dominant industry will be considered first, but with as little restriction to minor industries as may be possible; sudden changes in industrial conditions will be avoided by gradual adjustments after due notice; and where conflicting interests must be reconciled the question will always be decided from the standpoint of the greatest good of the greatest number in the long run."

As revolutionary as this might have sounded in 1905, "greatest

---

Edward P. Cliff on March 17, 1962, became chief of the U.S. Forest Service. When he delivered this paper, Cliff had been assistant chief of the service for 10 years, in charge of management divisions which handle the timber, watershed, range, wildlife, and recreation activities on all the national forests. He entered the Service in 1931 and held a variety of posts in the West before being assigned to the Washington office.

good of the greatest number in the long run" was not a new principle. It had its roots in the 18th century English philosophy of utilitarianism which had profound effect upon political, social, and economic reform in 19th century England and later in the United States. The beginning of utilitarianism is found in the writings of Bishop Cumberland in 1672. In 1720 Francis Hutcheson introduced the thought that the criterion of right action is its tendency to promote the general welfare and "that action is best which procures the greatest happiness for the greatest numbers." In 1817 David Ricardo worked out "the laws by which wages are regulated and by which the happiness of the greatest part of every community is governed." The doctrine of utilitarianism was popularized and brought to public attention by Jeremy Bentham. Later this philosophy was interpreted by John Stuart Mill, who set up a standard for happiness or good grounded on the permanent interest of man as a progressive being: "Good is to be judged solely on its probable consequences in relation to its anticipated results." Here are the ancestors of Secretary Wilson's "greatest good of the greatest number."[1]

Thus, it is evident that the philosophy appropriated by Gifford Pinchot in 1905 had its origin in Restoration England. Propounded by Bishop Cumberland, polished and popularized by Jeremy Bentham, and perfected by John Stuart Mill, this precept is now being perpetuated by the Forest Service in its concept of multiple-use management of the national forests. It is a cardinal criterion that guides decisions, choices, and judgments.

DEVELOPMENT OF MULTIPLE-USE PLANNING

Only in recent years has the phrase "multiple use" been applied to land-use planning. Principles of multiple use, however, have been practiced in resource and land management since 1905.

In 1910, Treadwell Cleveland, Jr., in his paper, *National Forests as Recreation Grounds,* said, "National Forests form as a whole by far the greatest national recreation grounds in the world. As forests are opened up progressively by more intensive economic use, they will become more attractive, more convenient and more accessible."[2]

In 1917, F. A. Waugh, a landscape architect, was commissioned by the Forest Service to make an extensive field examination and re-

---

[1]Richard Cumberland, *De Legibus Naturae* (1672); Francis Hutcheson, *Inquiry Concerning Good and Evil* (1720); Jeremy Bentham, *Principles of Morals and Legislation* (1789); David Ricardo, *Principles of Economics and Taxation* (1817); John Stuart Mill, *Essay on Liberty* (1859).
[2]Unpublished report.

port on recreation conditions. His description of the Forest Service processes he observed amounted to an early definition of what we now call multiple use. "For each particular case these utilities (uses) are weighed against one another and a plan of administration devised to adjust and harmonize, to the utmost point practicable, the various forms of use so that the largest net total of public good may be secured. When one must be subordinated to another, preference is given to that of highest value to the public." In 1918 he quoted a policy statement, "On the principal areas of the national forests, recreation is an incidental use; on some it is a paramount use; on a few it becomes the exclusive use."[3]

The Chief of the Forest Service referred to the importance of growing recreation use in his report of 1919 by saying, "The forests must be handled with full recognition of their recreational values, present and future. . . ." In his 1924 report the chief stated, "As a matter of fact, the most unsentimental inventory of the National Forests would have to set down recreational assets as scarcely less valuable than their economic resources."

Livestock grazing was well established before the national forests were created and since then has been recognized by administrative policy, by numerous appropriation acts, and by the Granger-Thye Act of 1950 as one of the important uses.

Over the years wildlife has received consideration along with all other renewable resources. Such early statements of policy as "National forest management contemplates production of the largest wildlife population consistent with use and needs of other resources and permanent food supply of animals, birds and fish. . . ." indicate awareness of the importance of wildlife in multiple-use management.

And so there is little really new about the multiple-use concept. What is new is the growing intensity of planning and application dictated by a rapidly expanding population and man's hunger for the essentials and amenities which can be made available on national forests.

In the 1930's, multiple-purpose land-use planning was under way in several national forest regions. Ten years later there was growing interest in formal planning and application, particularly on national forests adjacent to large population centers. Terminology varied: "integrated resource plans," "integrated land use plans," or "national forest land-management plans," were common titles. All referred to a

---

[3]F. A. Waugh, *Recreation Uses on the National Forests* (Government Printing Office, 1918).

system of management which considered using wild land for as many different purposes as reasonably possible and in compatible combinations. To coordinate effort and standardize terminology, the practice is now officially called "national forest multiple-use management."

Statutory Basis for Multiple Use

On June 12, 1960, the 86th Congress enacted Public Law 86-517, better known as the "Multiple Use-Sustained Yield Act." To some, it was a panacea for all the resource ills of the national forests; to others a device out of Dante's Inferno created to destroy esthetic and cultural values of primeval forests. It was well received in Congress and has been acclaimed by most people interested in the management of the national forests.

There were four basic reasons for enactment of this law:

1. There was need for statutory authority for multiple use which previously had been recognized only as a matter of administrative policy.
2. There was need for a similar directive for sustained yield which had also been in a policy status.
3. Several resources and services previously had never been named in basic legislation. It was considered logical and desirable to name all renewable resources and services in a single statute.
4. Multiple-use legislation was a natural component of Operation Multiple Use, the Secretary of Agriculture's "Program for the National Forests" sent to Congress in 1959.

Over many years a number of congressional enactments, appropriation language, court decisions, and statements had firmly given the implication that national forests were to be administered under the principle of multiple use. Since application had been established for over 50 years, it was considered timely for legislation clearly to specify authority and responsibility.

THE MULTIPLE-USE PLANNING PROCESS

The Multiple Use-Sustained Yield Act names the resources to be managed—recreation, range, timber, watershed, wildlife, and fish—but no priorities are designated. The purposes of the act are declared to be supplemental to, but not in derogation of, the purposes for which the national forests were established. The law directs that all resources be given equal consideration, but values should vary for particular areas. In application, relative values would be assigned resources for particular areas, but not necessarily in combinations which would give the greatest dollar return or the greatest unit output.

Since resource priorities are not specified by the act, the responsibility for determining and assigning priorities for particular areas rests with the Forest Service. This presents the problem of developing criteria to guide choices involving both materialistic and nonmaterialistic values, as both are recognized in the law. The number of uses of the same land which constitutes multiple use and the size of particular areas for planning and application also are not specified in the act. Because watershed values are inherent on all national forest lands, and basic policy requires that all national forest activities be managed to maintain or improve watershed values, current policy states that it takes more than two uses to constitute multiple use—watershed use and at least two others. These various uses need not occur on each acre of land but would be included in the program for a larger management area such as a national forest or a ranger district. The ranger district has been designated as the basic planning unit.

Determining key resource values and the desired combination of uses for particular areas is the most exacting task of a planner. Sound multiple-use policy and decisions can be developed from facts, valid assumption, thorough analysis, and logical conclusions. A planner must maintain objectivity. He is usually confronted by a variety of choices requiring professional knowledge of ecological factors—soil, water, vegetation, and climate—and the complex interrelationship of animal life, including people. Values subject to mathematical measurement frequently must be compared with, or weighed against, those which can be appraised only by judgment. Bridging the gap between the materialistic and nonmaterialistic worlds is a judgment process. It demands awareness and understanding of the culture in which we live, sensitivity to public needs, wants, and the economic and social values people currently place on resources and services.

Since management objectives are directed toward both economic and social goals, the bridge between the world of economic-natural sciences and the world of amenities must be crossed. Crossing this bridge presents many dilemmas, because lines are not clearly drawn. Any choice of values must be interpreted in terms of social and economic standards at a particular time. To illustrate—our culture is one of abundance, so recreation ranks high. In an economy of scarcity, recreation would rank much lower. During a national emergency or disaster, all values would change sharply.

In the process of analysis and evaluation to determine choice of combinations, data concerning each of the resources and management factors must be reviewed broadly and summarized concisely. It is of utmost importance that these summaries be correct and adequate, for conclusions, assumptions, and management direction based upon them are the source and support for multiple-use management decisions.

Analyzing basic data for a planning area consists of ascertaining what resources, uses, and site suitabilities exist, and what kinds and amounts of public needs, both current and anticipated, relate to these resources, uses, and suitabilities.

National Policy and Goals

In establishing national policy and goals, the Forest Service draws on information from such studies as the Timber Resources Review, the National Forest Recreation Survey, the water resources studies of congressional committees and others working in this field, and population projections by the Bureau of the Census. Regional guidelines and goals are based on more localized data and projections pertaining to each region. Forest and ranger-district planning is accomplished within the framework of national and regional policy and goals but is also based on analysis of the local resources and needs. Timber inventories, soil and water surveys, game surveys conducted in cooperation with wildlife agencies, range analysis data, recreation surveys, and all other sources of information bearing on local resource management situations are considered.

Evaluation consists of weighing all factors to arrive at judgments as to: (a) relative values in terms of human welfare of the various resources and uses; and (b) the combination and patterns of uses which will best meet public needs by giving desirable emphasis to various resources and making the land most productive.

The principal factors or criteria which are considered when making judgments and choices are:

1. Compliance with applicable laws and regulations.
2. National programs and goals.
3. Compatibility of various resource and use developments to each other and to broad objectives for the area.
4. Suitability of the land for a particular use or combination of uses.
5. Maintenance of land productivity.
6. Intangible as well as tangible values; social as well as economic factors.
7. Future and current public needs or desires for particular resources or areas.
8. Feasible opportunities to integrate orderly development of several resources and to place emphasis in accordance with specific objectives.
9. Professional knowledge, research findings, and experience, as they relate to particular resources.
10. Public attitudes, local economy, legislative climate.
11. Programs and activities of other agencies.

There are more factors. All must be considered in the analysis, but usually only a few are pertinent in a particular situation. One factor is rarely conclusive in itself. Choices are not usually black or white—yes or no—but rather a selection of alternative ways of doing things. In multiple-use planning there is no substitute for sound judgment. It would be a mistake to depend solely on formulas, equations, or built-in weights. All serve as a basis for the judgment process. Weighting is a value judgment itself and should be left to the man who has the decision to make at the time he must make it, preferably during planning. His knowledge, experience, insight, and awareness of local economic and social conditions become a part of the analytic process giving substance to decisions.

Multiple-use management planning for national forests is comparable to land-use planning of any kind. However, it differs in some respects because it deals with wild land in public ownership. Many features are adaptable to private land of similar character or to land controlled by other public agencies. Variations stem chiefly from the owner's or administrator's management objectives. As an example, the primary objective of an industrial owner of forest land is to grow timber for commercial use. The owner may be willing to permit fishing and hunting or other forms of recreation, but timber always receives top billing. On similar forest land in public ownership, the objectives of management would probably be quite different, and the weight given to various uses and combinations of uses would likewise differ.

Forest officers at all levels of administration participate in developing multiple-use plans for the national forests. At the national level, authorities and responsibilities are translated from law and delegated to national forest regions. Over-all national policies and goals are established. Manuals and handbooks provide guides for use within and between regions.

Regional Guides

At the regional level, more specific policies known as regional guides are prepared within national policy. They provide the framework within which ranger-district multiple-use plans are prepared. These guides may be designed for an entire region or for sub-regions, depending on similarity or disparity of conditions. As an example, southern California has been designated as a sub-region of the California region because it is so completely different from any other area in the state.

An informal system of land classification then comes into play. Homogeneous areas in which a paramount resource value or values can be recognized are identified, named, and described—but not precisely delineated. These areas vary in size. They may be continuous irregular belts or intermingled parcels of land. General management objectives and multiple-use policies are prepared by areas as guides for planning on the national forests and in ranger districts.

Designation of areas is important because it says in effect that certain resources generally have priority within the area, and in the management of other resources, nothing will be done which will be sharply detrimental to the key value or values. This does not mean that only subordinate resources will be modified—it may be necessary to modify all resources in some degree to attain the optimum combination of uses. For example, to enjoy full use of a municipal watershed where water is the priority value, recreation use and facilities may be modified in many respects so as to preserve water quality, but the community may have to accept lower-quality water and compensate by installing a filtration plant in order to enjoy the benefits of recreation on the watershed. Timber may be the key resource in a heavy stand of commercial timber; but under our system of management, timber culture is commonly modified to accommodate recreation and wildlife and to enhance water yield.

Determination of priorities does not signify exclusive use. It considers full multiple use to the extent possible, recognizing natural limitations inherent in any area.

Decisions in which one resource is favored over another are not always as critical as might appear. Should policy be that of single use, comparable to urban land-use planning, decisions might be harsh indeed. As an example, consider the apparent problem of favoring recreation over timber in recreation areas. In the Rocky Mountain region we have projected public needs for timber and recreation until the year 2000. The recently completed recreation survey and inventory indicate we can meet recreation requirements for camping, picnic areas, swimming sites, boating sites, summer homes, resorts, organization camps, and ski areas on the national forests of the Rocky Mountain region on about 2 percent of the land. Considering that this relatively small amount of land is not all forested, and that it is often necessary to harvest timber in recreation areas to maintain a healthy stand of trees, the decision is not particularly critical. District rangers or recreation specialists determine the desired landscape to be maintained within recreation areas, and timber specialists use their skill, experience, and knowledge to provide the desired recreation landscape. Some areas will be opened up to let in sunlight or provide space for facilities. Others will require protection from winds. Still others will need insect-risk and sanitation cutting to maintain timber vigor and thrift. Fully developed recreation areas may actually provide greater net growth than some timber stands not planned for harvest for many years.

When one old tree dies in a virgin forest, net growth may be canceled out on several acres for several years. In recreation areas these veteran, high-risk trees are usually removed as a safety measure. Dense stands of trees often must be thinned in campgrounds to provide public access. The remaining trees grow more rapidly with less competition for sunlight, water, and soil nutrients. Frequently reforestation is necessary to increase tree density or provide screening. The "social forests" in France, located adjacent to villages or towns, have been managed successfully for recreation and timber for generations.

Some combinations of resource uses naturally work well together, and only moderate effort is required to obtain harmonious management. To illustrate, clear-cutting in strips or blocks in even-aged timber stands increases water yield and improves big-game habitat. Other combinations are more difficult and require careful planning and greater supervision to prevent conflict. An example would be patch-clear-cutting near recreation areas wherein natural vistas are modified by silvicultural practices. Some recreationists vigorously oppose any form of timber cutting where the natural landscape is changed.

Putting Plans to Work

The ranger district is the administrative unit of execution. District multiple-use plans do not state policy. They contain management decisions which state how, where, and when policy guidelines will be carried out. Planning areas are more precisely delineated on large-scale maps, but they are not marked on the ground until plans are applied in the field.

A district ranger usually subdivides generalized areas into smaller units so that he can prescribe management decisions or coordinating requirements more precisely. The number of units on a ranger district is governed by differences in multiple-use complexities and need for intensive management. An example of this is an area where a combination of big-game use, timber harvesting, and livestock grazing in a key wildlife winter range requires intensive management. And so a unit would be delineated to enable the manager to quickly relate coordinating management decisions to this particular area.

Multiple-use decisions are spelled out guiding management of each resource within each unit to harmonize and improve multiple use. The coordinating decisions are then written into the appropriate functional plans. Specific prescriptions, jobs, and specifications are incorporated in project plans, contracts, and special-use permits.

A sheepherder might not know why he must avoid a newly reforested burn; a logger might not know why his contract requires him to windrow slash on a particular aspen timber sale or to chip slash or dispose of cull logs in a recreation area. But the tasks get done under close supervision of forest officers who are guided by requirements in the district multiple-use plan.

Our continued existence requires that we keep our natural environment productive of the essentials of life. An expanding population puts increasing pressure upon living space. An advancing technology uses up resources in increasing quantities. And last, outdoor recreation, with all its variations and opportunities, is a cherished and established requirement of American society. We in the Forest Service believe that multiple use offers the best hope of stretching the resources of a shrinking land base to meet the expanding needs of our people.

Resource Use and Metropolitan Sprawl

DE WITT NELSON

The dodo bird is dead. We cannot bury him for he is too long gone. We cannot praise him for we know so little of him. We have lost our opportunity to become acquainted with the dodo. It may seem that knowledge of him and his place in his environment is of small magnitude. That may be true; I do not know.

One would think this strange, awkward creature could have little bearing on our way of life. Yet acquaintance with the dodo might have contributed vastly to our lives, to our culture, and to our advancement. Another strange, eerie creature—the bat—has been of great value. Research on bats and their habits had been neglected until recent years. One important researcher was considered "bats" or, perhaps, "a dodo" for his interest in them. Yet study of the unusual navigating abilities of bats has contributed greatly to the rapid development of radar and like systems of non-visual navigation. And further knowledge of the methods of bats shows promise of contributing a means by which blind men may "see" with their ears. Had bats suffered the fate of the dodo, this facet of human advancement might have come more slowly or might not have come at all.

I do not pretend that the demise of the dodo can be charged directly to urban sprawl. Yet in a larger sense it can. For the dodo fell prey to man—to man, the social animal. What are we, at this time, losing from the vast potential of man's well-being and knowledge when the natural balance of our basic resources is disturbed by the sprawling monster of urbanization?

GROWTH OF URBANIZATION

Urbanization is not a new phenomenon, nor is it confined to man. The ants have their hills, the bees their hives, the birds their rookeries. Lewis Mumford, in his *Natural History of Urbanization*, traces its hu-

DeWitt Nelson is Director of the Department of Natural Resources, State of California. From 1925 to 1944, Nelson was a member of the U.S. Forest Service serving on many western forests and acting for two years as Civilian Conservation Corps liaison officer for the Ninth Corps Area, headquartered in San Francisco. In 1945 he was appointed State Forester of California and in 1953 he was appointed to his present post.

man origin to the gathering of men in caves to practice prehistoric magic rites. Certainly the Swiss Lake Dwellers and the American Pueblo Indians were urbanized. Ancient Rome had, at its peak, a population greater than present-day San Francisco, and there were many other ancient cities that could vie in population with our medium-sized ones.

Villages and Towns

In tracing the course of urbanization, one may discern five phases: the growth of the village, of the town, of the city, of suburbia, and the development of what has been termed "conurbia."

Simplest and generally smallest was the village. It was essentially a collection of farmers whose houses were grouped together. The limits of the village and the limits of its growth were directly controlled by the land and water about it: by what the land would grow and by the amount of usable water. Thirty years ago, four-fifths of the persons on this globe lived in these simple villages. Even in such densely populated regions as India, fully 90 percent of the people were village dwellers as late as 1940.

The town was primarily organized as a service area for farmers. The growth of the town, like that of the village, was also controlled by the land—by the available water and food supply within reasonable access.

Transportation Brings Cities

New means of transportation allowed the city to be born of the town. The city was able to extend its domination far beyond its agricultural hinterland, as it took its impetus from new large-scale sea and inland-water transport and from the construction of roads for horse-drawn wagons.

It is sometimes said that the city is the product of the industrial revolution. I will not argue it. But certainly the great population centers of the ancient world—Rome, Carthage, Alexandria—were large and populous enough to qualify them as cities, and certainly they utilized rapid methods of transport. The vast highway system of Rome is said to have destroyed the surrounding lands by accelerating erosion; the aqueducts so necessary to provide water gathered the natural run-off for many miles, parching the surrounding terrain; the public bath denuded the forests for fuel.

Some observers have claimed that the downfall of Rome, as well as the downfall of other ancient cities, including some of those within the New World, is directly traceable to the limit of the water supply.

When population and industry became so large that the demand for water exceeded the supply, the city was doomed. If this is true, we are fortunate that we can now develop water supplies and transport that precious commodity many miles to its point of use. Eventually, the conversion of sea water will augment local supplies for purposes other than agriculture.

Rise of Suburbia

A more modern thread in the pattern of urbanization is the emergence of "suburbia" as a significant force. Here in the United States, two types of suburbs have developed: the industrial suburb, relying on inexpensive land, adequate water supply, and cheap, speedy transportation of raw materials; and the "dormitory" or "bedroom" suburb, mainly dependent upon quick and easy transportation.

The industrial revolution was responsible for both. Industry itself developed the industrial suburb; we are all—or were, in our childhood—familiar with the mill town, the railroad town, the abattoir ("butcher town" or "slaughter town" we called them), or the steel town. In 1881, Andrew Carnegie moved his Bessemer steel plant from the metropolis to the suburbs—to Homestead, seven miles up the Monongahela from Pittsburgh. Granite City, outside St. Louis, was founded to house a granite-ware industry. Gary, Indiana, was created by the United States Steel Corporation. The little farming community of Hamtramck, in Michigan, was transformed when the Dodge Motor plant was located there; in the first decade of this century it had increased to thirteen times its original population, and today it is a city within the city of Detroit.

A famous community in my state has also mushroomed in the same fashion. In 1911, a motion picture was produced in a sunny temperance colony called Hollywood, a suburb of Los Angeles. Today Hollywood is engulfed by Los Angeles, although in some ways Hollywood engulfs the world.

As the English writer Dan Jacobson puts it in his *No Further West:*

> It is an ironic thought that the same industrialism which was responsible for the sudden massive development of cities in every industrialized society in the world is now—in California at least—offering the first real threat to the predominance of the cities.[1]

The most spectacular change in the past two decades has been the tremendous increase in the size of our "dormitory" or "bedroom" suburbs. One of the first bedroom communities to develop in this

---

[1]Dan Jacobson, *No Further West* (London: Weidenfeld and Nicolson, 1957), p. 57.

country was the town of Old Greenwich, Connecticut, where in 1850, a handful of hardy businessmen commuters jumped from the train as it slowed to cross a bridge.

The bedroom suburb was virtually the exclusive reserve of businessmen, the wealthy, and others on their own time schedule until the eight-hour day for most workers became a reality. Shorter work hours, coupled with speedier transportation, enabled the great bulk of the American middle class to move into the suburbs if they so wished.

The great bloating of suburbia in the past two decades is due to these two factors—better transportation and increased time—as well as two others of nearly equal importance: the spiraling of population and the decline of the central city.

Population Growth Brings Conurbia

No one knows for certain how rapidly the population of the world is increasing. Estimates vary with the investigator, but there is little doubt but that the population of the world has doubled in the last century. Dr. Glenn Seaborg has reminded us that, at our present rate of increase, in 1,000 years the earth will have standing room only! In California, the population in 1940 was 7,000,000; this has risen to a present total of over 16,000,000. In ten years it is expected to reach 23,000,000. California's population increase has been the most spectacular, but almost all of the 50 states have had an increase in population in the past score of years. This is due in large measure to what has been called the "unexpected fertility" of this generation of Americans.

Whatever the reason for the population increase, the fact remains and the result is the yeast-like expansion of the bedroom suburb out and beyond the central city. This new pattern of expansion—the pattern of farther and farther out—has given rise to a new type of urbanization.

When this pattern is repeated from several centers all active simultaneously, the result is the fusing of the suburbs of two or more cities until the entire urban mass becomes almost indistinguishable as individual units. Patrick Geddes observed this method of growth at work in Britain and termed the new urbanic mass "conurbia."

Los Angeles County today presents the aspect of a conurbia. One might make out a very good case for considering the entire seacoast from Boston to Washington and the urban reaches from New York to Philadelphia as virtual conurbias.

By 1980, it is anticipated that in California there will be one massive conurbia extending about San Francisco for a radius of 75 miles until it coalesces to the east with that from Sacramento, to form a still greater conurbia. Los Angeles, it is believed, will connect (as it nearly does now) with San Diego on the south and Santa Barbara on the north, making the whole south coastal plain and seacoast one megalopolis.

EFFECTS OF URBANIZATION ON NATURAL RESOURCES

What has the creation of this conurbian monster done to us? Are our large cities, like New York and Philadelphia, which are presently competing for the same water supply, or Los Angeles, competing for its water supply with the entire state of Arizona and with northern California, nearing the limits of their expansion, if not plotting their own doom?

Water, Air Pollution

How does urbanization affect the land, the water, and the air we must have for survival? Just as the village and the town were dependent upon the water and land about them, so our modern urbias, suburbias, and conurbias are dependent upon the natural resources they can command. It is true that modern methods of transportation have brought the resources of the whole world to our doorsteps, yet there are certain basic resources upon which we must depend and which we dare not squander.

In the process of urbanization, we have polluted the water and the air that sustains life. We have dimmed the sun with our waste.

Pollution of the air has long been an effect of urbanization and a cause of suburban spread. As early as 1661 one John Evelyn was proposing a method of curbing "the inconvenience of the aer and smoake of London."

Pollution of the water supply is another obvious result of overuse and carelessness. Rome drained its sewers into the Tiber. Two thousand years later, with all our modern knowledge of bacteriology, with all our urgent need for clean water, and with our American love of plumbing, we have not yet ceased to dump raw sewage into rivers and bays. Our newspapers and magazines daily reflect the concern of all of us for obtaining an adequate water supply and for decreasing the pollution of our water and air. Other speakers will deal more fully with this.

Loss of Agricultural Land

Less widely publicized is what is happening to the land itself. What is the impact upon those natural resources which are closely tied to mother earth and upon which the basic economy of our cities depends?

It is in this area that use and misuse of our natural resources must be more clearly defined, that advance planning must be implemented, if we are to achieve a proper balance between resource availability and metropolitan development, the city-farm balance. We must conserve these resources, using them wisely and well.

In California, one of our major problems is the engulfment of prime agricultural land by suburbia. Each day some 375 acres of our best soils are being taken out of production. About 140,000 acres annually are being converted to nonagricultural use. These losses have a serious effect on the whole nation, for California produces a number of crops that do not grow satisfactorily in other places. She produces the major portion or all of the nation's almonds, walnuts, dates, plums, prunes, apricots, avocados, peaches for canning, lemons, figs, wine grapes, early table grapes, olives, and artichokes. As each acre of these crops is taken from production, the state and the nation suffer a serious economic loss. The problem is not indigenous to any one state. As one travels over the country one sees this encroachment taking place around all of our cities. If this attrition of agricultural land continues in California, it is estimated that almost 3,000,000 additional acres will have been removed from agricultural production by 1980. It should be noted that, of California's 16,000,000 acres of land suitable for intensive agriculture, only about 6,000,000 acres are Class I and Class II soils.

At the present time many communities are sprawling by "shotgun" or "leap-frog" developments that not only take land directly out of farm use but also commit additional land to urban development. The great mobility of our population and the desire for "country living" have stimulated this practice. But this open-space environment is soon lost as the gaps are filled in by the horizontal growth of the city. Through this method the farmer can be forced to sell his prime land because of high taxes resulting from assessment according to its potential urban value, which increases as subdivisions sprawl into the area.

As stated by Elton R. Andrews, Planning Officer, State of California,

No responsible analyst believes that all of our prime farm land can be preserved. Most believe a vastly greater amount could be preserved if suitable metropolitan land policies were adopted. Not only would such land policies help to preserve agricultural land, they would also help preserve recreational open space adjacent to and within the metropolitan areas. This, in turn, would have a bearing upon our ability to solve problems of air pollution.[2]

Need for Planned Urban Growth

John E. Carr, Director of Finance, State of California, recently said that we need "civic birth control." Every city wants to get bigger and bigger.

At the outset each city, new or growing, should determine what kind of a city it wants to become. That is the time to plan. That is the time to zone for the various elements, which in combination make a city—business and residential areas, schools, parks, playgrounds, light industry, heavy industry, water supply, sewer systems, transportation, and communications. We must have planning, both short-range and long-range.

Physical planning and economic development go hand-in-hand. As our population grows, so must our job opportunities grow. Industry is looking for new features that were not considered 50 or even 25 years ago. The labor force of today is much more sophisticated. They want a decent neighborhood in which to raise their families; they want readily available week-end recreational opportunities, good schools, and comfortable homes not too far from their point of employment. Industries are looking for this combination, coupled with a healthy economic climate in communities that have demonstrated their fiscal responsibility.

Governments must examine themselves. In California we have 58 counties, 370 cities, and about 3,000 special-purpose districts, besides nearly 2,000 school districts, each serving local government. At a recent meeting in Washington, D. C., mayors of cities all over the world were in unanimous agreement that this elephantiasis of the urban areas demands a cure. Urban areas have outgrown effective local government, and they have spilled over into a class of small cities with multipurpose and single-purpose assessment districts. As a consequence, there are many legislative bodies where one would do, many fire chiefs and police departments where one would do, multiple water and sewer systems where one would serve better. These barriers to orderly, well-planned growth will be most difficult to remove. This problem is being studied by all levels of government, and certainly solutions will be evolved. The present "stop-gap" method results only in further splintering of government and pyramiding of taxes.

These problems and possible solutions are only examples of the

---

[2]Governor's Commission on Metropolitan Area Problems, *Metropolitan California* (Sacramento, 1961), p. 76.

complex job ahead. Probably the greatest task of all is to convince the proper authorities that complete planning is essential and, when once the plan is built, to see that it is implemented intelligently. No plan can remain static. It must be flexible and adaptable to change, but each change should be for the better.

Pressure on Forests

Let us look at some of the resources other than land that fit into the fabric of present-day living: our forests, minerals, wildlife, and wild-land recreation. They are not only a part of our economy but also an important factor in our social and family life.

The demand for forest products—lumber, plywood, particle board, and pulp products—continues to grow. The forests are being squeezed from all sides. Urban development, along with highways, power lines, reservoirs, and recreational development, is encroaching on many of our forest areas. It is predicted that 78,000,000 acres of commercial forest land will fall prey to such uses throughout the nation by the year 2000.

As our urban and industrial areas expand, more forest products will be needed. We must learn how to grow more trees per acre in a shorter period of time, and technicians must continue to develop more efficient methods for utilizing the whole tree. With our ever-improving methods of packaging and in this era of memoranda and carbon copies, our civilization is surely tied to the forest. Yet the forester is like the farmer except that his crop takes many years to grow and involves long-term risks of fire, insects, and disease. Under these conditions he cannot stand heavy tax burdens. Like the farmer, he too may be forced to liquidate this prime asset or dispose of it for other than forest production. The impact of taxes resulting from greater demands on the land by a growing population, both urban and rural, is being seriously felt by the timber producer.

Our forests are a reproducible resource, but if they are to meet the demands of the future they must be managed like any other crop, and a major proportion of them must be protected from encroachment. If this is to be accomplished, we must apply the principle of multiple use, not only on the public forests but also on those in private ownership.

Our watersheds, the keystone in our present water supplies, are falling prey to urbanization, through the development of highways, reservoirs, communities, recreation areas, and power facilities. As use spreads into these areas, the threat to denudation by fire increases. The effectiveness of a watershed is also lessened by the construction of roofs, pavement, and other compacted areas where fast runoff is encouraged and percolation into the soil is prevented.

Our wildlife are facing a similar, though in some ways more critical, dilemma. We give little thought to tearing up the "weeds" as we are likely to call them, to filling the marshes, or to draining the swamps. Yet each of these provides a habitat for wildlife. And each of them may consist of a rare—perhaps a very valuable—ecologic community.

Some living things survive better near civilization. From his hilltop, the coyote may be watching with anticipation the growth of the suburbs, for he grows fat on the kitchen middens of the towns. But others do not; they, like the dodo, are driven to extinction. Yet all of them are a part of our natural resources. We need them for the training of young scientists, if for no other reason. We must have natural laboratories in which our students can work; we must retain them in some measure for our scientists to study. Already, many of them are nearing the fate of the dodo.

As our communities grow and people are forced to live in more congested areas the demand for outdoor recreation increases. In fact, this demand is increasing at a more rapid rate than the population.

Outdoor Recreation Resources

California recently completed and published a report on Public Outdoor Recreation. Other states have made similar studies, as we have heard from Commissioner Wilm, and the Outdoor Recreation Resources Review Commission is currently studying the problem on a national scale.

Because there is a definite relationship between metropolitan growth and the need for outdoor recreation opportunities, it is appropriate that we review some of the findings of our study. Other reports I have read on the subject indicate that the problems are common to all in varying degrees.

This is an area in which long-range planning and strong financing by every level of government are essential. The problem of identifying the recreation responsibilties of each level of government and the coordination of all agencies in order to avoid duplication and gaps is of major significance. Leadership in this field from federal and state levels is of primary importance. Each year choice recreation lands are being lost for lack of planning, financing, and coordination. Even though the need for recreational opportunities is receiving greater attention, the competition for the public dollar denies adequate implementation of planning.

In the field of recreation there is urgent need for master planning in conjunction with all special-purpose plans, whether they be community, metropolitan, highway, industrial, or other. Special-purpose plans must be integrated in order to avoid serious conflicts in future development, as the following examples from our study indicate.

1. Nearly 50 percent of the automobile passenger miles traveled in California are for recreation and sight-seeing purposes. Surely this indicates the need for recognizing certain roads as scenic highways, where special treatment is given to location in order to preserve esthetic values; where adequate turnouts, overlooks, and rest areas are engineered into the original highway design. Highways and freeways are ravenous space-eaters. The smaller highways consume 20 acres per mile, and some of our larger freeways have gobbled up as much as 70 acres per mile.

2. As subdivisions spread and urban areas sprawl, more land should be set aside for open space, playgrounds, and recreation areas. There is great need for both youth and adults to have ready access to such areas. At present land values, developers are prone to ignore this need, and the children must continue to play in the streets.

3. Industry today is moving not only to potential market areas, but also to communities where employees may have pleasant living conditions. Recreation opportunities are a major factor in this selection.

In our studies we have found that *where recreation lands are most needed they are least available—in the metropolitan areas.*

Outdoor recreation is inseparably tied to open space and water. Sixty percent of our recreation activity-days are water-oriented, near rivers, lakes, reservoirs, and seashore. Unfortunately, these areas are in short supply as far as public ownership and public access are concerned. Too frequently there is insufficient upland area at beaches and other water fronts to meet parking, picnicking, and camping needs. This situation appears to prevail across the nation; it is particularly serious on the Atlantic and Pacific seashores.

In analyzing recreation needs in relation to time, income, and mobility, we established four zones of use and responsibility:

Zone I, within the community (two miles or less from the home), and Zone II, an area within about a 40-mile radius of the home represent the "day-use" or one-day round-trip zones within a convenient and economical travel limit.

Zone III recognizes the week-end or short-vacation travel period and rarely reaches beyond a 250-mile radius.

Zone IV reaches out beyond the 250-mile radius for the extended-vacation period.

Because a high percentage of all recreation is on a day-use basis and because most of the people reside in the metropolitan areas, the need for close-in facilities and opportunities becomes obvious. This

again points up the necessity for integrated planning and the build-
ing-in of recreation facilities as a community grows. This need is
being recognized by many communities and states. Pennsylvania, for
one, is planning a state park within a 25-mile radius of each of its
citizens. Other states are moving in a similar direction, but the population and the communities are growing faster than such plans are
being realized.

Minerals Affected by Urban Sprawl

I have not mentioned one class of our basic resources—minerals—
which also find themselves in conflict with the ever-expanding city
perimeters. Today the production of nonmetallic materials—the industrial minerals of limestone, sand, gravel, and gypsum—dominates the
mining activities in many areas. These extractive industries provide
much of the raw materials for housing and industrial projects. For economic reasons, they must be located close to their markets. For esthetic reasons, they are often forced far from the market. When the
latter occurs, the consumer must pay a much higher price. In the case
of sand and gravel, an additional 50-mile haul means adding 75 cents
per yard to the cost.

To meet this problem, some gravel companies, by utilizing screen
plantings and controlling the noise and dust from their plants, have
been able to establish a degree of compatibility with the communities. In other communities they are being tolerated because of their
convenient source of supply. Los Angeles County turned this into an
opportunity. As the gravel quarries are worked out, the county ac-
quires them for land-fill garbage disposal. When they are filled, the
county converts them into playgrounds and recreation areas. But this
may be fraught with the hazard of leaching pollutants into the ground
water supplies. Research is now being conducted on this problem.

URGENT NEED FOR INTELLIGENT PLANNING

Expanding populations and blossoming communities are bound
to have an impact upon our resources. Not only will they demand
more resource production but they will also engulf much of the resources upon which they are dependent. To meet this paradox of
growing need and dwindling supply will require skills in planning;
research and ingenuity in production and utilization methods; a
thorough knowledge and inventory of our resource potential, and a
dedicated leadership in protecting and husbanding both the known
and unknown values that we have.

Down through the ages man has been reckless with resources.

Too often we tamper with nature even though we know her laws can not be repealed. In the words of the late Aldo Leopold, a thoughtful conservationist, "men too wise to tolerate hasty tinkering with our political constitution accept without qualm the most radical amendment to our biotic constitution." Many times, objects and organisms of nature considered to be of little or no value, or of *unknown* value, prove to have great import in the lives of men.

I have circled back to the dodo. Had the creosote bush of our southwestern desert—certainly considered to be a plant of no particular value—been as extinct as the dodo, one of our young scientists could never have discovered that a chemical substance naturally exuded by the stems of the plant can keep oils fresh. And if the goatnut, another scraggly desert shrub, were gone, how then would we know of the power in the wax of its seeds to harden mineral oil? These are small things, but important.

A group of scientists from the University of California, appointed to study problems in the preservation of the scientific and scenic factors of the landscape, put it this way:

> *The most compelling reason for preserving any element of our natural landscape is that we know nothing about it.* Antibiotics, hormone sources, disease repellants, fibers, as well as knowledge that we may apply to other things, are hidden in great abundance in our natural landscape awaiting someone with imagination to discover them.[3]

Just as we should not withhold the best soil from our young farmers, so we should not withhold this laboratory from our young scientists.

Perhaps I have made it sound as if urbanization is all bad. If so, I have given a false impression, for I do not think this is true. I do think, however, that unplanned urban sprawl compounds many of the evils its dwellers seek to escape. The demand for suburbia—the demand for more elbow room, for more fresh air, for morally healthy communities in which to bring up our children—implies that we recognize the evils from which we attempt to escape. And by recognizing them, we have taken a long stride forward.

But if we are to have this elbow room, if we are to maintain ourselves in our high standard of living, if we are to breathe the fresh air, if we are to retain our sense of wonder at the world about us, we must take steps to establish a proper balance between our needs and the resources upon which we depend.

Some workers have suggested that our conurbias adopt a "regional

---

[3] Unpublished report prepared in conjunction with the California Outdoor Recreation Plan.

city" form of government, with plans formulated that take into account not just one city but all which come within the logical geographic confines of the urban mass. In some places, this is already in operation for some special purposes. Marin County, California, though it is not formally organized as a "regional city," has most of the aspects of one. Just this past year it won a "city of the year" award—the first time that award has been presented to an entire county composed of separate communities.

For transportation and certain other civic affairs, we already have in California regional government on an intercounty basis. I am aware also that this system has been used in certain midwestern states to great advantage. Some states have already cooperated on an interstate basis to provide such important special facilities as recreation. But special-area devices, good though they are, are not quite enough. We must move forward with over-all land-use planning on a statewide basis. Such a plan must take the problems I have mentioned, as well as the many others I did not cite, into careful consideration so that the best possible over-all land-use plan may be developed.

We can, of course, never have a final answer. We must have instead a developing framework that can accommodate new uses and new problems as well as old. We must aim high. We must intend to achieve the best. We must aim for a countryside that renews our sense of wonder and for cities of orderliness and beauty. We must, and I quote from a Forest Service Manual of 1905, "use well all the land." Although most of you are familiar with the words of one of our most talented architect-planners, Daniel H. Burnham, I should like to quote them in closing.

> Make no little plans; they have no magic to stir men's blood. . . . Make big plans; aim high in hope and work, remembering that a noble, logical diagram once recorded will never die, but long after we are gone will be a living thing, asserting itself with ever-growing insistency. Remember that our sons and our grandsons are going to do things that would stagger us. Let your watchword be order and your beacon beauty.[4]

---

[4]Quoted in Christopher Cunnard and Henry Hope Reed, *American Skyline* (Mentor, 1956), p. 153.

Columbia River Development: Some Problems of International Cooperation

JOHN V. KRUTILLA

If an international river is to be developed for maximum benefit, the people affected must recognize their common interest in the systematic development of the river and exhibit the maturity and patience needed to resolve conflicts in dividing the gains from cooperation. The problems are similar to those faced on interstate streams where political subdivisions are involved. Because of the importance of the recent Columbia River agreement by the United States and Canada, we take the occasion to examine this recent example of Canadian-United States cooperation.

The Columbia River rises in British Columbia. Its course and those of its tributaries show scant respect for the international border. (See map.) The total fall of the river from its source is about 2,650 feet, a little over half of which is in Canada.

There is virtually no development of the Columbia in Canada, although the head on the lower Kootenay, prior to its confluence with the Columbia, has been developed. In the United States, however,

---

John V. Krutilla is associate director, water resources program, of Resources for the Future, Inc., on whose staff he has served since 1955. From 1952 to 1955 he was an economist with the Tennessee Valley Authority. He has been a consultant to the United States Government, to the United Nations Economic Commissions for Latin America, Asia, and the Far East, and to The Ford Foundation. He has been visiting lecturer at universities in United States and Mexico.

This paper represents a progress report of the continuing research on the international aspects of the development of the Columbia River. Hence many of the data, all of the estimates, and even the conclusions should be regarded as good only to a first approximation, according to the author. He is indebted to John Herbert for assistance in preparing the paper and to Irving K. Fox, Henry Jarrett, and Allen V. Kneese for reviewing and commenting on an earlier draft. The work has benefited greatly from cooperation by members of the International Joint Commission and many of the technical personnel of the water resources agencies of Canada and the United States.

close to 800 feet of the 1,280 feet of head has already been developed, another 360 feet is under development, and the contemplated Wells and Ben Franklin projects will develop virtually the total fall below the border. In fact, in viewing the United States reach of the Columbia and tributary system, the head seems to have been developed disproportionately in relation to the storage. A great deal more storage is required for power as well as flood control. This is partly the result of the "partnership policy," which favored nonfederal expenditures in water-resource development, with the inevitable consequence that storage development was neglected.[1] In addition, many of the principal storage sites in the United States have been involved in a variety of controversies which have not contributed to an orderly development of a system that would keep head and storage developments in approximate economic balance.

It is evident that advantages may come from co-ordinated efforts by the two countries in the development of the Columbia. Initiative for exploring these possibilities was taken by the two governments in 1944, when they referred the task to the International Joint Commission, United States and Canada. The two objectives most germane to our present purpose were specified as follows:

It is desired that the Commission shall determine whether in its judgment further development of the water resources of the river basin would be practicable and in the public interest from the points of view of the two Governments, having in mind (A) domestic water supply and sanitation, (B) navigation, (C) efficient development of water power, (D) the control of floods, (E) the needs of irrigation, and (F) other beneficial public purposes.

In the event that the Commission should find that further works or projects would be feasible and desirable for one or more of the purposes indicated above, it should indicate how the interests on either side of the boundary would be benefited or adversely affected thereby, and should estimate the costs of such works or projects, including indemnification for damage to public and private property and the costs of any remedial works that may be found to be necessary and should indicate how the costs of any projects and the amounts of any resulting damage be apportioned between the two Governments.

An investigation was undertaken by the International Columbia River Engineering Board, which submitted a report to the IJC in

---

[1]See John V. Krutilla and Otto Eckstein, *Multiple Purpose River Development* (Johns Hopkins, 1958), chs. V (especially pp. 161 ff.) and IX, for a discussion of the lack of incentives for nonfederal interests to build adequate storage on the Columbia under partnership arrangements.

March, 1959.[2] While the investigation was extensive, the report must be regarded as preliminary, since it did not meet fully the directives of the 1944 reference.[3] Further analyses by the two governments individually and by joint work groups took care of some of the deficiencies and led to the negotiation of a treaty.

Toward the latter stages of the preparation of the IJC report, the two governments requested a special report from IJC with its recommendations on the principles to be applied in determining:

a) the benefits which will result from the cooperative use of storage of waters and electrical interconnection within the Columbia River System; and

b) the apportionment between the two countries of such benefits, more particularly in regard to electrical generation and flood control.

The need for such principles was apparent when it became evident that, to increase the benefits from the stream's development, costs would have to be incurred for storage in Canada that would increase the power developed over the head in the United States reach of the river.

The resulting report[4] is a judicious blend of engineering, economics, and diplomacy, which in the words of the Commission resulted from guidance "by the basic concept that the principles recommended herein should result in an equitable sharing of the benefits attributable to their cooperative undertakings and these should result in an advantage to each country as compared with alternatives available to that country."[5]

The two general principles which in effect subsume all of the others have a basic welfare economics flavor. The first expresses the general proposition that projects, irrespective of the border, be added to the system in the order of their economic merit so as to maximize net benefits. This may be referred to as the maximizing principle. The second refers to an equitable sharing of the "benefits or savings

---

[2]*Water Resources of the Columbia River,* Report to the International Joint commission, United States and Canada, prepared by the International Columbia River Engineering Board, 1959.

[3]For comments on some of the deficiencies, see John V. Krutilla, *Sequence and Timing in River Basin Development, with special application to Canadian-United States Columbia River Basin planning* (Resources for the Future, Inc., 1960).

[4]International Joint Commission United States and Canada, *Report on Principles of Determination and Apportioning of Benefits from Cooperative Use of Storage Waters and Electrical Interconnection within the Columbia River System* (December 29, 1959).

[5]*Ibid.,* p. 2.

in cost"[6] to each country. This represents an extension of the compensation principle of welfare economics because, since some of the storage to be built will be built in Canada for regulating stream flows over developed head predominantly in the United States, there would exist a dissociation of the locus of cost and benefits.

With these IJC principles at their disposal, negotiating teams chosen by the two countries proceeded to the agreement formalized in the treaty signed by Prime Minister Diefenbaker and President Eisenhower on January 17, 1961.

The treaty and progress report analyzing the treaty provisions[7] provide the substance and an interpretation of the agreement reached following protracted investigations, studies, and negotiations on the Columbia. It is not clear from these documents, however, how the conclusions proceed from the technical data of the engineering-economic investigations and the IJC principles for maximizing net benefits and achieving an equitable division of benefits from cooperative development. The principal task of this paper, then, will be to examine this question.

METHOD OF THE STUDY

The contribution of a project or set of projects to the output of the system will be in the form of a benefit stream extending over a substantial period of time. This fact complicates the problem of estimating the benefits of a project in a number of ways. First, there is the problem of obtaining appropriate discount rates by which benefits and costs accruing or incurred at different points in time can be made comparable. Second, there are all the problems of forecasting the power loads and demands for other services provided by the developed stream. Finally, there are difficult problems associated with what decisions will be made in the future as events and circumstances change; these decisions will affect the operation of particular projects in the system and, in turn, the benefits that may be expected to accrue from them.

If the various events now foreseen as future possibilities would affect the merits of all mutually exclusive projects proportionally, many of the imponderables could be dismissed as having negligible import for defining an "optimal" system. It is possible, however, that

---

[6]The savings being determined by the difference in costs between meeting developing loads through cooperative development as compared with meeting similar loads by the least-cost alternative sources of supply for power.

[7]*Analysis and Progress Report: Report to the Governments of the United States and Canada Relative to Cooperative Development of Water Resources of the Columbia River Basin* (October 19, 1960).

the economics of projects may be affected differentially, thus altering the relative merits of projects for inclusion in the ultimate optimal system. This complicates the identification of the most efficient combination of elements from among the mutually exclusive sets, as well as the nature and extent of the benefits to be shared.

Since one cannot perceive with certainty the combination of events which will obtain over the relevant planning horizon, I shall proceed as follows.

First, I shall attempt to identify the extreme values in the relevant range of possibilities for all variables that are influenced by imponderables of the kind discussed. In this connection, the potential change in system operation will be in response to requirements of the hydroelectric aspect only. But since power represents the preponderant share of the benefits from the system, the analyses can be carried out in terms of maximizing power benefits. Where results may be reversed by differences in flood-control benefits, in a choice between mutually exclusive projects, side calculations will be made to test the results of taking the additional purpose into account.

Second, I shall evaluate system elements and the sequence of project introduction on the assumption that conditions obtained are, alternatively, the opposite extremes of the relevant range, to ascertain whether the *relative* economics of particular projects are altered by changes in the value of variables within the probable range.

Finally, I shall use the results obtained to compare and perhaps help interpret the substantive provisions of the treaty to see if the treaty provisions can be demonstrated to proceed from the welfare economics principles stated in the International Joint Commission's statement of principles governing the cooperative undertaking.

DISCOUNT RATES AND OPPORTUNITY COSTS

Before attention is directed to the physical contribution of each project to the relevant system, it may be well to address the matter of making the stream of annual benefits comparable with the investment costs. This leads to the question of the interest rate and discount factor for time.

If water resources development is undertaken to maximize a river's contribution to welfare, the "interest rate" takes on a more complex function than an interest rate considered in a conventional financial role. In the latter, interest is considered as a practical "cost of money" and figures directly with amortization in the calculation of annual costs to be compared with estimated benefits or returns. In the former role, however, a certain rate, expressed as a percent, is used as a time discount to facilitate comparison of benefits and costs accruing or incurred at different points in time.

To complicate matters, there may be a departure between a private and a social rate of discount for time,[8] just as there are departures between private and social product in the water-resources field because the market does not provide for third-party costs and gains and other collective considerations in the prices resulting from market transactions.[9] The interest rate associated with government bonds and other financial transactions in the capital market reflects *private* rather than *social* rates of discount; even abstracting from the additional problem which arises if the capital market is imperfectly competitive, it is not the relevant rate for use in governmental undertakings.

A social rate of time discount can be, and is usually thought to be, lower than private rates. But if this is so, and such a lower rate is used to discount net benefit streams for purposes of comparison with capital outlays, a second matter requires attention in order that a low rate of discount for the projects' benefit streams does not result in the preclusion of more productive alternatives in the private sector. In order to evaluate the relative economics of all competing applications of capital—i.e., between the resource sector and the private sector as well as among projects in the resource sector—the same rate of discount must be used for all. A project or system increment can be justified only if the present value of its net benefit stream per dollar of investment exceeds the present value per dollar in the private sectors, *both present values being computed at the social rate of interest.*[10]

If the social time rate does not happen to coincide with the time preference revealed by the market (and there is no presumption that it will), the problem is complicated by the need to estimate two rates—the social time rate and the opportunity cost rate.

In the case of the social rate, we cannot appeal to the market, as it does not reflect collective preferences. Since there is not likely to be any national referendum held to settle this issue by the only means possible, we have to be content for the present with a "reasoned

[8]For a recent statement of the basis for a distinction between private and social rates of time preference, see William J. Baumol, *Welfare Economics and the Theory of the State* (Harvard, 1952), and an unpublished paper by Stephen Marglin.

[9]For discussion of this aspect of the problem, see Julius Margolis, "Secondary Benefits, External Economics, and the Justification of Public Investment," *Review of Economics and Statistics*, XXXIX (1957); and Krutilla and Eckstein, *op. cit.*, ch. III.

[10]An illustration may help clarify this matter. Let us assume that a proposed project, which is estimated to have a capital cost of $100 million, produces a

guess" as to what such a collective judgment might be, if it were possible to obtain an informed judgment on so technical a matter. Dorfman has suggested the rate might lie in the neighborhood of 4 percent, and Eckstein has implied that it may lie in the neighborhood of 2.5 or 3 percent.[11] Their judgments do not represent a satisfactory substitute for a correctly derived social time discount,[12] but since this objective is not attainable within the compass of this paper, we shall content ourselves with analyses using a social rate of discount within this range, noting whether variation will tend to reverse the findings among mutually exclusive projects.

In the case of the opportunity cost rate, the estimate will depend in part on how the Columbia River projects are financed, imperfections in the capital market which prevent returns from being equalized at the margin in the several subsectors, and the effectiveness of the national stabilization policy. This paper deals with only one of the possible financing alternatives—i.e., financing by means of governmental borrowing—and it assumes an independent and effective economic stabilization policy. Because this is an international project, the possibility of private development is excluded, and it is assumed that as a public undertaking the financing can be accomplished, and the plans for the development formulated, without capital or budget constraints.

The opportunity cost will vary depending on such factors as what public body assumes responsibility for the financing; whether

---

stream of benefits over time whose present value, discounted at the social rate of 2.5 percent, is $150 million. On this basis, we say that the project has a benefit-cost ratio of 1.5 to 1. But preclusion of the stream of social benefits from private investment by employment of capital in the public sector may result in an understatement of the social cost of the project. Suppose, for example, each dollar of private investment yields $0.05 per year in perpetuity at the margin. Thus the stream of benefits possible from an investment of $100 million in the private sector, when discounted at the assumed social rate of interest of 2.5 percent, gives a present value of $200 million. If investment of $100 million in the water-resources sector forces the nation to forego $200 million in the private sector, then the "real" or "opportunity" cost of the $100 million invested in the resources sector is $200 million, not the "money" or "nominal" cost of $100 million. Accordingly, if the public water-resource development displaces private investment on a dollar-for-dollar basis, a cutoff benefit-cost ratio of 2 to 1, rather than 1 to 1, is required to correct for the market's undervaluation of investment relative to consumption.

[11]Robert Dorfman, "Water and Welfare," paper presented before a joint session of the Econometric Society and the Regional Science Association, St. Louis, December 1960, p. 18. Otto Eckstein, *Water Resources Development; The Economics of Project Evaluation* (Harvard, 1958), pp. 103-104.

[12]For a suggested method see Maynard Hufschmidt, John Krutilla, and Julius Margolis, *Report of Panel of Consultants to the Bureau of the Budget on Standards and Criteria for Formulating and Evaluating Federal Water Resources Development* (Washington, D.C., July 1961), Section II.

the financing of Canadian development is undertaken at least in part in the United States capital market; if so, whether there are assumed to be differences in the exchange rate between the time of borrowing and repayment; and other technical considerations of comparable sort. Since these matters are dealt with in a study by Reuber and Wonnacott,[13] we can avoid a detailed discussion here. Suffice it to say that, based on the variety of potentially relevant assumptions with respect to the imponderables in the situation, opportunity cost rates emerge within the range of 4 to 5.5 percent.

THE CONSTANT STORAGE VALUE CASE

Now to consider the physical aspects of the problem. Under certain assumptions the use of storage in a hydroelectric system will not vary over time, thus providing a constant level of benefits. Under these circumstances, the set of relevant projects can be evaluated on the basis of their initial values in alternative sequences of introduction into the system. This has been done for the High Arrow-Duncan Lakes project,[14] the Libby project, and the Bull River-Dorr combination.[15] The Mica Creek project, being substantially larger than the others and requiring more time for construction than is compatible with meeting the projected load requirements, was purposely excluded as a relevant "first-added" alternative, but was included with the others for consideration in a "second-added" position. Of the upper Columbia storage projects, only Libby and Bull River-Dorr are mutually exclusive in a physical sense, i.e., they pre-empt sites to be occupied by their potential alternates. In addition, these two projects provide duplicating storage services, and only one of the two can be justified economically. For this reason they would be economically incompatible even if the reservoir areas did not partly overlap.

Table I presents the estimated physical gains in system output associated with the addition of each of the projects in different sequences on the assumption that the projects would be fitted into a regionally integrated, hydraulically coordinated system ignoring the international boundary. A number of things should be mentioned in this connection. Since the redevelopment of the lower Kootenay is

---

[13]G. L. Reuber and R. J. Wonnacott, *The Cost of Capital in Canada, with Special Reference to Public Development of the Columbia River* (Resources for the Future, Inc., 1961).

[14]A combination of two sites, the High Arrow Lakes and the Duncan Lakes projects developed for interdependent operation and for convenience, evaluated as a single unit.

[15]Also consisting of two sites which in combination may be treated as a single storage reservoir of equivalent capacity in the same reach of the river.

TABLE I. Estimated power contribution of selected projects added in different sequences in prospective Upper Columbia development (Case I).

Projects	Dependable capacity in megawatts	Annual usable energy in megawatt-years
FIRST ADDED TO BASE SYSTEM[1]		
High Arrow-Duncan Lakes		
At site	0	0
At W. Kootenay Plants[2]	111	73
At U. S. Base System Plants	1,832	1,118
Total	1,943	1,191
Libby		
At site	258	188
At W. Kootenay Plants[3]	344	212
At U. S. Base System Plants	1,380	860
Total	1,982	1,260
Bull River-Dorr		
At site	158	116
At W. Kootenay Plants[3]	344	212
At U. S. Base System Plants	1,380	860
Total	1,882	1,188
SECOND ADDED AFTER HIGH ARROW-DUNCAN		
Mica Creek		
At site	1,045	785
At Downie and Revelstoke[4]	1,125	838
At U. S. Base System Plants	1,168	600
Total	3,338	2,223
Libby		
At site	259	189
At W. Kootenay Plants[5]	266	185
At U. S. Base System Plants	588	300
Total	1,113	674
Bull River-Dorr		
At site	158	116
At W. Kootenay Plants[5]	266	185
At U. S. Base System Plants	588	300
Total	1,012	601
THIRD ADDED AFTER HIGH ARROW-DUNCAN AND MICA CREEK		
Libby		
At site	254	189
At W. Kootenay Plants[5]	266	185
At U. S. Base System Plants	280	130
Total	800	504
Bull River-Dorr		
At site	154	116
At W. Kootenay Plants[5]	266	185
At U. S. Base System Plants	280	130
Total	700	431

[1]Projects appearing as "Base System" in Annex B, Columbia River Basin Treaty.
[2]Includes additional units at Brilliant and Waneta and integration benefits in the Canadian system.
[3]Includes additional units at Brilliant and Waneta and complete Canal Plant.
[4]Downie Creek and Revelstoke Canyon are not estimated to be required much before 1980; accordingly as a first approximation the benefits are to be considered lagged a decade behind the initial occurrence at-site and at U.S. Base System plants associated with the construction of Mica Creek.
[5]Includes additional units at Brilliant and Waneta and complete new Canal Plant.

dependent upon storage of an amount equivalent to that of Libby or the Bull River-Dorr projects, the gains in power over the redeveloped lower Kootenay were attributed alternately to Libby and the Bull River-Dorr storages. Similarly, since the Downie Creek and Revelstoke Canyon head plants below Mica Creek reservoir would not be economic in the absence of the storage at Mica Creek, the power output of these plants is attributed to Mica as a component of the interdependent complex. Aside from these combinations, the estimated output was obtained in a straightforward manner, as each project or interdependent set was added incrementally to the base system of projects existing or currently under construction in the United States reach of the Columbia.[16]

Table II gives the value of the benefits at a social discount rate of both 2.5 and 4 percent from a constant physical output over a 50-year project life. The value per kilowatt of dependable capacity was based on studies of the Federal Power Commission in connection with the U. S. Corps of Engineers' recent Columbia River "308 review report."[17] Estimates of capacity values range from $15.32 to $18.28 per kilowatt to reflect an imputed interest rate ranging from 4 to 5½ percent for the thermal source (which would be alternate to the Columbia, and hence an index of benefits); energy values range from $29.12 to $29.61 per kilowatt-year for similar variation in interest charges.[18] Precise power values for each locality cannot be computed from the data available. Thus, although differences probably exist, this analysis attributes the same value for capacity and energy to the plants of both countries.[19]

---

[16]That is, the projects appearing as the "Base System" in Annex B, *Treaty Between Canada and the United States of America Relating to Cooperative Development of the Water Resources of the Columbia River Basin.*

[17]U. S. Corps of Army Engineers, *Water Resources Development, Columbia River Basin,* Division North Pacific (June 1958), II, App. C., pt. 2.

[18]The slight variation in energy values with changes in the interest rate results from the technique which the FPC staff employed to take account of the differences in distance from load center of generating units (hydro vs. thermal) reflecting in the energy rate differences in transmission costs and losses.

[19]Fuel cost estimates obtained for British Columbia steam alternatives range from 25 to 35 cents per million Btu's, whereas similar data for the Northwestern U.S. plants have ranged from 23 to 36 cents per million Btu's, depending on location of plant and fuel source. Similarly, while plant and equipment costs to Canadian utilities may run a little lower because equipment imported from England is likely to be used, these differences are not likely to be as great following the U.S. domestic price adjustments resulting from the identical bidding exposures. What differences in price of plant and equipment may remain will be offset to a greater or lesser extent by somewhat higher fixed charges on capital in Canada as compared with the United States.

TABLE II. Estimated power benefits of selected projects added in different sequences in prospective Upper Columbia River development (Case I).

Projects		Estimated benefits with	
Dependable capacity at _____		$15.32/kw	$18.28/kw
Annual energy at _____		29.12/kwy	29.61/kwy
		($ million)	($ million)
FIRST ADDED TO BASE SYSTEM[1]			
High Arrow-Duncan Lakes			
Discount rate of:	2.5%	1,810.7	1,958.8
	4.0%	1,371.6	1,483.6
Libby			
Discount rate of:	2.5%	1,849.8	2,015.1
	4.0%	1,401.2	1,526.3
Bull River-Dorr			
Discount rate of:	2.5%	1,760.9	1,903.3
	4.0%	1,333.5	1,441.6
SECOND ADDED AFTER HIGH ARROW-DUNCAN			
Mica Creek[2]			
Discount rate of:	2.5%	2,904.5	3,108.4
	4.0%	2,112.1	2,259.9
Libby			
Discount rate of:	2.5%	989.3	1,073.5
	4.0%	749.4	813.1
Bull River-Dorr			
Discount rate of:	2.5%	898.6	974.2
	4.0%	680.8	737.8
THIRD ADDED AFTER HIGH ARROW-DUNCAN AND MICA CREEK			
Libby			
Discount rate of:	2.5%	713.1	773.5
	4.0%	540.0	574.2
Bull River-Dorr			
Discount rate of:	2.5%	623.0	674.7
	4.0%	471.8	511.1

[1]See Table I, note 1.

[2]Since the Downie and Revelstoke head plants are not estimated to be in operation before the decade of the 1980's, the net benefit stream (annual benefits less annual O & M costs) is assumed to commence as of 1980, but its value is discounted to 1970 to render the benefits of both elements of the interdependent Mica-Downie-Revelstoke complex comparable to all other projects under consideration.

One further comment is required in connection with the values given for the Mica Creek storage and power project. Since the Revelstoke Canyon and Downie Creek projects are not economical because they lack the sort of regulation which storage at Mica Creek can provide, they were included as part of an interdependent complex with Mica. One complication arises, however. It is thought that power from the Mica Creek operation can be absorbed into a regional system by 1970, but the Revelstoke and Downie Creek projects might not warrant introduction much before 1980. Accordingly, their benefits were assumed to commence in 1980 but were discounted back to 1970 to make their value comparable with other projects.

Table III estimates the investment cost of each project on the basis of interest during construction of 2.5 and 4 percent. Since redevelopment of the lower Kootenay, referred to as the Canal project, is dependent on upstream storage capacity, the cost of this project is added to the costs of Libby and alternatively Bull River-Dorr, since the benefits were also attributed to these projects. A similar adjustment is made in connection with the costs of Mica, since the downstream Revelstoke Canyon and Downie Creek projects are interdependent elements of the entire Mica Creek complex. In the case of these projects, however, their 1980 investment costs have been discounted back to 1970 to render them comparable with their associated benefits, and with all other projects.

Estimates of the excess of benefits over costs for each project are given in Table IV. These are based on the extreme values of the opportunity cost range (4 to 5.5 percent) and the social discount (2.5 to 4 percent), and on the assumption that initial storage values will remain constant over the life of the facilities. This, of course, represents one extreme value in a range of potential storage values. But, under these sets of assumptions, it is not difficult to identify the projects that qualify for addition to the system at each stage.

The High Arrow-Duncan Lakes project is the most attractive for next addition to the base system, as it has excess benefits of about $150 million more than the next best of the remaining two relevant "first-added" possibilities.

TABLE III. Estimated investment cost of projects adjusted to 1970 base.

| Projects | Imputed interest during construction | |
	2.5 %	4.0 %
	($ million)	($ million)
FIRST ADDED TO BASE SYSTEM[1]		
High Arrow-Duncan Lakes	97.5	98.7
Libby	364.1	378.7
Bull River-Dorr	188.9	195.0
SECOND ADDED AFTER HIGH ARROW-DUNCAN		
Mica Creek[2]	474.8	464.7
Libby	358.2	372.3
Bull River-Dorr	182.6	188.5
THIRD ADDED AFTER HIGH ARROW-DUNCAN AND MICA		
Libby	362.3	372.3
Bull River-Dorr	182.6	188.5

[1]See Table I, note 1.

[2]Investment costs in the case of Mica represented not only the cost of construction and interest during construction but similar costs of Downie Creek and Revelstoke Canyon assumed to be built by 1980. The Downie and Revelstoke projects' investment was then discounted back to 1970 symmetrically with the benefits to put all benefits and costs of all projects on a comparable time basis.

TABLE IV. Estimated excess of benefits over costs of selected projects added in different sequences in prospective Upper Columbia development (Case I).

Projects		Estimated excess of benefits over costs with	
Dependable capacity at_____$15.32/kw			$18.28/kw
Annual energy at_____ 29.12/kwy			29.61/kwy
		($ million)	($ million)
FIRST ADDED TO BASE SYSTEM[1]			
High Arrow-Duncan Lakes			
B minus C with discount at:	2.5%	1,713.2	1,861.3
	4.0%	1,272.9	1,384.9
Libby			
B minus C with discount at:	2.5%	1,485.7	1,651.0
	4.0%	1,022.5	1,147.6
Bull River-Dorr			
B minus C with discount at:	2.5%	1,572.0	1,714.4
	4.0%	1,138.5	1,246.6
SECOND ADDED AFTER HIGH ARROW-DUNCAN			
Mica Creek			
B minus C with discount at:	2.5%	2,429.7	2,633.6
	4.0%	1,647.4	1,759.2
Libby			
B minus C with discount at:	2.5%	631.1	715.3
	4.0%	377.1	440.8
Bull River-Dorr			
B minus C with discount at:	2.5%	704.2	791.6
	4.0%	492.3	549.3
THIRD ADDED AFTER HIGH ARROW-DUNCAN AND MICA			
Libby			
B minus C with discount at:	2.5%	350.8	411.2
	4.0%	167.7	201.9
Bull River-Dorr			
B minus C with discount at:	2.5%	440.4	492.1
	4.0%	283.3	322.6

[1]See Table I, note 1.

The Mica Creek project stands out as the most attractive alternative for second addition. In this connection it is appropriate to indicate that the very substantial differences between Mica Creek and the competing alternatives (Libby and Bull River-Dorr) shown in the table require some adjustment. It is known that a substantially larger outlay for transmission facilities would attend the development of the Mica Creek-Revelstoke-Downie Creek complex, than necessary for, say, Libby. However, the magnitude of the difference between the Mica complex and its alternatives is so great that we need not fear a reversal of results from including the (yet undetermined) differential transmission outlays associated with these projects.

Finally, it can be seen that the Bull River-Dorr project appears to be superior to the Libby project as a "third-added" project. Transmission costs associated with Bull River-Dorr might exceed those associated with Libby, but the difference is not likely to reverse their positions.

THE DECLINING STORAGE VALUES CASE

A substantial body of technical opinion believes that storage values will diminish over time as the system load exceeds the hydro potential and a thermal component is added to the system.[20] As the thermal component of the system grows quite large in relation to the hydro, all the hydro energy that can be generated at any time is usable to replace fuel consumption in thermal stations. If hydro is used in this manner, storage will not be needed to regulate the generation of hydro energy for specific times of the year.

As the thermal component grows in response to developing loads, more hydro turbines and generators will be installed in the hydro dams in order to peak the thermal plant, which will be most efficiently operated in the base of the load at as close to 100 percent plant factor as possible. This additional hydro capacity can generate more energy from unregulated flows, and therefore the benefit of storage is further decreased.

Finally, in the region of the Columbia power system, as the thermal component of the system builds up to the estimated 2010 year load conditions, there will be more thermal energy available than is required to meet the load during critical streamflow conditions. Prime power will therefore no longer determine capacity benefits, and the value of storage will be further diminished. After all three conditions occur, the benefits of storage are reduced to only the value of the energy represented by the water which would be spilled in the absence of the storage.[21]

If the hydroelectric component will be converted to use in this fashion, we would expect the power values of a particular storage project to change rather than remain constant over time. Crude estimates of the changes in capacity and energy attributable to the projects in question are presented in Table V. The initial estimates remain for 1970, but different values are shown for 1985, 1995, and 2010, the years selected to illustrate the changed relationship in the pattern of project uses. Since we are interested in extreme values, the estimates are based on the estimated maximum levels of load growth provided by the Federal Power Commission,[22] with corresponding estimates for

---

[20]U. S. Corps of Army Engineers, op. cit., I, 50-54.

[21]Actually this represents an overstatement because storage is useful to an extent to complement thermal operations so as to permit maximum capacity factor on efficient thermal plants in the system and minimize use of the less efficient thermal plants. See Ross N. Brudenell and Jack H. Gilbreath, "Economic Complementary Operations of Hydro Storage and Steam Power in the Integrated TVA System," paper presented at the AIEE Summer Meeting, Buffalo, N.Y., June 22-27, 1958.

[22]U. S. Corps of Army Engineers, op. cit., III, App. C.

TABLE V. Estimated power contributions for selected projects in different sequences for selected dates, taking account of assumed changes in system operation in response to growth over time of system's thermal component (Case II).

Project	1970		1985		1995		2010	
	Dependable capacity (megawatts)	Annual usable energy (megawatt-years)	Dependable capacity (megawatts)	Annual energy (megawatt-years)	Dependable capacity (megawatts)	Annual energy (megawatt-years)	Dependable capacity (megawatts)	Annual energy (megawatt-years)
FIRST ADDED TO BASE SYSTEM[1]								
High Arrow-Duncan Lakes								
At site	0	0	0	0	0	0	0	0
At W. Kootenay Plants[2]	111	73	111	73	119	73	119	73
At U. S. Base System Plants	1,832	1,118	1,557	845	1,520	780	0	290
Total	1,943	1,191	1,668	918	1,639	853	119	363
Libby								
At site	258	188	258	188	320	188	791	228
At W. Kootenay Plants[3]	344	212	344	212	451	212	451	212
At U. S. Base System Plants	1,380	860	1,040	750	1,000	755	0	200
Total	1,982	1,260	1,642	1,150	1,771	1,155	1,242	640
Bull River-Dorr								
At site	158	116	158	116	196	116	630	125
At W. Kootenay Plants[3]	344	212	344	212	451	212	451	212
At U. S. Base System	1,380	860	1,040	750	1,000	755	0	200
Total	1,882	1,188	1,542	1,078	1,647	1,083	1,081	537
SECOND ADDED AFTER HIGH ARROW-DUNCAN								
Mica								
At site	1,045	785	1,080	785	1,340	785	2,784	785
At Downie and Revelstoke[4]			1,125	838	1,704	838	1,704	838
At U. S. Base System	1,168	600	1,175	360	980	295	0	160
Total	2,214	1,385	3,380	1,983	4,024	1,918	4,488	1,783

Libby							
At site	259	189	258	188	320	188	791	228
At W. Kootenay Plants[5]	266	185	266	185	332	185	332	185
At U. S. Base System	588	300	595	175	500	140	0	90
Total	1,113	674	1,119	548	1,152	513	1,123	503
Bull River-Dorr							
At site	158	116	158	116	196	116	630	125
At W. Kootenay Plants[5]	266	185	266	185	332	185	332	185
At U. S. Base System	588	300	595	175	500	140	0	90
Total	1,012	601	1,019	476	1,028	441	962	400
THIRD ADDED							
Libby							
At site	254	189	258	188	320	188	791	228
At W. Kootenay Plants	266	185	266	185	332	185	332	185
At U. S. Base System	280	130	188	115	170	105	0	50
Total	800	504	712	488	822	478	1,123	463
Bull River-Dorr							
At site	154	116	158	116	196	116	630	125
At W. Kootenay Plants	266	185	266	185	332	185	332	185
At U. S. Base System	280	130	188	115	170	105	0	50
Total	700	431	612	416	698	406	962	360

[1] See Table I, note 1.
[2] Includes additional units at Brilliant and Waneta and integration benefits in the Canadian system.
[3] Includes additional units at Brilliant and Waneta and complete Canal Plant.
[4] Downie Creek and Revelstoke Canyon are not estimated to be operating until 1980; accordingly the benefits are to be considered lagged a decade behind the initial occurrence at site and at U. S. Base System plants associated with the construction of Mica Creek.
[5] Includes additional units at Brilliant and Waneta and complete new Canal Plant.

TABLE VI. Estimated power benefits of selected projects added in different sequences in prospective Upper Columbia River development (Case II).

Projects		Estimated benefits with	
Dependable capacity at_____		$15.32/kw	$18.28/kw
Annual energy at_____		29.12/kwy	29.61/kwy
		($ million)	($ million)
FIRST ADDED TO BASE SYSTEM[1]			
High Arrow-Duncan Lakes			
Discount rate of:	2.5%	1,263.1	1,365.6
	4.0%	1,032.9	1,117.7
Libby			
Discount rate of:	2.5%	1,540.7	1,670.0
	4.0%	1,208.8	1,310.6
Bull River-Dorr			
Discount rate of:	2.5%	1,433.6	1,549.5
	4.0%	1,130.9	1,221.9
SECOND ADDED AFTER HIGH ARROW-DUNCAN			
Mica Creek[2]			
Discount rate of:	2.5%	2,920.0	3,167.6
	4.0%	2,109.0	2,284.0
Libby			
Discount rate of:	2.5%	906.8	990.1
	4.0%	694.1	757.2
Bull River-Dorr			
Discount rate of:	2.5%	800.1	872.7
	4.0%	616.2	671.7
THIRD ADDED AFTER HIGH ARROW-DUNCAN AND MICA			
Libby			
Discount rate of:	2.5%	725.9	790.7
	4.0%	544.1	591.0
Bull River-Dorr			
Discount rate of:	2.5%	619.4	673.3
	4.0%	466.2	506.3

[1]See Table I, note 1.

[2]Since the Downie Creek and Revelstoke Canyon head plants are estimated not to be in operation before the decade of the 1980's, the net benefit stream (annual benefits minus annual O & M costs) is assumed to commence in 1980, but its value is discounted to 1970 to render the time stream of the interdependent Mica-Downie-Revelstoke complex comparable with respect to time with all the other projects under consideration.

the Canadian areas of the regional power market. The more rapid the rate of load growth, of course, the more quickly will the hydro become insufficient to meet power demands, and the more quickly will the thermal component be brought into play with the attendant—and most pronounced—decline in storage values. The estimates are based on the assumption that the hydro projects will operate in a system developed to meet growth in loads corresponding to the maximum used in the FPC studies.

Examination of the data confirms what would be suspected. The projects with the highest ratio of storage to total values suffer relatively more in the comparisons. High Arrow-Duncan, for example, which is a pure storage project, generating all the power attributable to it predominantly at the head plants in the United States, is the most adversely affected in this analysis. The Bull River-Dorr and Libby projects, by comparison, have installed capacity at site and can be converted to peaking plants as the hydro system is converted to operate as a peaking supplement to the thermal base load plants. Accordingly, the capacity and energy values of these projects do not decline as greatly.

The system was not regulated to the load annually, as this involves an effort quite outside the scope of this paper. Rather, selected dates were taken, and the interstitial period values were estimated crudely by simply distributing the 1985, 1995, and 2010 point estimates five years in each direction. That is, the 1970 estimated values were assumed to hold for the decade of the seventies, the 1985 estimates were assumed to remain constant from 1980 to 1990, etc., as a crude approximation. The same capacity and energy values per kilowatt used in the previous section were applied to obtain annual values in monetary terms. These are shown in Table VI, again discounted to the year 1970 in all cases at the two rates of discount. Finally, the same investment is used as in the previous case. However, since the storage projects with capacity at-site would have to install additional capacity in later years when they would be used as peaking plants, the excess of present value of benefits over costs given in Table VII tends to be overstated somewhat compared with High Arrow-Duncan.

As the storage values decline, the High Arrow-Duncan project, which is exclusively a storage project, is affected disproportionately relative to combination head-storage projects. The Libby and Bull River-Dorr projects are able to maintain higher annual values in the later years relative to the earlier, than is the case with High Arrow-Duncan.[23] Accordingly, in the extreme case of declining benefits from storage coupled with a low social discount that gives relatively more weight to future benefits, the relative economics of the projects appears altered. The Bull River-Dorr project's excess benefits exceed those of the High Arrow-Duncan project significantly in this case.[24]

---

[23] Although there remains also the possibility of installing some capacity for energy at both Arrow Lakes and Duncan.

[24] The modest amounts by which the Bull River-Dorr project's excess benefits exceed the High Arrow-Duncan project's excess benefits for the 4 percent social discount lie well within the range of error of our crude estimates of power contribution of particular projects in the more distant years, and cannot be interpreted as significant. Identical observations are warranted in the case of the difference between Libby's excess benefits and those of High Arrow-Duncan at the 2.5 percent discount rates.

TABLE VII. Estimated excess of benefits over costs of selected projects added in different sequences in prospective Upper Columbia River development (Case II).

Projects	$15.32/kw 29.12/kwy	$18.28/kw 29.61/kwy
Dependable capacity at_____		
Annual energy at_____		
	($ million)	($ million)
FIRST ADDED TO BASE SYSTEM[1]		
High Arrow-Duncan Lakes		
B minus C with discount at: 2.5%	1,165.6	1,268.1
4.0%	934.2	1,019.0
Libby		
B minus C with discount at: 2.5%	1,176.6	1,305.9
4.0%	830.1	931.9
Bull River-Dorr		
B minus C with discount at: 2.5%	1,244.7	1,360.6
4.0%	935.9	1,026.9
SECOND ADDED AFTER HIGH ARROW-DUNCAN		
Mica Creek		
B minus C with discount at: 2.5%	2,445.2	2,692.8
4.0%	1,644.3	1,819.3
Libby		
B minus C with discount at: 2.5%	548.6	631.9
4.0%	321.8	384.9
Bull River-Dorr		
B minus C with discount at: 2.5%	617.5	690.1
4.0%	427.7	483.2
THIRD ADDED AFTER HIGH ARROW-DUNCAN AND MICA		
Libby		
B minus C with discount at: 2.5%	363.6	428.4
4.0%	171.8	219.5
Bull River-Dorr		
B minus C with discount at: 2.5%	436.8	490.7
4.0%	277.7	317.8

[1]See Table I, note 1.

Before this conclusion is finally accepted, however, the difference must be subjected to an additional test. When a "lower than opportunity cost" social time discount is used, the yields in the opportunity cost sector must be discounted at the same rate. Since we have used weighted average perpetuities of 4 and 5.5 percent estimated to be relevant in the opportunity cost sector, the benefit streams in the project sector when discounted at a social rate of 2.5 percent must show an incremental benefit to cost ratio of 1.6 to 1 and 2.2 to 1, respectively, before the present value of the incremental benefits will exceed the present value of the perpetuities when discounted at the social rate.[25] Accordingly, we use this method to make our comparisons. Since the ratio of the difference in benefits between High Arrow-Duncan and

[25]That is, $\frac{4.0}{2.5}$ and $\frac{5.5}{2.5}$ respectively.

Bull River-Dorr to corresponding incremental costs exceeds this threshold value in only one instance, we can dismiss all the other instances. Table VIII presents the relevant threshold ratios and the corresponding incremental benefit-cost ratios for each instance in the declining benefits case.

Under the circumstances, which of the two projects should be selected for first addition? In only one combination of extreme values does Bull River-Dorr appear the more attractive. Moreover, some supplementary factors should be given weight. We have assumed the most rapid rate of growth projected by the FPC in order to obtain extreme values for the decline in storage values. At this rate the output of the High Arrow-Duncan project would be required in the mid-sixties, well before either the Libby or the Bull River-Dorr project could come on the line. Since a two-year difference in the construction time of High Arrow-Duncan, compared with Bull River-Dorr, is sufficient to dispose of this case, High Arrow-Duncan appears superior when this factor is taken into account.

Finally, there is an additional small difference in flood-control benefits. High Arrow-Duncan has no local flood-control benefits comparable with the Libby or Bull River-Dorr project. However, it has much more storage and produces more flood control in the lower reaches of the Columbia. This also tends to tip the scales in its favor.

Accordingly, High Arrow-Duncan is accepted for first addition for three reasons: (a) the understatement of costs for transmission outlays and future installation of additional capacity for Bull River-Dorr as compared with High Arrow-Duncan; (b) the time difference in the availability of benefits; and (c) the somewhat larger flood control benefits from the High Arrow-Duncan project.

Once the differential impact of declining storage values on a purely storage project has been disposed of, the declining value of storage does not alter the relative economics of the other plants with

TABLE VIII. Threshold values and corresponding benefit-cost ratios.

	Social discount of 2.5%	Social discount of 4.0%
Threshold B/C ratios when perpetuity is 4.0%	1.6:1*	1.0:1
Actual incremental B/C ratios	1.9:1*	1.0:1
Threshold B/C ratios when perpetuity is 5.5%	2.2:1	1.4:1
Actual incremental B/C ratios	2.0:1	1.1:1

*Threshold value significantly exceeded.

capacity installed at site. Mica Creek continues to be "second-added" by a large margin, and Bull River-Dorr "third-added."

It must be emphasized that these conclusions are only first approximations. More refined machine simulations for the more distant years and analysis of differences in complementary investments, etc., are desirable. Without these, the choice of High Arrow-Duncan over Bull River-Dorr as "first-added" on the assumption that the value of storage will decline to a maximum should be regarded as tentative.

THE RELEVANCE OF THE EXTREME CASES

What is the relevance of the analysis in terms of extreme values? Since neither of the extremes is likely to obtain, the significance of the analysis is the added security to be derived from results that indicate that the selection of the optimal elements of the system and the sequence of their introduction are independent of the values the variables are likely to take in the imponderable range. Aside from meeting this objective, it is desirable to speculate on the most probable values that may be expected based on a consideration of some governing factors.

First, it seems unlikely that the storage in the Columbia power system will continue to be utilized in precisely the fashion that attends regulation for maximizing prime power after the system evolves into a predominantly thermal system. The system will be operated to an increasing degree for peaking; and, with increased installation of capacity, less unregulated flow will be spilled. In order to maximize effective head,[26] less reservoir capacity will be reserved for storage. This appears consistent with historical experience; it does not contradict the TVA experience, for example. Experience with other projects, however, is not entirely comparable. The combined hydro-thermal systems now in operation with hydro used for peaking are much smaller than the Columbia system will be when hydro becomes basically a peak-load operation. Even the TVA hydro system is diminutive by comparison. The Columbia's Grand Coulee project alone, with the third powerhouse built, would have ultimate capacity comparable to the entire TVA hydro system. To operate plants of such size for peaking without regard for effects downstream, particularly in reaches without slack water, seems to be a dubious prospect. Then, too, the operation of hydro in an integrated system assumes either (a) that

---

[26]For the combination projects having generators along with storage. Exclusively storage projects like High Arrow-Duncan, however, are not adversely affected by head loss, and therefore their use for regulation should be maintained at a high level.

the thermal will be operated and managed by the same entity as the hydro or (b) that flexible, yet binding, institutional arrangements can be made to coordinate management of the storage, hydro-generating capacity, and thermal components that are distributed among a number of ownerships. This is a prime necessity in the Columbia system if efficient operations are to be achieved. To date, however, despite the requirements of licensing provisions, such arrangements do not exist.

Given the above considerations, it is probably more likely that the hydro component of the system will be operated in a manner which represents a compromise of various economic and social objectives rather than in a manner consistent exclusively with meeting power requirements. What the time profile of storage values will be, therefore, remains an imponderable. But the value of storage is likely to decline less than indicated in our extreme case.

TREATY RESULTS AND WELFARE ECONOMICS PRINCIPLES

If our analysis of the relative merits of the several upper Columbia projects with storage is correct, there is a discrepancy between the welfare economics principles articulated in the International Joint Commission general principles and the treaty results. That is to say, while the High Arrow-Duncan projects seem supportable as the most attractive for first addition, and little question can be raised about the inclusion of Mica second, there remain doubts regarding the inclusion of Libby in lieu of the Bull River-Dorr alternate. Other things being equal, it appears that Bull River-Dorr would substitute economically for the Libby project, and failure to have it do so will not maximize the system benefits.

Why this discrepancy between maximization and the treaty results occurred cannot be known for certain. One factor which may have been instrumental is that the Bull River-Dorr project would inundate a larger proportion of the limited arable land in British Columbia than would Libby, and that this was considered locally quite undesirable. Secondly, the Bull River-Dorr project is compatible with, and might be considered integrally associated with, the potential diversion of the Kootenay into the headwaters of the Columbia in the vicinity of Columbia Lake, in order that the flow occur over a substantially greater Canadian head. Such an operation, however, providing a sizeable amount of storage in the Bull River-Dorr-Luxor complex of installations, is known to have met with some expression of disfavor locally. The Columbia Lake region has a unique recreational potential which would be most adversely affected by such a violently fluctuating impoundment as would characterize the operation of the storage reservoir located at the highest elevation in the system.

Another reason, of course, was that British Columbia may have heeded the gentle entreaties of its good neighbors from Montana to "share the projects," maximization to the contrary notwithstanding. Or perhaps both factors were influential. Local opposition alone, however, would have as much force in eliminating Bull River-Dorr as a relevant alternative as domestic opposition in the United States on the part of some groups has been in eliminating Nez Perce as a relevant alternative at the present time. In fact, the IJC principles (pp. 5-7) are explicit in protecting each country from the "tyranny of economic merit."

But so much for the consistency between the IJC principles and the treaty results with respect to the selection of efficient projects. These appear capable of being rationalized on the basis of the IJC principles.

How do the provisions for sharing of benefits conform with the principles of compensation? To answer this question would require a substantial effort to: (a) determine what each country could achieve by way of power supply and costs employing its best alternative relying on its domestic resources, excluding cooperation; (b) determine what share of power would be required from the collaborative effort in order to leave it comparably well off; and (c) then address the question of an equitable division of the residual, or the savings realizable through cooperation. This, needless to say, exceeds the scope of this paper. However, some insights might be gained by more casual comparisons.

The treaty provides that the downstream power gains in the United States from storage regulation in Canada, as well as the flood losses averted, are to be divided equally between the countries. Downstream gains in British Columbia on the lower Kootenay from storage regulation at Libby, on the other hand, are to be retained in full by Canada.[27] Since approximately a third of the total benefits from the Libby project accrue to Canada, the question occurs whether or not the benefits accruing from Libby in the United States justify the costs to the United States.[28]

The data in Table IX indicate that if Libby is added after High

---

[27]In this instance Canada provides flowage rights for the upper portion of the Libby reservoir without cost to the United States which, however, represents only a minute fraction (4 to 5 percent) of the value of the downstream benefits in Canada from the storage regulation provided by Libby.

[28]The treaty provisions with respect to Libby are permissive rather than mandatory.

TABLE IX. U. S. benefits and costs of Libby and Knowles projects third added after High Arrow-Duncan and Mica Creek.

Projects	Case of Constant Storage Values ($ million)		Case of Declining Storage Values ($ million)	
	A[1]	B[2]	A[1]	B[2]
Libby				
Present value of net benefits discounted at:				
2.5%	463.24	504.03	463.58	506.67
4.0%	350.87	381.76	347.12	378.89
Capital costs (less British Columbia flowage costs)	325.17	338.20	325.17	338.20
Knowles				
Present value of net benefits discounted at:				
2.5%	425.69	461.20	427.71	465.92
4.0%	322.43	349.32	324.05	352.43
Capital costs:	272.62	286.72	272.62	286.72
Incremental benefit-cost ratios	A[1]	B[2]	A[1]	B[2]
2.5%	0.7:1	0.8:1	0.4:1	0.4:1
4.0%	0.5:1	0.6:1	0.3:1	0.3:1

[1]Estimated benefits with dependable capacity at $15.32/kw and annual energy at $29.12/kwy.
[2]Estimated benefits with dependable capacity at $18.28/kw and annual energy at $29.61/kwy.

Arrow-Duncan and Mica Creek, it is inferior to an alternative, the Knowles project on the Pend Oreille, from the United States viewpoint. The incremental benefit-cost ratio is substantially below unity in comparing the differences between the two projects. When the local flood-control benefits in the Bonners Ferry area are added to power benefits for Libby, in none of the eight cases does the incremental benefit-cost ratio exceed the required benefit-cost threshold values to justify Libby as third added from the United States point of view.[29] Canada, however, would stand to gain $150-200 million from an incremental Canadian cost of about $50 million.

There is another, and perhaps more significant point with respect to the compensation principle in the division of benefits. This relates to the pre-emption of the site values of United States storage sites by the superior Canadian sites. The Corps of Engineers major water plan

[29]It is true that, although the Canadian projects provide upwards of 20 million acre-feet of storage, "credit" is taken for only 15.5 which would affect the absolute amount of benefits imputed to Libby. But, the contribution of Knowles also would have to be calculated on the basis "as if" it were being added after only 15.5 million acre-feet, since the 15.5 million acre-feet credit is not offered by Canada as a *quid pro quo* for Libby.

calls for only about 20 million acre-feet of additional storage for flood control and power production combined.[30] In the absence of cooperative development, the United States could develop a number of storage sites which, although economically inferior to the Canadian projects, would provide benefits exceeding their costs. However, once 20 million acre-feet of Canadian storage have been added, the benefits of the United States projects are drastically reduced, since the value of incremental storage drops sharply after the addition of 12.5-15.5 million acre-feet to the base system. This represents a displaced value—or a United States opportunity foregone—which should be considered if the compensation principle of welfare economics is to apply.

The nature of the pre-emption of United States storage resource values by Canadian storage is illustrated in Table X, which gives the estimated contribution of selected United States storage projects if built before, as compared with after, the 20 million acre-feet of Canadian storage. It is apparent from the physical output data that the Canadian storage added first greatly reduces the value of subsequently added United States storage projects. To obtain a crude estimate of the value of United States storage resources displaced by Canadian storage, Table XI gives the present value of three projects *with* and *without* prior addition of Canadian upper Columbia storage. These projects represent only about 6.5 million additional acre-feet of storage, roughly half the amount that can be accommodated without drastically reduced incremental benefits per unit of additional storage. Even so, the value pre-empted by additional Canadian storage for just the three storage projects would range between $0.7 billion and $1.4 billion.

There is in addition to the displacement of storage resource values the pre-emption of currently excess peaking capacity, some of which was built in anticipation of United States storage projects. If something like 1.5 million kilowatts of capacity will be utilized for peaking the Canadian prime power, an additional investment of something like $200 million in capacity is called for to meet peaking requirements associated with United States hydro projects added after the Canadian projects. The pre-empted values for just the three storage projects and the peaking capacity, therefore, will range from $0.9 to $1.6 billion, exceeding the United States share of upper Columbia Canadian storage benefits ($0.8 to $1.5 billion) as shown in Table XII. A qualification must be entered at this juncture, however. The data here employed assume benefits from 20 million acre-feet of

---

[30]U. S. Corps of Army Engineers, *op. cit.*, I, 34.

TABLE X. Estimated power contribution of selected U.S. projects with storage when added to U.S. base system prior to and following High Arrow-Duncan and Mica Creek Canadian storage projects.

Projects	1970		1985		1995		2010	
	Dependable capacity (megawatts)	Usable energy (megawatt-years)	Dependable capacity (megawatts)	Usable energy (megawatt-years)	Dependable capacity (megawatts)	Usable energy (megawatt-years)	Dependable capacity (megawatts)	Usable energy (megawatt-years)
Knowles								
Pre-Canadian	1,249	819	1,081	755	1,220	739	589	320
Post-Canadian	459	299	379	325	620	276	589	210
High Mountain Sheep								
Pre-Canadian	1,195	603	1,116	682	1,592	697	1,725	606
Post-Canadian	714	469	685	633	1,194	631	1,725	597
Bruces Eddy								
Pre-Canadian	496	196	438	216	474	201	276	180
Post-Canadian	195	128	195	186	253	186	276	175

TABLE XI Estimated reduction in value of power from selected U.S. storage projects following addition of High Arrow-Duncan and Mica Creek storage.

Projects		Estimated reduction with	
Dependable capacity at_____		$15.32/kw	$18.28/kw
Annual energy at_____		29.12/kwy	29.61/kwy
		($ million)	($ million)
Knowles			
Constant storage value case			
benefits discounted at:	2.5%	772.88	833.77*
	4.0%	585.39	631.51
Declining storage value case			
benefits discounted at:	2.5%	542.56	683.61
	4.0%	445.92†	480.11
High Mountain Sheep			
Constant storage value case			
benefits discounted at:	2.5%	319.67	354.27*
	4.0%	242.13	268.53
Declining storage value case			
benefits discounted at:	2.5%	198.32	221.55
	4.0%	166.20†	185.57
Bruces Eddy			
Constant storage value case			
benefits discounted at:	2.5%	175.25	194.84*
	4.0%	132.74	147.58
Declining storage value case			
benefits discounted at:	2.5%	107.01	120.04
	4.0%	88.06†	100.96

High total _____$1,382.9 + $200.0‡ = $1,582.9
Low total _____$ 704.2 + $200.0‡ = $ 904.2

*Individual estimates marking high extreme of the range.
†Individual estimates marking the low extreme of the range.
‡Cost of replacing pre-empted peaking capacity.

storage in Canada preceding storage in the United States and an equal division of the resulting downstream gains. While the treaty (Art. vii., sec. 2-b) makes explicit the evaluation of Canadian storage as next added, it allows credit for only 15.5 million acre-feet, which tends to redistribute the benefits by an undetermined amount.

CONCLUSIONS

What then is the advantage to the United States from cooperative development of the Columbia, given the distribution of benefits? This analysis indicates that there will be no economic advantage to the United States; in fact, the total cost of power is likely to be greater over time through cooperative development than through reliance upon United States resources alone. It is true that the increment of power supply obtained through cooperative development can be obtained with a lesser immediate outlay than an equal increment obtained from

TABLE XII. Estimated value of U.S. share of power benefits from Upper Columbia Canadian storage.

Projects		U.S. share of power benefits with	
Dependable capacity at_____		$15.32/kw	$18.28/kw
Annual energy at_____		29.12/kwy	29.61/kwy
		($ million)	($ million)
High Arrow-Duncan			
Constant storage value case			
benefits discounted at:	2.5%	859.80	929.72*
	4.0%	651.24	704.19
Declining storage value case			
benefits discounted at:	2.5%	535.22	632.26
	4.0%	481.49†	520.61
Mica Creek			
Constant storage value case			
benefits discounted at:	2.5%	501.59	545.41*
	4.0%	379.92	413.11
Declining storage value case			
benefits discounted at:	2.5%	332.51	363.24
	4.0%	274.94†	300.46
High total _____$1,475.1			
Low total _____ 756.4			

*Marks high extreme of the relevant range.
†Marks low extreme of the relevant range.

development of United States resources. However, successive increments of supply following Canadian storage will require substantially larger outlays and increased costs for the United States than if the United States were to have proceeded independently. Thus a temporary advantage to the United States appears to be offset by a longer-range increase in costs over what the United States could have done relying upon its own resources.

There could, of course, be reasons other than economic for proceeding with cooperative development. For example, the Columbia settlement may have been only a minor element in the grand strategy which considers United States-Canadian relations in a broader context (defense and other); and restricting the analysis to resource issues in the Columbia basin may constrain the issue too narrowly to explain the treaty. Whatever the dominant factors involved, however, it is clear that a complete analysis would reveal that it may be difficult to reconcile the treaty results with the welfare compensation principle articulated in the IJC's statement of principles directed toward this issue.

Physical and Biological Obstacles to Economic Growth: Measures Needed to Reduce Them

E. G. DUNFORD

Land and water are the basic resources that underlie economic growth and provide all the elements of man's existence. It is the nature of man, however, to try to modify the interaction of these resources to achieve greater efficiency and more production. We have been moderately successful. But our aim is for still greater and more efficient production despite physical and biological obstacles which I will touch upon briefly in this discussion.

PHYSICAL AND BIOLOGICAL OBSTACLES

Our efforts to reap economic and social gains from our natural resources have been hampered by three major obstacles: (1) for any given area, land and water are extremely variable in supply and physical characteristics; (2) we do not have adequate inventories of our resources; and (3) we do not fully understand the nature of physical and biological systems and therefore lack complete knowledge of how to manage them.

Variability of National Resources

One of the most obvious characteristics of nature is heterogeneity. The atmosphere surrounding the earth, the configuration of the earth's land mass, location of water bodies, and distribution of forests, deserts, and plains differ greatly. Soil mantles exhibit wide differences in depth, structure, mineral content, productivity, and stability. Vegetative cover ranges from dense rain forests to sparse desert growth.

Water supplies are also characterized by inherent maladjustments which result in something less than optimum use and economic good.

E. G. Dunford has been a member of the U.S. Forest Service since 1935. He now heads the division of watershed management research of the Pacific Northwest Forest and Range Experiment Station, head-quartered at Portland, Oregon.

One example is the characteristic pattern of moisture supply in the Pacific Northwest as shown in the state of Washington. Generally, this is a region of abundant precipitation. But roughly 95 percent is received during nine months; the three summer months are usually a period of drought. Supply is not uniform by area, either. Parts of the Olympic mountains receive an average yearly precipitation of 180 inches, while Hanford, east of the Cascade Range, receives only 6 inches annually. No other state in continental United States has a wider variation in supply.

Once it is received on the land surface, water supply is further complicated by variations in amounts diverted to evapotranspiration. Meteorological forces governing rates of evapotranspiration are not necessarily in harmony with those which produce precipitation in any given area. Thus, where rates of evapotranspiration are high, precipitation is often low, and the residual water available for streamflow may be reduced to zero except during occasional storms. Similar quantities of moisture in areas of low evapotranspiration opportunity may produce perennial streamflow.

Streamflow is further governed by wide variations in the soil mantle and underlying rock. These provide natural storage reservoirs which temporarily hold large supplies of water. At one extreme, tight rock formations overlain by thin soil mantle provide greatly restricted storage and transmission opportunity. Streamflow tends to be erratic and highly responsive to precipitation. The other extreme is a deep, well-developed, aerated soil lying over deeply fissured and fractured parent material. Here, streamflow is well regulated, less subject to sudden increases from precipitation, and well sustained during dry periods.

The Umpqua River drainage in southwest Oregon offers a good example of natural differences in watershed characteristics. This 4,000-square-mile watershed, which heads in the Cascade Range and empties into the Pacific Ocean, has two main forks of about equal area, both yielding roughly equal amounts of yearly average streamflow. The North Umpqua, however, receives much of its supply from fissured basalt formations overlain by pumice, while waters in the South Umpqua are delivered from tighter soil and rock formations. Flows in the North Umpqua are better regulated. The ratio between average maximum winter flow and average minimum summer flow is 176 to 1, whereas comparable relationship in the South Umpqua is 2,833 to 1.

As a general rule, obstacles to economic development in a watershed are proportional to degree of fluctuation in streamflow. Water-using activities are determined by available water supply during periods of low flow. Frequently, these are periods of greatest demand for irrigation, domestic use, recreation, and some types of seasonal industrial activities. Supplementary storage and other costly water-management works have been the traditional methods of meeting this problem.

Peak flows create additional barriers to development. When peak discharges attain sufficient volume to cause economic loss, they become floods. It is obvious that peak flows are characteristic of all streams, but degree of flood damage depends on extent of economic development in the normal flood plain. By the same token, the intensity of agricultural, urban, and industrial development is restricted in these zones by the probabilities of flood occurrence. Any attempt to intensify the use of flood-plain areas is made at the expense of costly structures for control and storage.

Incomplete Resource Inventory

In spite of increasing efforts, we are handicapped by incomplete inventory of our resources. Surveys of forest resources in the United States have been improving greatly in the past 30 years, but we need more accurate appraisals of our growing base and better methods of assessing growth potential and predicting future supplies. Our knowledge of vegetative cover on uncultivated lands is much less complete. We know even less about what types of soils we have in uncultivated lands. Classification and mapping of wildland soil types is in its bare beginnings, far behind our progress on cultivated areas. Our knowledge of water supply is also incomplete. For any given land area we need more accurate information about the total average annual precipitation, the relative proportions which appear as streamflow, the amounts that are returned as vapor by evapotranspiration, and finally, how much is retained in the soil or in groundwater reservoirs.

Lack of Basic Information

Paralleling the requirement for better resource inventories is a need for more complete understanding of processes which govern interaction of land and water. We should have more thorough knowledge of soils, particularly in the vast uncultivated areas where soil characteristics have been virtually unexplored. Such information is needed if we are to improve productivity of forest and range lands, curtail damaging erosion and sedimentation, and manage water supplies which are stored and distributed in the soil mantle. Much more must be learned about the use of soil moisture by vegetation and about the influence of vegetative cover on streamflow. Evaporation and transpiration processes hold many mysteries which, if cleared up, might open the way to more efficient use of water. Increasing efficiency of vegetative production on noncultivated land is another challenge. Productivity of forest lands, for example, could be increased if principles of genetic selection were as highly developed as those for some of the horticultural crops.

MAN AGGRAVATES NATURAL OBSTACLES

Man's works on watershed lands tend to increase natural maladjustments in water supply and quality. Use of water by vegetation is altered, characteristics of the soil mantle are modified, and natural quality of streams, lakes, and groundwaters are lowered by waste products.

Streams have traditionally been used to carry away waste products from all of man's activities. Polluted waters harm fish habitat, recreation, irrigation, and public health. Sediment from soil erosion reduces the quality and usability of water for many purposes.

Natural regulation of streamflow and stability of soil are affected by any activity that decreases the opportunity of precipitation to enter the soil mantle. Water affected by this change finds its way to streams as surface flow with consequent change in timing and volume of stream discharges. Paved areas and compacted soil are the prime causes of rapidly moving surface flow, leading to erosion and erratic behavior of streams.

Stream discharges are further influenced by major changes in vegetative cover. Since vegetation uses a large part of the total water received as precipitation, major increases or decreases in vegetative cover will influence the amounts of water remaining for delivery downstream.

Cultivation, for example, is a major land use causing widespread changes in the natural relationships of plants, soil, and water. When uncultivated land is converted to agricultural purposes, change occurs immediately. There is greater opportunity for evaporation; in some irrigated areas 50 percent of the water reaching the root zone is lost by evaporation from the soil surface. Pattern of soil-moisture use is also changed. Tillage practices employed in dryland farming have permitted more efficient use of available soil moisture at certain times of the year but lowered its use at other times. Irrigation tends to raise water tables, create drainage problems, and cause accumulation of soluble salts. Return flows of irrigation water generally result in lowered quality of streamflow on account of increased sediment load and temperature.

When soil is laid bare, there is also greater risk of surface runoff and erosion. Repeated cultivation often creates a plow layer, a zone of accumulation below the surface which restricts downward movement of water. Lands devoted to intertilled crops or in clean-fallow condition are particularly susceptible to surface runoff and erosion.

In addition to cultivation, a high percentage of the land surface in the United States is devoted to tree growing. On most of these forest lands, harvesting of forest products is progressing at a sustained pace. Removal of forest crop appears to cause some temporary and localized release of additional streamflow which persists until the areas are revegetated. We lack complete information concerning these effects, but in the absence of data one hears many theories. Some observers are certain that timber cutting is the cause of destructive flooding; others say logging causes springs and small streams to dry up.

It is apparent that logging can cause some temporary changes in a watershed. Wherever soil is cleared of vegetation and scraped, scoured, and compacted, erosion can be caused by water moving over the bare surface. Poorly designed logging roads are usually the main sources of postharvest erosion.

Uncontrolled fire is another enemy of watersheds, especially conflagrations which consume all living vegetation and reduce the organic content of the soil. Thus exposed, soil is highly susceptible to erosion because it receives the full impact of rainfall. Loss of organic material reduces its ability to withstand the pounding force of raindrops; soil particles are more easily moved, sorted, and carried away by water. Controlled burning as practiced in some forest-management operations exerts less drastic influence if fires occur while the soil and litter are moist. There is not full agreement concerning the consequences of such practice, and it is a subject needing more investigation.

Rangelands are important areas of water supply, but because of excessive concentrations of livestock and competition for forage between stock and game, the great bulk of our important ranges are overgrazed. Soil compaction has resulted from trampling, and forage production has decreased, with consequent reduction in the natural return of organic material to maintain good infiltration qualities. The total effect is to reduce opportunity for precipitation to soak into the protective mantle. Erosion and loss of range productivity are inevitable results.

There are other activities on water-producing lands which decrease the usability of water in some manner. Some of these are mining, recreation, powerline construction, reservoir clearing and construction, and highway and airfield development.

RESEARCH NEEDED TO REDUCE OBSTACLES

We have come a long way in the science of land and water management. A review of our progress in the past 30 years will reveal dramatic improvements in farm practice, range and forest management, and control and use of water. Techniques are available for carrying out additional improvements as soon as economic demands dictate. Other measures have not passed the theoretical stage and remain to be evaluated quantitatively.

There is growing recognition that research is not keeping pace with increasing demand for production from our resources. This lag has resulted, in part, from a nationwide lack of basic research on principles and processes in the complex interrelationships of soil, water, plants, and animals. Consequently, we lack "why" and "how" answers to problems that can be solved only by basic research. The following is only a partial list of research projects requiring this fundamental approach:

1. Evaporation from land surfaces
2. Use of water by transpiration
3. Storage and movement of water in soils
4. Properties of soil associated with erosion
5. Genetic improvement of trees
6. Nutrient cycle in plants and soil
7. Physical and chemical properties of water
8. Energy distribution in natural environments
9. Sediment transport by water

I have emphasized the importance of research because it is an essential step toward economic growth. In the final analysis, resource management will be appraised in an economic framework leading to optimum combined uses of land and water. I should hasten to add that intangible values will continue to motivate some types of resource management. Yet, there is evident need, insofar as possible, to appraise physical and biological resources in quantitative terms. These data can come only from intensive research.

OBJECTIVES OF WATERSHED MANAGEMENT

Supply

Faced with growing needs for water, man has attacked water problems first with the most obvious solutions: storage of surplus supplies and diversion from areas of oversupply to those of under-supply. He has by this means increased the usability of water and made more efficient use of the land. Storage and diversion have also created electric power and made water available for more domestic and industrial use.

Increasing dependence has also been placed on natural storage, especially that provided by groundwater aquifers. These supplies are not generally subject to losses by evaporation and seepage.

Most water-supply systems can be improved to curtail water losses. Many communities, for example, have found that as much as 50 percent of the water pumped in their systems can not be accounted for. Canal losses are also common to every irrigation system, although modernized techniques are available to curtail waste of this kind. Recycling of nonconsumed water offers a method for more efficient water use. Methods are being perfected for using subsurface reservoirs with impervious enclosures to provide for treatment and reuse in a closed system. These methods hold promise in areas where the need is greater than the supply.

Multiple Use

If it is within our power to "control" part of our water supply by vegetative management, we must weigh carefully the alternatives for achieving highest use. At various times proposals have been made to cut timber or other forms of vegetation to make more water available for downstream uses. Two factors, it seems to me, will guide decisions in this type of watershed management. First, we must learn, through more experimental data than we now possess, the actual amounts of water that will be gained by the process, realizing that reduction of transpiration may lead to greater losses in evaporation. A second question would be one of weighing the loss of timber production against gains in irrigated crop production or other uses made of water released by removing vegetation.

Demands for the products of land and water have outmoded single-minded management for water, or timber, or recreation, or for any other individual use of land. The day of locked-up municipal watersheds, for example, is coming to an end. To an increasing extent, they will also be needed for production of forest crops and for some forms of recreation as well as for domestic water.

The same principle should cause us to examine carefully our major water-control structures. I strongly suspect that some water-management projects would show less favorable cost-benefit ratios if we were to equate the true economic loss incurred by their construction with the gains attributed to their installation.

In a broad sense, one could say that watershed management is the allocation of basic resources in accordance with their highest combined use. Since water is one of our three basic resources, one can argue that watershed management does, indeed, encompass a broad scope. To think of it only as management of water in streams, lakes, and ditches is a very narrow and restrictive view—a concept that has led us to some uncoordinated and ineffective water-control projects. If, on the other hand, we look upon it as the coordinated management of land and water, it becomes clear that we are dealing with the whole watershed, whatever its size and location and irrespective of ownership, land-use patterns, lines of responsibility, or political boundaries.

Obstacles to Growth

GLENN L. JOHNSON

The topic originally assigned to me was "Social and Economic Obstacles to Economic Growth." For reasons which I hope to make clear later, I have elected to modify that title to read simply "Obstacles to Growth."

My procedure will be about as follows. I shall first discuss the problem of knowing what we mean when we talk about "social and economic" obstacles to growth as contrasted to the "physical and biological obstacles" discussed by Mr. Dunford. I shall then speak briefly about the meaning of "growth." I shall then have to address myself to certain problems in the philosophy of science and in philosophic value theory which I shall have raised in discussing the meanings of "social and economic obstacles" and of "growth." Finally, I shall present a way of looking at obstacles to growth which I think is more productive and far less restrictive than some of the formal views commonly expressed. This way of looking at obstacles to growth will, I think, be quite in accord with what some of our most effective workers are doing in the field of resource utilization.

THE MEANING OF "SOCIAL" AND "ECONOMIC"

The presence of the two words, *social* and *economic*, in my original assignment implied that I should be able to distinguish between an economic and a social obstacle. I cannot, either practically or in the abstract.

I have just spent six weeks trying to evaluate the United States economic and military aid program to Thailand. In this connection, I often encountered practical discussions about social, economic, and/or political growth and was unable to distinguish among the three. This was true whether I tried to make the distinction factually, in terms of the pecuniary versus the nonpecuniary, in terms of the normative, in terms of the individual versus group action, or in terms of different bases for making choices.

Glenn L. Johnson is professor of agricultural economics at Michigan State University. His teaching career followed five years' association with the Bureau of Agricultural Economics, U.S. Department of Agriculture.

When we talked about social as contrasted to economic facts, I found that there were very few, if any, facts of economic significance which did not also have social significance. Similarly, when we tried to find facts which were of social consequence, I found that they almost invariably had economic consequences.

Sometimes an attempt is made to distinguish between the economic, on one hand, and the social and political, on the other, in terms of the pecuniary versus the nonpecuniary. This basis for distinction is extremely unsatisfactory to the economist whose work deals more with consumption than production economics. The economist working with consumption economics is ordinarily dealing with the attainment of nonpecuniary values. As such, he would certainly object violently to having consumption economics excluded from the field of economics and classified as social or political.

At other times, attempts are made to distinguish between the social and economic on the basis of the nature of values involved. Economic value is alleged to be something different from social or political values. Here again one encounters the same difficulty as on the factual side. The so-called social and political values turn out to have economic significance while the so-called economic values are of great social and political significance. The distinction is about as useful as that between a woman and a human female.

Others attempt to distinguish between the economic and the social and political on the basis of the distinction between individuals and groups. This distinction is very unsatisfactory to the economist who deals with the economics of the behavior of individuals and groups, the latter being termed macro-economics.

Some distinguish between the economic and the social and political on the basis of the distinction between the free-enterprise system of making choices and other methods. This, of course, is a very unsatisfactory view to those economists who have elected to work with socialistic and non-free-enterprise organized economies. They have demonstrated clearly that economics, in its broader sense, applies to such organizations as well as to free-enterprise organizations.

Mr. Dunford's assignment to discuss biological and physical obstacles implies that both he and I should be able to differentiate the social-economic and the physical and biological. Again, I cannot.

Physical and biological obstacles are not obstacles unless the cost of overcoming them exceeds the value of the benefits gained by overcoming them. This begins to sound very social-economic to me, and the essential distinction between the social-economic on one hand and the physical and biological on the other eludes me.

Another difficulty which arises in trying to distinguish between the social and economic, in one instance, and the physical and biological, in another, is that the physical and biological are increasingly man-made and made as a matter of conscious policy. This begins to sound political and socio-economic. Again, the distinction between social and economic, on the one hand, and the physical and biological on the other, becomes elusive. Another difficulty one encounters in attempting to make this distinction is the essentially human characteristic of knowledge about the so-called physical and the biological. Knowledge is a human phenomenon and is, by the nature of knowledge, quite social.

Thus, I am going to refrain, for the remainder of this paper, from contrasting the social-political-economic with the physical and biological. The one simple title, "Obstacles to Growth," will have to be sufficient to cover what is sometimes referred to as social-economic, physical, and biological obstacles to growth.

THE MEANING OF GROWTH

Originally, I was supposed to talk about economic growth but, as is apparent from the preceding pages, I would have difficulty distinguishing economic from other kinds of growth.

There is another difficulty involved in talking about plain growth, however. Growth of nations, regions, and societies is commonly defined as "an increase in ability to satisfy wants." The difficulty with this definition can be illustrated by considering the consequences of a course in music appreciation. A course in music appreciation increases the wants which can be satisfied with a given amount of resources, whereas the definition we are considering tends, almost universally, to apply only to instances where wants are held constant while the means of satisfying wants are increased.

It appears to me that a better definition of economic growth would be the following: "Growth is an increase in the quantity of wants which can be satisfied." This definition includes in growth an increase in both (1) the means of satisfying wants and (2) the wants which can be satisfied with a given amount of means as a result of normative development and education of the individuals in an economy. In short, growth in tastes, wants, and preferences is, according to this definition, as important as growth in the means to satisfy wants. Growth, then, also occurs when a man learns to appreciate nature, sanitary facilities, music, justice, boating, relaxation, and solitude, to mention only a few of the things which we can learn to appreciate.

SOME PROBLEMS IN THE PHILOSOPHY OF SCIENCE
AND IN PHILOSOPHIC VALUE THEORY

My tampering with the meaning of "social" and "economic" led me to talk about normative matters or, more simply, questions of "goodness" and "badness." Such discussion opens up a Pandora's box of problems in philosophic value theory and in the philosophy of science. I appreciate the enormity of the area which I am opening up for discussion, for I am in the middle of a sabbatical leave program devoted to a study of methods for working with values in solving farm management and policy problems.

Basically, I find that most common formal positions in the philosophy of science and in philosophic value theory are unduly restrictive. None of the positions seems to me to be complete enough for work on obstacles to growth.

One of the most popular current positions is positivism, including logical or rational positivism. This position is particularly popular with the physical scientists and with the mathematically and statistically oriented social scientists who are trying to imitate their counterparts in physical science. This position excludes the possibility of objective knowledge of goodness and badness and hence avoids addressing itself to answering questions of purpose, value, or objective.

Less commonly encountered in scientific work is what I call "outright normativism," which also seems unduly restrictive. Outright normativism addresses itself to answering pure questions concerning "goodness" and "badness." There are many forms of outright normativism, including emotivism and intuitionism, both of which seem unduly restrictive within normativism, not to mention their inadequacy for producing the factual concepts so often required for solution to practical problems in resource utilization.

Modern welfare economics theory is a modified form of positivism commonly used by economists. Mr. Krutilla's paper, with its analysis of the International Joint Commission's work on the Columbia Basin problem, dealt with modern welfare economics. That commission worked (presumably) within the framework established by modern welfare economics. Modern welfare economics recognizes the economist's inability to produce interpersonally valid or comparable utility measures and, hence, refuses to reach judgments about what should be done if as many as one person is made worse off in order to benefit another. As a large proportion of the important resource-development problems of this world involve making some people worse off in order to make others better off, this position seems far too restrictive for work on resource-utilization problems.

A fourth position commonly encountered among economists, particularly those of the institutional school, is what I call the "John Dewey form of pragmatism." In addition to applying a test of workability, this form of pragmatism is based on the dual presumption that the *values* of ends and means and the *natures* of factual and normative concepts are both interrelated. Though this position is far less restrictive than the other three mentioned, its very complexity can become restrictive. The assumed interdependencies between means and ends and between factual and normative concepts make this philosophic position complicated. At the same time, these assumed interdependencies prevent the pragmatist from utilizing either positivism or outright normativism in situations where these two approaches seem appropriate. Those of you who are acquainted with Wisconsin institutionalism and Wisconsin land economics will recognize that John R. Commons and, later, Leonard Salter were profoundly influenced by John Dewey's pragmatism as it appeared in his early writings and as it was finally summarized in his *Theory of Inquiry*.

I find a distinct need in my research for a method of utilizing the contributions of the above four and other related philosophies without submitting to their accompanying restrictions. The view of man and his problem-solving activities which I shall present in the next section is a way, I think, of utilizing those contributions without submitting to their inherent restrictions.

A WAY OF LOOKING AT MAN AND HIS PROBLEM-SOLVING ACTIVITIES IN CONNECTION WITH OBSTACLES TO GROWTH

I find it advantageous to view man and his problem-solving activities according to the following points. While these points reflect a formally different view of man than is reflected in many of our courses in research methodology, I think some people will derive comfort from the correspondence between these points and the activities of competent researchers on resource-utilization problems.

1. Man is viewed as both an individual and as a social being. Hobbes, Locke, Rousseau, and, to a lesser extent, Mill viewed man as an individual deriving whatever significance he has from his individualism. On the other hand, Plato, Hegel, and Marx regarded man as a social being deriving whatever significance he has from being a part of a larger social organization.
2. Man and groups of men are viewed as problem solvers.
3. Problem-solving or rational activity, on the part of man and groups of men, is envisioned as an attempt to find the right action to take as a solution to the problem. Right actions are viewed as compromises among man-conceived normative concepts of "goodness" and

"badness" in view of man-conceived positive concepts about the present, the conditional future, and the unconditional future. Subproblems of problems of finding the right action to take involve questions of pure fact and questions of pure value, for the attention of the pure positivists and pure normativists, respectively.

4. Man's processes of inquiry are regarded to be essentially the same whether he seeks factual or normative concepts. Objectivity is viewed as involving, fundamentally, a willingness to revise concepts (either factual or normative) on the basis of tests of consistency, clarity, and workability. Thus, man is viewed as capable of working with both factual and normative concepts contrary to more restrictive philosophies, such as positivism.

5. Man is viewed as a creative being capable of conceiving of a nonexisting reality and of creating or inventing in the image of such original concepts. He is also viewed as creative in the additional sense that he can conceive of nonexisting values and instill them in himself, in others, and in society; freedom and justice being examples. He is also viewed as being creative in the sense that he can conceive of nonexistent, decision-making procedures and then invent or bring into existence institutional arrangements for implementing the decision-making arrangements, democracy being a case in point.

6. The problems which man seeks to solve are viewed as typically complex, requiring descriptive or factual concepts, normative concepts, decision-making systems, and inventive, creative activities for their solutions. The descriptive, factual concepts come from the sciences of economics, sociology, biology, physics, political science, chemistry, etc. The normative concepts come from a wide range of disciplines involving theology, philosophy, economics, political science, sociology, and biology. Decision-making arrangements are studied in economics and political science. Inventive, creative activities occur with respect to physical arrangements, norms, and decision-making arrangements.

When man is conceived as I have suggested here, obstacles to growth become mainly the limitations of man—limitations in his ability to know and in his ability to create. This does not mean that there are no obstacles that man cannot overcome. It means that the obstacles which cannot be overcome exceed man's total capacity to know and to create. Resource limitations, of course, reflect man's inability to create.

The concepts of man and of his problem-solving activities embedded in the above points serve, I believe, to liberate us from the undue formal restrictions and complications of various philosophic positions which sometimes dominate us almost as a matter of accident in our educational histories. This freedom is likely to involve much more objective attention to questions of "goodness" and "badness" without the guilty feeling that we are propagandizing. With respect to water and land utilization, I refer to attention to conservation values, recreational values, the values of sanitary facilities, and the values of public investments in power production, which of course involves the value of productivity in its most fundamental sense.

The above concept of man and his problem-solving activities will keep us, I believe, from confining our efforts to one aspect of a group problem while referring to other aspects as obstacles rather than engaging in *complete, creative* attacks on problems. This will, I think, conform with the work of our present competent researchers in the field of resource utilization. I have little patience with the sociologist who complains that crass "economic motives" stand in the way of his favorite sociologic solution. Similarly, I find that the technologist who argues that economic and political obstacles prevent the construction of his ideal structures has simply not completed his problem-solving activities by taking into account the so-called political and economic considerations.

I could continue with this list almost indefinitely, but the point would always be the same. Solutions to problems of growth are complex things requiring creative, factual, and normative work from many disciplines. So long as information from one discipline represents an obstacle, the solution is not at hand and the job has not been completed.

Engineering Research in the Development of Water Resources

WALTER H. PRICE

The social, economic, political, scientific, and engineering problems involved in supplying potable water for our rapidly expanding population are so great that all segments of our society must assist in solving them. This paper will deal only with those engineering problems that are related to the development and construction of water storage and distribution projects and those which can be solved through research.

Should the present birth rate be sustained, the population of the United States will increase to 214 million by 1970, to 260 million by 1980, and to 1 billion by the year 2050, a date some of our children will live to see. This increasing population will use more water per capita. Hence, by the year 2000, just 39 years from now, our water demands are expected to be three times what they are today. The report of the Select Committee on National Water Resources of the United States Senate states that more than $200 billion will have to be spent during the next 20 years on all types of water resources facilities if this country is to continue to grow and prosper and to have an ample supply of good quality water.

The state of California, alone, expects to spend nearly $2 billion on some of the essential features of its water plan during the next 10 years. This is nearly half as much as the Bureau of Reclamation has spent in all the 17 western states during its entire 59 years of existence. Parenthetically, it is interesting to note that California will probably spend more than three times this amount for highway construction during the same period.

In the water-deficient areas of the West, where our consumptive use is high because of needed irrigation, we must develop our available supply to the fullest, and find ways and means of conserving this supply and using it more efficiently. The Bureau of Reclamation has

Walter H. Price is chief research engineer, Bureau of Reclamation, for which agency he has worked since graduation from Tulane University in 1930 with a degree in civil engineering.

listed over a thousand water projects which are feasible of development in the 17 western states by the year 2000. These and other projects will involve dams, canals, tunnels, pumping plants, pipe lines, bridges, and power plants. In order to build these structures most economically, we must advance in our engineering knowledge and improve our construction methods.

RESEARCH ON ROCK AND SOIL BEHAVIOR

In general, dams have already been constructed at the most favorable sites. As a result. we must know more about the limitations of the remaining sites so that dams may be built with economy and safety. At the Seventh International Congress on Large Dams, held in Rome in June 1961, much discussion centered around test methods for determining strength, moduli of elasticity, and imperviousness; and means of reducing water pressures in cracks of rock foundations. Rock bolting, grouting, and other procedures for improving foundation rock quality were also discussed.

The urgency of having such information had been made clear by a disaster in France about a year and a half before. On December 2, 1959, at about 9 p.m., the Malpasset Dam in southern France collapsed and released a flood that caused the death of well over 300 people and wrecked or damaged more than 2,000 homes. Local authorities estimated total damage at between $4 and $5 million. The collapse was attributed to movement of the rock abutments.

Since that time, increased attention has been given to dam foundations. When I was in Italy for the Congress, I inspected the recently completed Vaiont Dam, which is 860 feet high, the highest arch dam in the world. Because of the comparatively high deflection of the abutments observed during the first partial filling of the reservoir behind the dam, reinforcement was deemed advisable. I saw extensive work in progress to provide reinforcement with high-strength cables, anchored 125 feet into the face of the abutment rock.

It is expected that, in the immediate future, much more emphasis will be placed on the development of the science of rock mechanics and on the necessary attendant research. The Bureau of Reclamation has been doing a relatively small amount of research on rock in the laboratory and at job sites, and this work will be expanded.

In many instances, more economical storage and more efficient hydro-power production can be obtained with less evaporation per unit volume of storage by constructing high dams. An example is the proposed Oroville Dam, to be built on the Feather River as a key structure of the California water plan. A fill-type dam was selected because it is the most economical, and because the Oroville site was not believed suitable for any type of concrete dam of the height required for this development. The Oroville structure will be a fill dam with an impervious earth core; 735 feet high, it will contain 80 million cubic yards of material. Oroville will be 350 feet higher than any existing rockfill dam and about 200 feet higher than Trinity, which is the world's highest earthfill dam. Oroville will be 9 feet higher than Hoover, the highest concrete dam in this country.

Russian engineers announced at the Congress in Rome that they had under construction a rockfill dam on the Vakhsh River, southeast of the Caspian Sea, that will be 990 feet high.

So that structures of such unprecedented heights may not be wastefully overdesigned or dangerously underdesigned, it is essential that information be obtained through research for predicting their behavior under operating conditions. Small-scale laboratory specimens preclude the determination of the strength of rockfill material of the types used in dam construction, and tests must be devised and performed to determine the behavior of the rockfill under the high pressures developed in the high dams now being designed and constructed. Also, the behavior of undisturbed samples of soil removed from a large mass and subjected to conventional tests in the laboratory may be quite different from the mass itself. Hence, testing procedures for evaluating the in-place behavior of large soil masses must be developed.

Other problems related to behavior of large soil masses are observable where subsidence has resulted from lowering the groundwater by pumping. Such subsidence has occurred in many areas and is of considerable consequence where buildings and irrigation works exist or must be constructed. A large portion of Mexico City has sunk about 28 feet during the last 50 years and is continuing to sink at a rate of 6 inches per year because the city's water demands continue to lower the groundwater level. Areas of several hundred square miles in the San Joaquin Valley of California are sinking at rates of ½ to 1½ feet per year because pumping is lowering the groundwater. Some sections of this area have sunk more than 18 feet.

In addition to deep subsidence caused by pumping, a surface subsidence also occurs in some areas of the San Joaquin Valley due to consolidation of the low-density soils of this arid region upon initial wetting. In one test section near the area that must be crossed by water conveyances that will deliver water to southern California, the ground settled 10 feet in one year of ponding. Additional investigations are needed to predict and control these subsidences.

RESEARCH TO REDUCE LOSSES FROM CANALS AND RESERVOIRS

One of the major expenses in the construction of an irrigation system is the cost of canal linings to reduce water loss by seepage. Seepage losses as high as 50 percent have occurred in some unlined canals. The Bureau of Reclamation, through its lower-cost canal lining investigations conducted in cooperation with water users, universities, and industry, has developed linings that are less expensive than those previously available. However, there is still need for a cheaper lining or soil sealant for sealing the many miles of unlined canals already constructed and for reducing the cost of future construction. Progress is being made in this direction.

Recently a new type of chemical sealant was tried in a 6.6-mile reach of a canal on the Eden Reclamation Project in Wyoming. The sealant is a petroleum-based emulsion, of which nearly 45,000 gallons were donated by the California Research Corporation for the test. The emulsion was introduced into the flowing water of the canal and carried into the soil of the bottom and side slopes by the water seeping from the filled canal. Measurements taken before application of the sealant showed that, of the 27.7 cubic feet per second of flow entering the 6.6-mile test section, only 7.9 cubic feet reached the lower end. Forty-eight hours after treatment, the seepage had been reduced by almost two-thirds. The permanency of this treatment has yet to be determined. Other sealants, such as SS-13, manufactured by the Brown Mud Company, and "cationic asphalt emulsions" from the Armour Industrial Chemical Company, are being tested in cooperation with the suppliers and with other agencies.

The loss of reservoir capacity through sediment deposit cannot be overlooked. When the Imperial Dam closure was made, the reservoir behind it had a capacity of 85,000 acre-feet. Its capacity now is less than 1,000 acre-feet. The Guernsey Reservoir of the North Platte River Project in Wyoming and Nebraska has lost one-third of its original capacity during the 30 years since the dam was completed. Many other examples could be given of reservoir capacity loss due to sediment deposit and the clogging of canals of irrigation systems by sediment.

It is apparent, therefore, that additional research is needed to find economical means of reducing the movement of sediment from the watershed without appreciably reducing the streamflow through evaporation and evapotranspiration. Research is also needed to find more efficient ways of keeping the sediment out of irrigation canals and controlling its deposition in the stream.

Reducing Evaporation

Every year 14 million acre-feet of water are lost from lakes and reservoirs of our 17 western states by evaporation. Research has demonstrated that a layer of the compound hexadecanol, which spreads over the water surface to a thickness of one molecule, will materially reduce evaporation. Reductions as high as 75 percent have been obtained in the laboratory. Large-scale tests have been made at Lake Hefner near Oklahoma City, Lake Mead behind Hoover Dam, and Lake Sahuaro near Phoenix, Arizona. Tests are now being conducted at Cachuma Reservoir in California and Utah Lake in Utah. These field tests are made to develop methods of application and to determine the life and behavior of the layer under field conditions.

Lake Sahuaro was almost completely covered with a film on a number of occasions during the test, and evaporation was reduced by as much as 22 percent during a one-month period. The average reduction at Lake Sahuaro was about 14 percent because of the difficulties in keeping the lake covered. When the wind is above 15 miles an hour the hexadecanol is swept off the surface. In certain areas of Australia where the wind seldom exceeds 5 miles an hour, reductions in evaporation up to 50 percent have been reported.

Seven universities are cooperating with the Bureau of Reclamation in conducting research in the various phases of the evaporation-reduction problem. These researches range from a study of the influence of evaporation-reducing substances on fish and wildlife, here at Colorado State University, to a study of the fundamentals of the evaporation-reduction phenomenon.

A powder spray of hexadecanol is now on the market for heated swimming pools. It is sold to reduce loss of heat resulting from evaporation. Hexadecanol is nontoxic. In fact, it is used in many cosmetics, such as lipstick and hand creams.

Cutting Transpiration Losses

It has been estimated that one acre of salt cedar will transpire up to 7 or 8 acre-feet of water a year. In cooperation with the Department of Agriculture and three universities, the Bureau of Reclamation is investigating means of eradicating and controlling this water-wasting plant, which inhabits sizeable acreages in the West.

The Bureau is also cooperating with the Department of Argiculture in the study of means of eliminating aquatic weeds which clog our canals and reduce their water-carrying capacity. Several years ago, in cooperation with the Agricultural Research Service, we discovered a chemical which is quite effective in the control of aquatic weeds in small canals, but we have not yet found a means of controlling their growth in large canals.

RESEARCH ON GROUNDWATER AND BRACKISH WATER

About 20 percent of our present water supply is obtained from groundwater sources. Because surface supplies will become increasingly more difficult to develop, it is believed that the demands on groundwater sources will increase rapidly until almost 50 percent of our supply will come from these sources. Research is needed to find economical means of recharging aquifers, controlling salt water encroachment, and reducing loss of fresh water to the sea.

Demineralization

The Bureau of Reclamation is cooperating with the Office of Saline Water in the study of the electrodialysis process of demineralizing water. In this process an electrical potential is placed across a bank of selective membranes through which the water is pumped. The process is believed to have great promise for removing salts from brackish waters such as are found in many areas of the West.

A field test station is located at the Dalpra farm near Longmont, Colorado, where brackish water from a well is being demineralized. Visitors are welcome at this station and our laboratory in Denver.

The Office of Saline Water now has under construction at Webster, South Dakota, an electrodialysis plant which will produce 250,000 gallons of potable water per day. In the process, raw water will be demineralized from about 1,800 ppm total solids to a product water of about 250 ppm total solids. The demineralizing portion of the plant at Webster was made in Japan where the process was developed principally to recover salt from the sea, rather than for making fresh water.

Cost is still the limiting factor in demineralizing water. Water is delivered to the taps of the home in Denver, Colorado, for about 6 cents per ton. At the present stage of development, brackish water can be demineralized by the electrodialysis process for about 24 cents a ton.

Corrosion damage to metals is estimated to cause a loss of 5 to 6 billion dollars a year in the United States. The reduction of this annual expense would obviously be a financially worthwhile research effort. Irrigation and power projects have much metalwork in the form of gates, penstocks, and conduits, and the bureau is performing a limited amount of research on protective coatings, cathodic protection, and methods of evaluating the severity of the corrosion which will be experienced.

HYDRAULICS AND MATERIALS RESEARCH

Hydraulics is still an inexact science despite a long history of laboratory and field research. If you visit our laboratory in Denver, you will see hydraulic models of spillways and outlet works in operation because experience has shown that a better design can be arrived at through model tests than through computations alone. Recently we have discovered that the coefficients derived from experience and tests of small lined canals cannot be extrapolated and used accurately for the design of large lined canals. Field research is now being performed to explain this nonconformity of accepted relationships and to supply data for the design of large canals. One canal of river-size, having capacity up to 9,000 cubic feet per second, is now being planned for the Texas Basins Project. It would extend from the Sabine River in northeast Texas to the lower Rio Grande in the southwest, a distance of 450 miles.

The Bureau of Reclamation is also conducting a continuing program of research on concrete as a material and on the improvement of methods of concrete design. We are investigating new uses of materials. For the first time, soil cement will be used in place of rock riprap on Merritt Dam in Nebraska. Research showed that this could be safely done in this area, which is devoid of suitable rock for riprap. The bureau is also studying the engineering properties of soils to better predict their behavior in engineering structures. Asphaltic materials are being studied for canal linings and facings of dams and embankments. Plastics are investigated as they become available on the market and certain epoxy resins have been found suitable for bonding new concrete to old in the repair of old structures.

As one of the largest producers of hydroelectric power in this country, the bureau is interested in all developments in this field. Of particular interest is research into the transmission of power at ultra-high voltages and the use of hydroelectric generators of a size larger than we now have in this country.

I have not previously mentioned one of the most pressing problems which call for the attention of the nation's research engineers and scientists: the control of pollution. It is well known that waste water is used over and over again in areas of dense population. Between Sioux City and St. Louis, the waters of the Missouri River are believed to be re-used sixteen times. Such re-use builds up concentrations of detergents and dissolved solids, as well as contamination from overloaded, inefficient sewage-treatment plants along the stream. No single means offers greater possibility of adding to supplies of usable water than does the control of pollution. To this we must direct increased attention.

As many of you know, most appropriations for Reclamation Bureau work are in the form of monies repayable to the federal treasury. That allocated for irrigation is repaid without interest, and that allocated for power, with interest. As an example, two-thirds of the monies that will be appropriated to the Upper Colorado Basin Project will be repaid with interest.

In 1961, Congress for the first time made an appropriation in nonreimbursable funds for research in engineering methods and in materials, to be conducted or underwritten by the bureau. The $300,000 so appropriated is only a small fraction of funds needed to support properly the kinds of research outlined in this paper, which are crucial to the development and conservation of the West's water resources. But it is a beginning.

It is desirable that much of the research which the government supports through the bureau should be performed in the universities. Here it will serve a double purpose. It will help to produce the needed knowledge. It will also create a stimulus to research that may bolster the sagging enrollments in civil engineering courses. The proportion of entering engineering students to all freshmen in the nation's universities dropped from 10.8 percent in 1957 to 7.3 percent in 1960. This drop must be stopped if we are to have manpower competent to meet the engineering challenges in water-resource development in the next 40 years.

BROAD ATTACK ON WATER PROBLEMS

It is obvious that extraordinary efforts will be called for within our lifetime to meet our water demands, and that these efforts must include the application of new scientific ideas and technical measures, as well as new attitudes in the economic and social spheres of water-resource development. It is important that the public be made aware of the seriousness of the impending water shortage and the fact that it requires up to 20 years to plan, design, and build huge, complicated projects such as the Texas Basins Project and the California plan.

In conclusion, I quote from the report of the Senate committee which I mentioned early in this paper.

> The water crisis is not something to be feared for the future. It is here now. It urgently demands immediate attention from all segments of our economy—governmental and nongovernmental. The American people must proceed with the programs and provide the governmental mechanisms to assure more and faster water resource development.[1]

---

[1] U.S. Senate, Select Committee on National Water Resources, *Report,* Jan. 30, 1961, p. 144.

Soil-Water-Plant Research

ROBERT S. WHITNEY

Basic research on soil resources involves the use of all physical and biological sciences. Investigations range from studies of the origin of soil and its description as a naturally occurring body to studies leading to its characterization as a bio-colloidal system. Research is directed toward an integration of the physical, chemical, and biological aspects of this dynamic medium of plant growth. The ultimate goal of all such studies, perhaps, is to provide a basis for efficient use of the soil and water resource and to insure the permanency of agriculture.

DEVELOPMENT OF SOIL SCIENCE

From the beginnings of agriculture, man has sought to identify the factors involved in plant growth and the relationship of these factors to the soil in which the plants grow. Major advances awaited the development of the sciences of chemistry and physics and the foundations of plant physiology, microbiology, and laboratory and field experimental methods.

By the beginning of the twentieth century, or shortly thereafter, agricultural scientists had learned much about soil-water-plant relations. The productive soil was being regarded as a three-dimensional system consisting of solids (minerals and organic matter), liquid (water), and gases (air). Experimentation usually involved Liebig's law of the minimum and Baconian methods. Effects of physical characteristics of soils on plant development, erodibility, and moisture retention and movement were being identified. Micro-organisms other than bacteria were found to be present and significant, and the soil was found to have colloidal properties. The necessity of a continuous oxygen supply in the root zone was recognized.

This whole complex body was recognized to be an organized product of mineral weathering with characteristics dependent not only on the kind and amount of minerals but also on climatic, vegetative, and topographic features. While differences in soil characteristics

---

Robert S. Whitney is professor of agronomy at Colorado State University, specializing in soil chemistry and reclamation of saline-sodium soils. In 1960 he was a member of a special mission on salinity research sent by the Agricultural Research Service to the U.S.S.R.

were found to occur even over short distances, enough similarity of profile features was recognizable to enable man to classify them into groups, series, types, and phases. Such genetic classification systems have more or less persisted. However, systems now in process of development are based on characteristics of soils *per se* and presumably will permit the categorization of all soils found world-wide.

To most soil scientists, the profile is sacred. It is a product of perhaps hundreds of years of soil-forming processes, and mutilation of its ideal features by man or erosion is a catastrophe. It is recognized that the surface horizon contains most of the organic matter and nutrients, and that the sub-surface horizons are zones for water storage and a source of some of the plant nutrients. Throughout its depth, the colloidal clay mineral fraction is a thing to be studied by the physicist and physical chemist insofar as consistency, cohesiveness, water-energy relations, ion adsorptive and exchange capacity, and other properties are concerned. Its microbial population and the effects of the living organisms on organic matter and nutrient transformations are of importance to the microbiologist. The soil solution or liquid phase with its soluble nutrient content is a challenge to both the plant nutritionist and the chemist. Soil is a beautiful thing to those with properly oriented eye. But after all, it is a thing to be used—protected yes, but used.

Original researchers on soils sought the factors involved in plant growth by rather empirical methods. Try this and, if plant growth responses occur, recommend it. Unfortunately, a treatment for Soil A often does not work for Soil B, and the research has to be repeated to find the factor which is limiting growth in Soil B. This method is still being used to some degree.

Fortunately, however, owing to the availability of new techniques, refinement in experimental procedure, and the availability of computers capable of handling mass data, research attacks are changing. A considerable portion of the studies are designed to seek the explanation of phenomena—the "whys," not just the "what happens." There probably will always be the trouble-shooting type of research, but support is becoming more and more available to the soil and plant scientist to investigate a phenomenon just because he is interested in it. More of such support is needed in this field, since it is now evident that it is possible to identify and evaluate the parameters of natural phenomena. Eventually, it is hoped to obtain mathematical expressions which will fit any situation in any soil. This is one of the objectives of basic research. It is quite apparent now, however, that if precise explanations of even the common phenomena involving soil-water-plant and aerial environments are to be forthcoming, the joint efforts of many disciplines will be required.

WATER PROBLEMS ON THE FARM

Many soil-plant problems facing agriculture must be solved if we are to ensure adequate food and fibre supplies to meet future demands of our rapidly expanding population. No problem is more important than ensuring an adequate water supply. Of concern to the soil and plant scientist are the problems associated with efficient use of water on the farm since it apparently will be necessary to stretch the use of existing supplies. Some of the research now in progress eventually will be applicable to conservation of water and maintenance of water quality after it reaches the farm either through irrigation or natural precipitation. The possibility of reducing losses of water in storage and in transit to the farm is well recognized, but apparently the tremendous saving in water that may be possible at the farmstead level has not been emphasized sufficiently or fully recognized. Certainly it is the scientist's responsibility to explore such possibilities, even if at the moment solutions may seem to be somewhat impractical.

In general, the farmer knows how to do a fairly good job of irrigation, but he may not be able to do his best because of the type of his delivery system, uneven topography, or labor costs. Any one of these factors can and usually does result in water waste. Excessive use of water results in loss of water itself, loss of plant nutrients through leaching, poor plant growth, development of drainage and salinity problems, poor physical condition, and often lower-quality ground and return-flow waters due to contamination with salts and even pesticides.

Land Preparation

In order to minimize runoff loss and obtain uniform distribution of water, much land can be leveled to certain specified grades or be left at a uniform grade in all directions. Implications of this practice as to water-saving are obvious. But what about the effect of grading on the soil? The profile becomes truncated in certain areas, and additional soil is added as "fill" on otherwise undisturbed soil. Plants may be growing on subsoils in some parts in the field and on mixtures of surface and subsoils or even normal surface soils in others. Without further corrective treatment, uneven and spotty plant growth usually occurs even though water distribution is good. Research at Colorado State University and other experiment stations has shown that spotty plant growth is due mainly to lack of available plant nutrients and, in some cases, poor physical condition of the exposed subsoils.

Fortunately, through laboratory, greenhouse, and field studies, corrective measures have been identified that are economical in view of the saving of water and labor effected by such land treatment. While much still remains to be discovered in this connection, we can, with considerable confidence, encourage the agricultural engineer and farmer to proceed with grading plans and re-orientation of the water application systems. Often drastic changes in the landscape can be made with ultimate success. While continued maintenance of land so prepared is necessary, plant growth equal to or better than that occurring on the original undisturbed soil profile has been reported. Actually, such preparation constitutes a permanent improvement of the land from the standpoint of water conservation for generations to come. The deleterious effects of water wastage can thus be minimized.

Irrigation Application—Amount and Time

Even with carefully prepared land surfaces, there still remain problems of how much water should be applied and when.

For efficient use of water, we are concerned with production per unit of water. The amount of water to apply depends on many factors such as the water-holding capacity of the soil, the amount of water left in the profile at time of application, the nature of the plant (especially its rooting habit and depth), and the salinity status of the soil and water being used. Time of application is related to the total soil-moisture stress as well as to the stage of growth of the plant, and specifically to the internal water balance of plant tissues. Something is known about all of these factors, but better means of evaluating them are needed.

Measurements of the state of soil moisture are of two kinds: those that are based on the energy condition of soil water; and those that measure the amount of water in a given mass or volume of soil. Some techniques are now available to evaluate the state of soil moisture, but simple methods for detecting internal water deficits of plants in the field (which result in wilting) are practically non-existent. More effective equipment for evaluating soil-water and plant-water balance is needed as a means of helping the farmer to determine the best time to apply water.

Data from the Experiment Station at Colorado State University illustrate possible savings in water that may be obtained by proper timing of application of water to corn. Certain plots received four irrigations, a common practice, the last one falling in late August; other plots were irrigated three times, the late application being eliminated. The area receiving 12.8 inches of water in four irrigations produced 152 bushels of corn per acre, while the area receiving 9.6 inches of water in three irrigations produced 147 bushels. Four irrigations thus produced only five bushels per acre more than three irrigations, hardly a significant difference. It has been repeatedly shown that the late irrigation of corn often can be eliminated, thus saving the water and cost of application.

Plant Nutrient Level

Further efficiencies in the use of water are influenced by the supply of plant nutrients and by physiological responses of plants. In the study referred to above, 4.9 bushels of corn per acre-inch of water were produced on unfertilized land, while application of adequate nitrogen fertilizers resulted in production of 7.4 bushels of grain per acre-inch. Similar experiments on grassland meadows showed marked reduction in amount of water used to produce a unit of dry hay as the level of available nitrogen was increased. In studies by the Agricultural Research Service at Yuma, Arizona, 14 acre-inches of water were required to produce 1 ton of alfalfa hay on an acre of soil deficient in phosphorus, while only 8 acre-inches were required per ton of hay on soil receiving adequate phosphate fertilizer.

Soil Evaporation Losses

Evaporation from the soil surface is one of the main ways in which water is lost. It is estimated that, of the amount of water that reaches the root zone under irrigated conditions, up to 50 per cent is lost by evaporation. Losses may be even greater in non-irrigated areas. In the summer fallow region of the Great Plains, it is estimated that at least two-thirds of the rainfall is lost by evaporation. In a 20-inch rainfall belt, reduction of evaporation loss by only 8 per cent would result in a saving of 1 inch of water, which is equivalent to an increase of 3 inches of precipitation under normal evaporative conditions.

Some data are available which show the effects on plant growth of extra water saved for use when evaporation losses are reduced. The evidence indicates that there is a great possibility of reducing the amount of water required to produce crops and increase crop yield. Unfortunately, there now seems to be no very practical means of reducing evaporation losses from soil surfaces either under irrigated or non-irrigated conditions, other than mulching or soil compaction. However, a few other methods have been investigated recently.

Several investigators are studying the effects of plastic covering between rows of planted crops. Rain reaching the plastic covers runs to the furrows where it concentrates and penetrates to considerable depths. A greater portion of this water will remain in the soil and be used by plants than when the rain moistens the entire soil surface uniformly but to a shallower depth, where it is more subject to evaporation. The plastic reduces evaporation from the soil area covered. By preventing weed growth, it also eliminates loss by transpiration from the weeds.

By and large such treatments are uneconomical now, but the potential of this or other methods needs to be investigated. In fact, intensive research is needed to develop ways of obtaining deeper storage of water from light rains, in order to reduce evaporation losses.

Dr. Sterling R. Olsen and associates, of the Agricultural Research Service, have just provided results of a preliminary experiment based on another possibility of reducing evaporation loss. In these studies potted soils with no plants were treated with hexadecanol, and water loss over time was compared with that from untreated soils and open pans. The results given in Figure 1 show the possibility of reducing water loss by such treatment. The data represent only a 10-day period, but certain treatments showed continuing benefit several months later. The cost is prohibitive now, but the results warrant further studies of this type. Basic to such investigations is elucidation of principles of saturated and unsaturated flow of liquid water, vapor movement, and the interactions of atmospheric and soil environments.

Transpiration Losses

Another approach to water conservation on the farm is reduction in transpiration loss from plants. It has been estimated that 20 to 50 per cent of the water that falls on an area is used in the process of transpiration from plants. The amount of water evaporated from leaf surfaces is tremendous, and it varies from 400 to 1,000 pounds for each pound of dry plant material produced. Only a fraction of a per cent of water taken up is elaborated into plant tissue; the balance is lost from the plant. The amount transpired varies, of course, with plant species, climate, and soil properties.

Development of methods for reducing transpiration loss will depend on clarification of the process of water uptake by plants, its movement through the plant, and its loss to the atmosphere. Methods suggested include: use of chemicals that are taken up by roots, which might reduce evaporation once they are transported to leaves and stems; external waterproofing of plants; and genetic development of

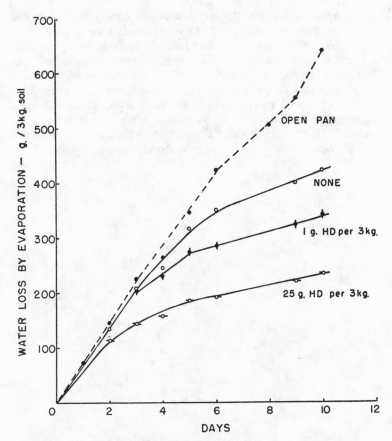

FIGURE 1. Effect of hexadecanol (HD) on water loss by evaporation from uncropped soil. (Sterling R. Olsen and associates, Soil and Water Conservation Research Division, Agricultural Research Service.)

varieties that require less water to grow and reproduce. Very little work is under way on such studies. It would seem that further attack on these methods, particularly the genetic approach, might prove to be fruitful.

SUMMARY

Evidence has been presented which shows that tremendous saving of water on the farm is possible and that efficiencies can be effected. The practicality of techniques developed from fundamental research will depend on how short the water supplies become in the future and on the economic situation at the time. The indication now is that it is possible drastically to alter some soils physically in order to permit efficient water application and use, and that the resulting soil can be returned to normal productivity. Numerous other possibilities have been suggested as ways of making more efficient use of irrigation water and natural precipitation at the farm level. Land and water planners for the future should encourage further basic research by soil and plant scientists with the objective of finding ways of "developing" water on the farm in order to stretch existing supplies.

Integration of Natural and Social Sciences in Developing Natural Resources

RALEIGH BARLOWE

Most human knowledge can be classified in three general areas: the natural sciences, the social sciences, and the humanities. Natural science deals with the physical and biological features of the universe or, as Seligman has observed, "with the phenomena of the universe in which our world forms so tiny a speck."[1] Social science is concerned with human affairs, with "the activities of man in relation to the group or groups with which he associates."[2] The humanities in turn deal with man's culture and with "manifestations of his spiritual existence."[3]

This paper emphasizes the integration of the first two of these three bodies of knowledge as they apply in the development of natural resources. Before going on to this subject, a few comments are in order concerning the nature of the natural sciences, the social sciences, and our concept of natural resources.

NATURAL SCIENCES AND SOCIAL SCIENCES

Natural science is composed of two major sub-areas: the physical sciences which deal with inanimate nature and the biological sciences which deal with life and living matter. Among the physical sciences, we ordinarily list subject-matter areas such as astronomy, chemistry,

[1] Edwin R. A. Seligman, "What Are the Social Sciences?" *Encyclopedia of the Social Sciences* (Macmillan, 1930), I, 3.
[2] Wilson Gee, *Social Science Research Methods* (Appleton-Century-Crofts, 1950), p. 4.
[3] Waldo G. Leland, "Recent Trends in the Humanities," *Science*, LXXIX (March 30, 1934), 281.

Raleigh Barlowe is professor and head of the department of resource development at Michigan State University. His long career as a teacher has been varied by service with the U.S. Department of Agriculture and with the Food and Agricultural Organization of the United Nations.

physics, geology, and quite often mathematics. The biological sciences include such areas as botany, zoology, physiology, genetics, and pathology. Both the physical and the biological sciences started with a few basic classifications and added new ones as the frontiers of knowledge were pushed back. Both can look to basic cores of so-called pure science and also to wide-scale applications and developments in engineering and the applied sciences. Both also have subject-matter areas such as biochemistry and soil science that involve a combination or overlapping of the physical and biological sciences.

Like natural science, social science embraces a broad group of sub-areas. It includes some century-old subjects such as history, jurisprudence, and politics (political science), along with the newer disciplines of economics, sociology, anthropology, social psychology, and cultural geography. Developments in knowledge have contributed to the emergence of new social sciences such as penology and gerontology. Human interrelationships also have contributed to the rise of related hybrid areas such as education, ethics, geography, and medicine that involve an intermixing of social science with segments of the humanities and the natural sciences.

The three-fold classification of knowledge into the natural and the social sciences and the humanities has relevance for certain purposes. But it represents only one of many ways to cut the pie of knowledge. Other schemes are often used when we talk generally about subjects such as the development of natural resources. These other approaches frequently call for the integration and intermixing of ideas and concepts that have their roots in different classes of knowledge.

THE CONCEPT OF RESOURCES

A need for some integration of the concepts of the natural and the social sciences can be observed in the definition of the term "resource." In common parlance, we often think of a resource as involving physical or biological objects or, in Webster's words, "a new or a reserve source of supply or support." Viewed in another context, however, it appears that this concept of a resource has little significance to us as human beings until the physical objects in question are considered in relation to man's needs and desires and the state of his technical know-how. Fish and game were not food resources for man until he acquired knowledge of their edibility and of the means of capturing them. More recently, the oil of the Middle East, the coal of West Virginia, and the iron ore of the Mesabi Range became resources in an economic and human sense only when man became aware of their existence and also developed ways and means of using them. On this subject, the Encyclopedia Britannica observes:

> The parts of the environment useful to man are resources. For anything to be sufficiently useful to be a resource, three conditions must be fulfilled: (1) it must be adaptable to satisfying some want of man . . . ; (2) man must have learned how to use the potential resource; and (3) the potential resource must be available for an agreeable expenditure of other resources.

Zimmermann argues that:

> The word "resource" does not refer to a thing or a substance but to a function which a thing or a substance may perform or to an operation in which it may take part, namely, the function or operation of attaining a given end such as satisfying a want. In other words, the word "resource" is an abstraction reflecting human appraisal and relating to a function or operation . . . . Resources are living phenomena, expanding and contracting in response to human effort and behavior. They thrive under rational harmonious treatment. They shrivel in war and strife. To a large extent, they are man's own creaion. Man's own wisdom is his premier resource—the key resource that unlocks the universe.[4]

Reese expands upon this concept of resources as a product of human effort and behavior.

> Resources, it is argued, do not occur in nature, but rather are the product of man's science, technology, and knowledge. From this point of view, resources may be defined as that part of man's environment which can be used to provide food, shelter, clothing, tools, energy, or recreation. At the present time only a small part of our total environment can be used in this fashion, but this portion has been and can be increased as man advances in knowledge, and as his science improves. . . .

> While at any given time the supply of a particular material or group of resources may be limited, there is reason to believe that over the long run the total supply of resources can be expanded as knowledge increases new sources of supply [and] new methods of extraction as in the case of fuel where wood was followed by coal, then oil, natural gas, electricity, and perhaps in the future by nuclear fission or solar energy. And finally, there is a real possibility of a whole new field of artificial products of which the synthetic fibers and plastics are just a beginning. One cannot even rule out the exploration and exploitation of a whole series of new worlds in outer space.[5]

---

[4]Erich W. Zimmermann, *World Resources and Industries* (revised ed., Harper, 1951), p. 7.

[5]Jim E. Reese, "The Impact of Resource Development on America's Economic Development," in *Resource-Use Policies, Their Formation and Impact* (Conservation and Resource Use Education Project, Joint Council on Economic Education, 1959), p. 6.

When viewed as a product of human knowledge and need, the concept of resources becomes a mingling ground for the natural and the social sciences. Natural and man-made resources involve inanimate and living objects which are subject to all the laws of natural science. But their development and use for human purposes is affected at almost every turn by the many social-science considerations that motivate man in his decisions and behavior.

INTEGRATION BIAS OF LAND ECONOMICS

To ask a land economist to discuss the integration of the natural and social sciences in the development of natural resources is a bit like asking a clergyman if going to heaven is good. Most land economists have a strong bias toward integration of the natural and the social sciences. Richard T. Ely and George S. Wehrwein, two of the more prominent early teachers and writers in land economics, always started their classes by stressing the fact that man's use of land or natural resources takes place within a three-fold framework.

The three elements were described as the physical, the economic, and the institutional.[6] Together they were taken to mean that human decisions regarding the development and use of land resources always involve an intermixture of considerations concerning: (1) the extent, location, and nature of the physical and biological resource base; (2) the economic benefits and costs associated with expected development and use programs, and the impact of our price and credit systems on these operations; and (3) the many governmental, legal, and other societal arrangements that influence human behavior.

Emphasis on this three-fold framework has been continued in the teaching and writings of most of the present-day land economists. Indeed, there has been some tendency to expand upon Ely and Wehrwein and to think in terms of a four-fold framework. This broader concept stresses the physical and biological, the economic, and the institutional elements and separates out a fourth, the technological, which recognizes the impact of man's emerging stock of technical know-how on his ability to develop and use natural resources.

This three- or four-fold framework approach is simply another way of saying that the development and use of natural resources involves the interrelation and integration of the natural and the social sciences. In a world where decisions are made by and for people, it is hard to envisage any other situation as applying.

---

[6]Cf. Richard T. Ely and George S. Wehrwein, *Land Economics* (Macmillan, 1940), p. v.

INTEGRATION ESSENTIAL FOR AREA DEVELOPMENT

One of the easiest ways to visualize the joint roles that factors rooted in the natural and the social sciences play in resource development is to view the problem in terms of potentialities and accomplishments in area development. A brief look at conditions in different parts of the world is enough to indicate that some areas and regions have enjoyed more development and growth than others. Further examination shows that these differences can often be explained in terms of natural and social resources.

Bountiful supplies of natural resources provide an excellent base for economic development and growth if they are used by people of intelligence and drive who operate with economic, political, and social institutions that favor growth. Among the more important of these institutions are political order and stability, education and training of future workers, incentives for work and for efforts directed at maximizing returns and satisfactions, social acceptance of the desirability of productive labor, and widespread opportunities for personal advancement and progress.

History shows that areas that have combined these types of institutions with their natural-resource base have generally experienced growth. On the other hand, those areas that have suffered from political instability, low levels of living, limited opportunity for education, and few open roads for individual advancement, have usually stagnated even if they have had a good resource base. Until recent years, the resources in these areas have usually been developed by outside interests, if at all.

With our current emphasis on international economic development and the liberation of colonial areas, it is hoped that these areas will enjoy growth. But it must be recognized that the desired economic growth will not come by itself. Emphasis must be placed on the development and acceptance of economic, political, and social institutions favorable to growth. Without a favorable institutional climate, efforts to stimulate economic growth will bear little fruit.

Institutional arrangements can and often do have a more far-reaching impact on area development than the local natural-resource base. This does not mean that natural resources are unimportant. No one expects the rise of an industrial economy on the frozen wastes of Greenland or the deserts of Saudi Arabia. But countries such as Great Britain, Belgium, and Japan, which have other requisites for development, have demonstrated ability to develop strong economies based on importing and processing raw materials and then selling them as finished goods in world markets.

When one considers the over-all picture in natural-resource development, it is obvious that neither the natural nor the social sciences can provide a basis for resource development without help from the other. Difficulties can easily arise in assigning primary responsibilities to one or the other. When one faces the prospect of converting a desert into an expanse of irrigated fields or of taking mineral ores from the earth and processing them to provide tools and machinery, the problem can be viewed as one for the natural scientist or engineer. But when consideration is given to the emphasis now placed on concepts of benefits, costs, political acceptability, and the ultimate distribution of the returns expected from projects, one may also agree with Zimmermann that "the study of resources belongs in the social sciences, but the synthesizing work of the social scientist must rest on the findings of both natural and applied scientists."[7]

EXAMPLES OF PRIMARY CONCERN WITH THE NATURAL SCIENCES

This belief in the necessity for integration of the natural and the social sciences is not universally accepted. Within the physical and biological sciences there are many scientists, technicians, and even engineers who are primarily, if not exclusively, concerned with what is physically possible of accomplishment rather than with the economic, political, and social implications of their actions. There is the chemist intent on preparing a new compound, the physicist devising means to split the atom, the biologist seeking a cure for some disease, and the architect or engineer who converts new ideas as to design or form into structures.

In the back of his mind, each of these individuals is concerned to some extent with the cost of his project and with the hoped-for acceptance of his product or findings. It is usually assumed that the findings will bring new contributions to knowledge, that they will bring a many-fold return on their cost as they have so often done in the past. Throughout most of their working hours, however, these people can think almost exclusively in terms of the natural sciences without paying any particular heed to our world of social relations.

Sometimes, as during periods of national emergency, scientists and engineers are encouraged to expand on this approach and to move full speed ahead in pushing forward the realm of the possible. Crash programs are initiated to increase arms production, to devise improved weapons, to develop an atomic bomb, to make the nation first to place a man on the moon. Public opinion in these instances usually favors

---

[7]Zimmermann, *op. cit.*, p. 16.

programs of action and progress, or victory at any cost. It is in periods like these, when we operate on a blank-check or cost-plus basis, that some of our most spectacular scientific advances are made. It was in such a period during World War II that our military engineers were able to boast: "The difficult we do; the impossible takes a little time."

Crash programs with liberal financing may be needed to put a spaceman in orbit, to find a cure for cancer, or to devise a cheaper method for the desalinization of sea water. With the development of natural resources and with most peacetime activities, however, it is normal policy to think in terms of the bargaining and price calculations of the market place.

Under peacetime conditions, governments and corporations, like individual families, ordinarily find it desirable to live within their means. Scientists and engineers often find public or private employment on projects that call mostly for thinking in natural-science terms. But most employers are concerned with the development of products they can sell in a competitive market. Profit margins are often small; emphasis is given to efficiency and economy in plant or agency operations; care must be taken to abide by public regulations; attention must be given in market analyses to consumer tastes and attitudes. Some funds are plowed back into basic research and product development, but emphasis is often placed on devising or developing new products for which market demand may be anticipated.

Peacetime operations always bring more emphasis on the perennial questions: "Will it pay?" and "Can it pay off in the next few years?" They also tend to bring more concern with governmental procedures and regulations and more demands for public services. Operators generally find that they must think more in social-science terms and relatively less in terms of the strictly physical aspects of production.

Most people with a natural-science orientation accept this situation as a normal aspect of life. Some, however, fret from time to time because of the limitations our economic and political systems place on their activities and aspirations. The late Frank Lloyd Wright was an example of the latter group. Those familiar with his writings will recall that he frequently castigated our economic system, politicians, government officials, lawyers, and the police as artificialities that contributed to capitalistic centralization and that prevented realization of the "usonian democracy" he associated with his Broadacre City.[8]

---

[8]See, for example, Frank Lloyd Wright, *The Living City* (Horizon, 1958), pp. 31-35.

PROBLEMS WITH THE SOCIAL SCIENCES

Turning our point of emphasis about, it should be recognized that we also have many social scientists who are reluctant to give much consideration in their analyses to the natural sciences or to our natural-resource base. Economic theory, for example, is premised for the most part on a series of assumptions that create a wide gulf between the thinking of the theorist and the conditions of the real world.

Use of abstractions in economics, sociology, and other social sciences can be defended as a chemist justifies the use of test tubes or the physicist justifies the use of a vacuum chamber in his experiments. Abstractions, based on the assumption that most variables can be held constant, are used to isolate principles in human behavior. This is a worthwhile undertaking. But the real test of these principles comes when one relaxes his assumptions to see how his principles operate in real life.

At this point, people dealing with resource problems often have legitimate grounds for complaint. Many social scientists have become so enamored of their excursions into pure theory, of the logical rigor and conceptual precision of their theories, and of the mathematical games they have devised that they quite forget to relate their theories to the problems and behavior of real people. Precision and rigor are highly desired characteristics in social-science reasoning. But these attributes should be combined with a broad knowledge of empirical data. Too often it appears, as Taylor has observed, that:

> . . . precision and rigor are most easily and commonly achieved by clear but simple and narrow minds with very limited, inadequate knowledge and awareness of the infinite diversity and complexity of the real, empirical world, i.e., minds that can contentedly choose and strictly adhere to a few clear and simple abstract assumptions, rigorously develop or deduce their logical implications, and accept the resulting systematic theory as an adequate analysis and representation of a real social economy. For a mind with both a relatively full knowledge and awareness of the rich content of reality, and a strong sense of the importance of truth-to-fact and not only truth about logical implications, it is always very difficult and often impossible to formulate or spell out all that is "felt" to be probably true about the real, empirical subject matter, in a fully precise and rigorous logical theoretical system.[9]

Great forward strides have been made in all the social sciences in recent decades. This progress has brought specialization within the sciences. A few specialists have focused much of their attention on

---

[9]Overton H. Taylor, *A History of Economic Thought* (McGraw-Hill, 1960), pp. 88-89.

the political, sociological, and economic aspects of natural resources, but many others give little attention to relationships between their disciplines and the development and use of resources.

Political scientists often find it more glamorous to become authorities on international problems or on government in some distant area than on local government or natural-resource problems at home. Sociology has its people who prefer to soar at the higher theoretical levels with model concepts rather than to deal on a more pedestrian level with people in local communities. Economists now give more emphasis to location analysis and to the wise use of resources over time than they did a few years back. But much of their theory still rests on the assumption of perfect or near-perfect competition in a one-point world where goods and services move instantaneously without cost or friction to a market where price equilibrium is attained through a balancing of the forces of supply and demand.

All things considered, there are probably just as many social scientists as natural scientists who would prefer to work in a world where consideration need not be given to the complications posed by the subject matter and the findings of other fields. Development of natural resources, however, calls for integration of the contributions of both the natural and the social sciences.

RESOURCE DEVELOPMENT PROCESS

How do we get resource development? Obviously, the problem goes beyond application of the knowledge of any one discipline. One must know something of the laws of physics and also of geology, hydrology, biology, economics, political science, and many other fields. Abstract concepts must be adapted to the conditions at hand and be interwoven with ideas from other disciplines. Theoretical models such as Sir Thomas More's vision of Utopia or the economist's assumptions as to perfect competition must often be set aside for the simple reason that they assume a world where resources are already developed.

Individual operators engaged in the development of natural resources need an appreciation of both the natural and the social sciences. Success for them frequently requires knowledge concerning the nature and potentialities of their resource base, technical know-how relative to the development and use of this base, the talents of a businessman in proportioning inputs and maximizing returns from both production and marketing activities, ability to get along with people, recognition of the working rules of society, and an awareness of the impact of government and other institutional factors on their operations.

Public officials and businessmen operating in conjunction with others can often rely on the expertise of their staff and associates. But they themselves need broad comprehensions of development problems. Top-level administration calls for use of a macro approach that enables them to see the forest as well as the trees.

Integration of the natural and the social sciences starts with the basic rationale for resource development. An individual, a company, or a public agency owns a resource or singles out one that it may acquire or control. Consideration is given to the nature and development potential of the resource. With a tract of land, attention may be focused on its area, shape, climate, location with respect to other resources, water facilities, possible mineral deposits, and the flora and fauna found on the land or capable of being supported by it. Thought also is given to the development potential of the site—to the flow of goods, services, and income that may come from the sale of existing resources such as timber, oil, or residential building lots, or from development of the site for the continuing production of beef animals, farm crops, office rental space, or outdoor recreation opportunities.

Evaluation of the development potential of a resource calls for careful weighing of its physical and biological production possibilities along with its economic and other institutional opportunities. Characteristics of the resource, the uses to which it may be put, the market demand situation, and the community or society in which it is found may either favor or discourage development.

There is no point in trying to develop farm land or a winter resort if the land in question lacks the requisite physical qualifications. By the same token, prospective developments may be ill-advised if there is little economic demand for the products envisioned. Low-cost building sites could be platted in abundance throughout eastern Colorado, but the demand for new housing in this area is definitely limited. Large tracts of farm land in the United States could be used to grow potatoes or onions, but market demand limits the areas needed for these crops. Similarly, many areas could be used profitably for the production of marijuana, were it not for public regulations against growing and selling it.

The development potentials associated with a resource vary with the time and circumstance. Development programs involving shifts to higher and better uses ordinarily appear more feasible in prosperous times than in periods of market depression and economic uncertainty. Technological advances have a way of enhancing the potentials of those resources that experience greater demands and also of lowering the potentials for resources for which substitutes are found.

Population growth, the rise of cities, transportation facilities, industrial expansion in the area, and the phenomenon of urban sprawl all have a marked impact on the demand for resource products and facilities. Developments of this nature often trigger the development of new resources and frequently the redevelopment of numerous sites for emerging higher and better uses.

Even when allowances are made for differences in time, technical know-how, and market demand, important differences often arise between individual analyses of the economic potential of a given resource. Some operators are willing to shoulder a heavier burden of risk than others. Some have more imagination, more managerial ability, more operating capital, or a better credit standing.

Once the operator has appraised the development potential of his resource, he will consider the costs and benefits associated with different levels of development. If his calculations show an excess of benefits, measured in straight dollar terms or in some composite of monetary income and personal satisfactions, above his expected costs, he may proceed with the development process. Very often, however, he may hold back for reasons of caution, lack of faith in his calculations, desire to secure more return on the "sunk" costs of some existing investment, or a willingness to speculate on the eventual emergence of some higher and better use.

THREE FACETS OF RESOURCE DEVELOPMENT

Throughout the integration process, it is important to keep in mind three facts: (1) resources are developed primarily for human use; (2) social-welfare considerations dictate that resources should be developed or redeveloped in a co-ordinated manner that emphasizes their over-all highest and best use; and (3) developments should promise sufficient returns to more than cover their construction and operating costs.

When we emphasize the fact that resources are developed primarily for human use, we recognize that there is little point in developing resources for their own sake. Harrison Brown has pointed out that

> . . . if at some future time the average concentration of copper in copper ore were to drop to 0.01 percent, and if there were still an acute need for copper, there would be little question but that the metal could be extracted in high yield. . . . Given the brainpower and the energy, the people of the world could, if need be, support themselves entirely with the leanest of ores, the waters of the oceans, the rocks of the earth's crust, and the very air around them.[10]

[10]Harrison Brown, James Bonner, and John Weir, *The Next Hundred Years* (Viking, 1957), pp. 90, 92.

Copper, aluminum, and other metals could now be extracted from low-grade ores. But, given our present supply and demand situation, there is little point in pushing this type of resource development beyond experiments that prove the technical existence of these opportunities.

As human beings, most of us like to get our money's worth. Both as private investors and as taxpayers, we like to feel our dollars are invested to good purpose. This means that, with both public and private resource development, we assume that rational planning will lead to the undertaking of only those projects which promise to produce a surplus of benefits above costs.

This concern over benefits and costs can be viewed either from an over-all or an individual-project basis. In an over-all sense, it is important that the right decisions be made in the initial development of resources. Most developments freeze the pattern for years to come. Mistakes have been made in the past. Individual programs have been pushed through, often at the expense of other resource owners and of communities that could have realized more benefits from the use of alternative development plans.

Social-welfare considerations dictate that emphasis be given to programs that foster the co-ordinated development of the entire resource base and to programs that may emphasize multiple-purpose rather than single-use developments. Broad macro views of resource problems are needed on the part of the public and private officials who plan these co-ordinated developments. Considerable understanding of the issues also is needed in working out problems posed by dissociation of benefits and costs and by differences in public and private objectives.

When we turn our attention to the problem of benefit-cost analysis as it applies to individual projects, it is easy to conclude that benefits should always exceed costs. All sorts of complications arise, however, when one tries to explain what is or is not included in the concept of benefits and of costs, what emphasis should be given to intangible and extra-market values, the frequent dissociation of benefits and costs, the treatment given to separable segments of benefits and costs, and various other aspects of benefit-cost analysis.

This is not the time for a detailed probing of the issues in benefit-cost analysis. Yet it may well be observed that much of the integrating of the natural and the social sciences in public water-resource development comes to a head in our benefit-cost analyses. It is here that the engineer and the economist come together. Dollar values are placed on the benefits and costs associated with the projects planned by engineers, and decisions are made as to whether projects can produce a positive benefit-cost ratio. More integration of ideas at an earlier planning stage, the preparation of more alternative development plans assuming projects of varying scale, and adjustments in the standards used in calculating benefits and costs could have significant effects on the conclusions reached with many projects.

Two aspects of benefit-cost analysis strike me as being particularly deserving of further inquiry. One concerns our past tendency to limit this type of analysis. The second concerns the limited recognition we give to intangibles and extra-market values. If benefit-cost analysis provides a meaningful guide for public decisions concerning water-resource developments, why not apply it with other types of public expenditures? True, some cities use a type of benefit-cost analysis in their justifications of urban renewal. But why don't we apply this approach to our public expenditures for national defense, for highways, for education, for soil conservation and agriculture? An obvious answer is that these expenditures involve too many intangibles. But are these intangibles any more unfathomable than those associated with water-resource developments? Aren't we really requiring a rigid test of economic feasibility with some types of resource-development investments but not with others?

Far-reaching changes in the methods used to calculate benefits and costs would probably appear in order if we required benefit-cost analyses in justifications of other types of public expenditures. Monetary benefits could be claimed for expenditures on national defense, modern highways, and the like. But would these benefits be the most important ones? Personal satisfactions stemming from individual and group feelings of security could provide a major justification for expenditures on national defense. In like manner, the satisfactions and feelings of relief which drivers experience on our limited-access highways may provide greater justification for highway expenditures than any detailing of the dollar value of the time and transportation costs saved.

Intangibles and extra-market values receive considerable weight in the justifications for many of our expenditures. The crash program we are operating to get a man into space provides an excellent example. A variety of scientific benefits are claimed for our space program; but the major reasons for urgency are national prestige and our uncertainty as to the possible advantages or opportunities that will come with the conquest of space. Time alone will tell the value of this program. From our point of vantage, however, intangible benefits such as national prestige, contributions to knowledge, protection against possible uses of space as an avenue for world domination, and the hoped-for development of more powerful, more efficient, and less costly rockets may very well justify our program.

Turning back to the subject of natural-resource development, one might ask why more consideration is not given to the intangibles associated with water and other resource developments. Experience shows that these developments have often contributed quite handsomely to national defense. They have often had a catalytic effect on economic growth. They are providing new outdoor recreation resources at a time when we expect a tremendous surge in demand for these facilities. Consideration has been given to these types of benefits in recent years. But isn't it time to give more emphasis to ways and means for placing realistic values on the satisfactions associated with these types of benefits?

A SUMMARY VIEW

As the end of this paper looms in sight, a few summary observations appear in order. Integration of factors rooted in the natural and the social sciences has been viewed here as a necessary condition for resource development. Actually, we have little choice as to whether we are going to integrate the natural and the social sciences. In a world populated by people, some type of integration must take place if we are to have resource development. The really important issue centers in the quality of our mix of natural and social science factors. Some combinations of factors lead to more production and higher levels of development than others. This is true for nations and communities and also for individual projects and operators.

At the national and international level, it is essential that nations and peoples combine adequate resources, technical know-how, and workable institutional arrangements if they expect to achieve economic development and growth. It is worth noting in this respect that we have done a somewhat better job in our international development programs in exporting technical know-how than in helping the so-called underdeveloped areas to restructure their social and economic institutions. Yet the ultimate success of our foreign aid programs will probably depend as much or more on the development of local institutional climates favorable to economic growth as on our provision of technical knowledge and financial aids.

Closer to home, the same general principle applies. High-quality combinations of factors from the natural and the social sciences are needed to permit maximum levels of resource development at minimum costs. Public and private projects must be justified on economic and social as well as on technical grounds. Community development, multiple-use objectives, and maximization of social welfare all call for co-ordination in the planning of natural-resource developments. And wise planning cannot be accomplished without integration of many phases of knowledge grounded in the natural and the social sciences.

Welfare, Economics, and Resources Development

HENRY P. CAULFIELD, JR.

The words which have been used to specify this discussion—*welfare, economics,* and *resource development*—no doubt evoke in each of our minds different images of fact, different structures of thought, different senses of value, and different notions as to the relation of the content of each of these words to that of the others. Nevertheless, as teachers, researchers, and professional public servants devoting our varied skills to the field of natural resources, I am sure that we must have a high degree of common awareness of the significance for us of each of these words and of the interrelationship of their meanings. This discussion, I take it, is to see what common ground actually exists and also what real differences we have.

I propose to make my initial contribution to the discussion by answering three questions:

What are the images of fact, structures of thought, and senses of value that each of these words evokes in the minds of persons intellectually concerned with natural resources?

What are the general relationships which must or should obtain between the content evoked by these words?

What should we do, as intellectuals, to try to perfect social welfare?

THE SIGNIFICANCE OF OUR TERMS

Resource Development

By reference to "resource development," rather than to "natural resources" or "nature," this part of our subject—as I see it—is already

---

Henry P. Caulfield, Jr., is assistant director of the Resources Program Staff, U. S. Department of the Interior. An economist specializing in natural-resources development, he is on leave from Resources for the Future, Inc.

The views expressed in this paper are solely those of the author. They do not necessarily reflect those of either the Department of the Interior or Resources for the Future.

loaded. The concept, the relevant content of which really needs exploration first, is "natural resources" or, as it would have been said in the 19th century and before, "Nature," with a capital N.

Nature, as a "unity" and a substitute for the orthodox Judeo-Christian deity; man in a state of nature as naturally good (as in the thought of Rousseau); and communion with nature as a source of moral renewal—all of these ideas have long been held valid by an educated élite and others in our society, at least since the impact of Emerson and Thoreau in the middle of the last century. They are still so held today. Nature untouched is thus considered, on grounds of a natural theology, to be a fundamental social value. Nature as a source of esthetic and exhilarating pleasure is a parallel value in terms of its operational impact.

These values have been traditionally viewed by Americans as non-utilitarian or, as we might say here, anti-developmental. Gifford Pinchot had no use for them. His celebrated difference with John Muir in the Hetch Hetchy controversy of 1913 relating to Yosemite National Park turned, at least in intellectual terms, on the differences between the two men with respect to these values. The Echo Park controversy is one of many recent reminders of their reality and political potency. Our current professional effort to measure these values is another reminder.

Ecology is another prevalent mode of thought relating to natural resources of which account must be taken. For ecology, nature is naturally in a state of dynamic balance. Disturbance of this balance beyond critical limits produces, in many instances, irreversible changes. Such changes, in the view of many persons imbued with ecological truths, are bound to be bad. Ecology thus leads to strong resistance to use of nature, except in such a way as will not destroy its balance. Ecology also leads to strong efforts to overcome, at whatever cost, the depredations of man. High social value is placed upon maintaining nature's balance because such balance is a good in itself and because the existence of future generations depends upon it.

The last major intellectual opposition to development of natural resources is concerned directly with their "running out." In the crudest form of this opposition, projected physical requirements are related to known reserves of currently usable quality, and the doom of future generations is predicted. This type of thought has brought forth the neo-Malthusian vs. faith-in-technological-advance issue of our time.

Underlying the concern with this issue is the value that the current generation places upon its moral responsibility to future generations for resource supplies. The Judeo-Christian belief that man is but the steward of God in the use of God's earth and that each generation must account for its use of the earth's resources is the moral factor involved here. This social value, which calls for denial in the present so as to honor responsibilities to generations yet unborn, of course runs counter to the time preference assumed by economists to be involved in individual valuation of goods and services.

Proposals for resource development—in the context of these social-value considerations, the realities of the physical inter-relatedness of things in nature, and the state of scientific or engineering knowledge —become involved in one of two factual situations or a combination of both:

> —complementarity in the use of resources, where two or more uses can be made of the same resource more cheaply than if each use were based on a separate resource; and
> —conflict in the use of resources, where real choices among social and individual values have to be made—one value cannot be obtained in whole or in part if the other is.

Economics

The foregoing summary, in matter-of-fact terms, of the problem of *values* in the use of resources clearly invites discussion of the role of economics in the solution of the problem. For economics, in its normative form, thinks of itself as pre-eminently qualified to solve value problems. For some economists, no doubt, the whole concern with resource use should be viewed as subsumed within economic thought. If this line of thought is followed, resource-use problems fall within the special competence of economists for final analysis leading to inevitable conclusions before which all should bow.

That economic thought as a normative scheme for the determination of human welfare, that competitive private enterprise which economic thought idealizes, and that economic analysis as a professional practice can and do make substantial contributions to efficient solution of value problems of a free society (including value problems in resource use), I do not doubt. But this paper is not the occasion to justify these beliefs. What is important to bring out here, rather, are the major difficulties of normative economic thought generally, and some of the difficulties in the application of this thought to resource problems. These difficulties, as I see it, underlie many decisions that society has actually made to arbitrate value problems in the field of resource use—indeed, in much of economic life—through the political market places rather than the economic market places of our times.

These difficulties are not new to most of you and some have already been alluded to previously in this conference:

1. In many instances, the creation of resource values involves costs, but the values created cannot effectively be internalized by firms and marketed only to those who are willing to pay an appropriate fee. Instead, once created, they are available to all; for example, smog-free air. Thus, if these values are to be created, they must be created by public enterprise and covered by taxes.

2. In many instances, resource use involves costs external to development firms involving compensation to others, or extra costs to the firm to prevent external costs, but this is so only when public policy intervenes and compels the firm to bear such costs. Costs borne by firms for abatement of pollution are an example.

3. In some instances, the time preference expressed through available interest rates in the private sector does not coincide with the social time preference expressed in the political market place. The public role in soil conservation is a response, I believe, to this difference.

4. Logical necessity, in the conclusions of most normative economic thought, is predicated upon the assumption of "perfect competition." Problems of monopoly are thus put to one side. However, the public does not ignore problems of monopoly and it does care about the overall structure of the economy, despite its protests that interference will breed inefficiency. The 160-acre limitation in reclamation law is an interference that reflects a social value.

5. Logical necessity, in the conclusions reached within most normative economic thought, rests on the assumption that income and wealth distribution prior to a given economic action are in some sense "proper" and, in any case, will not be different after the action has occurred. The public historically has not accepted this assumption. The most obvious examples of public concern with the distribution of income and wealth are estate and inheritance taxes and the progressive income tax. With regard to natural resources, the public concern with "give-away" of natural resources, except to homesteaders and mineral prospectors, is a clear example.

6. Normative economic thought in which efficiency is being maximized is a static scheme of thought which is indifferent to space; regional inequalities in economic development are what they should be, and need not be a concern of public policy. The special concern and action of the federal government with the economic growth of the West is a clear indication that something more than the "invisible hand" was needed, or at least the public has clearly thought so.

Admission of these difficulties does not mean (for me at least) abandonment of economic thought in the solution of problems of value.

The field cannot be left to a combination of the natural sciences and political action. Rather, as has been said by others in this conference before me, a synthesis of the thought and skills of economists and natural scientists should present society with technically feasible choices for action, reflecting all relevant differences in social valuation.

Welfare

Welfare, in any sense meaningful to society as a whole, is clearly not just the sum of the net values obtained by individuals in the economic market place, where each individual makes his own, presumably unique, subjective valuation, which is reflected objectively in prices and costs. The political market place is the forum where collective values—common, majority and minority, regional, and other group values—are expressed and realized through the political process. Viability of any society, to say nothing of anyone's concept of the "good society," depends upon the realization of welfare through both markets!

THRUSTS TOWARD CREATION OF RESOURCES POLICY

In the American political market place over the past 150 years, as I have attempted elsewhere to summarize the history of natural resources policy, there have been what I have called "policy thrusts." These have been substantial policy drives trying to realize different objectives at the same time. Three such thrusts have been identified, and all detailed objectives in policy history have been taken to be subsumed under one or the other of these three.[1]

Development thrust, which clearly has been the strongest of the three, expresses the desire for economic development—collective and individual. Both the public reluctance to fetter private enterprise either by direct regulation or by public competition in exploitation of the public domain, and also the public enthusiasm since the Civil War to develop water resources through the federal government are clear expressions of this thrust—even though, in a sense, they are somewhat contradictory. The western regional orientation of this thrust as it realized itself in positive public policies is of particular importance to note.

Progressive thrust expresses the popular response to the emergence of "trusts," large organizations generally, "monopoly profit," and the apparent maldistribution of income to farmers and laborers in com-

---

[1]See Henry P. Caulfield, Jr., *The Living Past in Federal Power Policy,* Resources For the Future, Inc., annual report, 1959, pp. 24-33. This article summarizes the author's perspective on natural resource policy history. He is developing this perspective in a book.

parison to those who are profiting most from industrial development. The progressive income tax is the most obvious policy expression of this thrust. But the antitrust laws, public-utility regulation, public and cooperative power, and federal policies for lease, rather than sale, of public lands containing oil and gas are other important examples. The spirit of Henry George, if not the letter of his views, has animated much public policy concerning natural resources.

Conservation thrust expresses most potently the reaction by an educated élite, initially located in the East, to natural-resource "exploitation" generally. I have already alluded to the specific contents of this thought in my discussion of natural resources. In summary, despoliation of wilderness and natural beauty is deplored because of the importance of man's communion with nature as a means of moral regeneration. Also, the "exploitation" manifest in private disregard of long-run costs to society believed evident in the findings of ecologists is a segment of this thrust. And lastly, concern for the long-range adequacy of the natural resources available to man, the fear of a running-out of resources, has animated the conservation thrust.

These then—the development, progressive, and conservation thrusts—have been historically, and in large part still are today, the forces in the political market place which are at work forging natural-resources policy. As individuals, our total welfare derives from the subjective valuations we make and realize through the political market place, from those we make and realize through economic markets, and from those values we create within ourselves without direct benefit of either market.

If, intellectually, we would contribute to the achievement of welfare—as regards natural resources or more broadly—we must do more than pursue natural science and technology. We must do more than pursue the social sciences and achieve an interdisciplinary operational synthesis with the natural sciences. We must engage in social criticism, grounded in knowledge of past and present realities projected into the future, with a view to arriving at specific value judgments, derivative of social thought and values, including ethical postulates, that each of us takes to be valid.[2]

---

[2]See, as an effort in this regard, Irving K. Fox and Henry P. Caulfield, Jr., "Getting the Most Out of Water Resources," *State Government*, XXXIV (Spring 1961), 104-111.

Welfare Economics and Resource Development

JOHN F. TIMMONS

My remarks will first draw on certain elements of welfare theory as related to resource use and then suggest how welfare theory may provide an interdisciplinary approach to resource-use problems. Finally, I shall develop the outlines of a possible extension of welfare theory into what I term a "dissociation theory of irrational resource use" or an "association theory of rational resource use."

WELFARE ECONOMICS IN RELATION TO RESOURCE USE

In the context of this presentation, welfare economics is concerned with possible reorganization of resources that will leave the community involved better off without leaving any members thereof worse off. This includes the minimax concept of minimizing dissatisfactions and maximizing satisfactions. Major problems and limitations in the application of welfare theory are measurements of utility and disutility, and interpersonal comparisons of utility as pointed out by Lionel Robbins over two decades ago.

The economist has no monopoly on the appraisal of welfare aspects of resource developments unless the appraisal is so restrictive that it is meaningless. The engineers, the agronomists, the political scientists, and representatives of many other disciplines also are involved. Our problem then is to explore further possibilities of interdisciplinary research in welfare aspects of resource developments.

The development of welfare theory, stemming from discussions in the early 1930's by Hicks, Allen, Kaldor, and Hotelling of Pareto's relative optima, spelled out the meanings of Robbins' denial of interpersonal comparisons of utility and methods of making policy recommendations based on welfare theory in light of this denial. Out

Since 1947 John F. Timmons has been professor of economics at Iowa State University, where he is also on the staff of the Center for Agricultural and Economic Adjustment. He is in charge of work on agricultural problems in Peru, undertaken by Iowa State University under contract with the U.S. Agency for International Development.

of these discussions grew: (1) the compensation principle; (2) the necessary and sufficient conditions for optimal allocation of resources, as popularized by Hicks, Reder, and others; and (3) the marginal cost pricing controversy reviewed by Nancy Ruggles.

Bergson,[1] in 1938, helped clarify the welfare controversy engendered by the Robbins criticism. The welfare function of Bergson, later popularized and further developed by Samuelson, is so broad as to include everything. This general welfare function is reduced to an economic welfare function including only productive factors, their allocation, and the allocation of goods among individuals.

Value Propositions

Bergson states the general conditions for a position of maximum economic welfare for any economic welfare function followed by three sets of restrictions which are value propositions.

Group one restrictions are the *Lerner conditions*. A shift in a unit of any factor of production (not labor) from one production unit to another leaves the economic welfare function unchanged if other elements of the welfare function are held constant. Maximum conditions may be stated in terms of production functions.

Group two restrictions are the *Pareto-Barone conditions*. If an individual consumed goods and performed work in combinations indifferent to him, the economic welfare function would be constant. This is the well-known independence of consuming and working units. Group one restrictions are also assumed to exist.

Given these two groups of restrictions, production conditions may be stated in terms of indifference functions and production functions. Whatever the ratios of equivalence between commodities and work, the marginal rates of substitution must be the same for all. Since homogeneous factors are assumed, the marginal physical product for all workers is equal. The maximum position, given the fundamental value propositions, is one in which no improvement of the economic situation for one person can occur without making another person worse off. These value propositions appear fundamental to the recent welfare reasoning stemming from welfare writings in the post-Robbins period.

The third group of value propositions are the *Cambridge propositions* regarding equal shares. If the incomes of any two persons are equal and if the price and wage rates are fixed, the transfer of a

---

[1] A. Bergson, "A Reformulation of Certain Aspects of Welfare Economics," *Quarterly Journal of Economics* (1938), 310-334.

small unit of the share of one to the other would leave the welfare function unchanged.

The three groups of value propositions given above are not only sufficient but necessary for derivation of maximum conditions presented in welfare studies. These value judgments are not necessary to welfare analysis, but *necessary only to a particular group of maximum conditions.* If the individuals' indifference functions and the firms' production functions are known, they give sufficient information concerning the economic welfare function for determining the maximum position (if one exists). Any set of value judgments may be introduced. All that is necessary is compatibility with the community. This the social scientist can investigate.

INTERDISCIPLINARY APPROACH TO RESOURCE PROBLEMS

Welfare economics serves as a frontier which provides opportunity for bringing together disciplines from both social and physical sciences. The physical sciences provide the physical possibilities of resource use, the physical production functions, and the coefficients assigned to resource productivities within probability estimates. The economic model not only relies heavily upon the kind and quality of physical data but also helps to suggest the kind and quality of physical data needed to analyze resource use. The relevant range of physical possibilities for economic analysis is usually much more restricted than the total range of physical production possibilities. The total range is continually being expanded through physical research such as the work summarized by Professor Whitney.[2] The relevant range for economic consideration is continually being altered through changing costs, prices, and institutions.

In the social sciences, welfare economics suggests a matrix of interdependence between law, political science, sociology, psychology, and anthropology. Through the conjoint contributions of these disciplines, welfare may be more accurately identified and measured. Through these disciplines—particularly that of law—limitations in welfare shifts between people and groups may be obtained. For example, the Fifth and Fourteenth Amendments to the Constitution provide a legal basis for the application of the compensation principle. "Burdens" and "bounties," from the time of Jeremy Bentham down through Roscoe Pound and other students of jurisprudence, are very similar to the costs and benefits of the economists.

Thus, the application of welfare theory in appraising resource developments focuses on resource use which takes place within a frame-

---

[2] See pp. 147-154 above.

work of three dimensions: (1) the physical dimension, which specifies the physically possible limits that are continually being expanded
through extension of knowledge; (2) the economic dimension, which
specifies the economic feasibility of alternative production possibilities and which also continually changes as price and cost relationships
change; and (3) the institutional dimension, which is a creation of
man and can be altered by man to enhance his welfare.

DISSOCIATION AND IRRATIONAL RESOURCE USE

Basic to welfare theory is the idea of a planning and management
agent, which may be a state legislature, a federal congress, an irrigation district, or any other decision-making unit. Basic to this concept of the decision-making unit is the possibility of a resource reorganization that will enhance the welfare of the group. Within this
idea is the assumption, also basic, that the burdens and bounties, or
costs and benefits, or utilities and disutilities are perfectly associated
in the mind of the planning agent. From the group welfare perspective, any dissociation of these dichotomies can provide motivation
for the malallocation of resources.

Dissociations engendering malallocation of resources are of two
types, interspatial and intertemporal. Interspatial dissociations occur
whenever the consequences of a change in resource use by one participant are experienced by other participants spatially separated from
the one changing his resource use. Intertemporal dissociations occur
whenever the planning horizon of a participant is less than the length
of the planning period required for optimum resource allocation.

An example of interspatial dissociation of benefits and costs may
be drawn from a watershed development. Let us assume that a structure on an upstream farm will yield discounted benefits of $500 and
that the cost of the structure is $250. Let us also assume that dis-
counted benefits of only $100 accrue to the farm upon which the
structure must be located, the remaining $400 being distributed
among downstream beneficiaries. Investment in this structure would
be economic at the watershed level since discounted benefits are
double the construction cost. But the upstream farmer would not be
interested in building the structure alone since his return on an investment of $250 would only be $100. Spatial dissociation of benefits
from costs due to property lines would prevent this improvement from
being made.

An example of intertemporal dissociation of benefits and costs
may be illustrated by a leasing arrangement of 1-year duration without

compensation provision. Let us assume that net returns to the farm firm would be maximized over an optimum planning period of 10 years if a current investment were made in the construction of terraces. The landlord would be willing to bear only 50 per cent of the construction costs, since the terms of the lease are such that the tenant, or subsequent tenants, would reap 50 per cent of the benefits over the 10-year period. The current tenant, however, would not be willing to pay half of the construction costs, since his secure expectations would be limited to one-half of the benefits that would be obtainable in one year only. Possible dissociation of benefits accruing over time from costs incurred by current resource contributors probably would prevent this investment from being made.

Solutions to interspatial and/or intertemporal dissociations such as these lie within the theory of welfare economics, and particularly in application of the compensation principle whereby dissociated costs and benefits of resource developments may be reassociated in the minds of the planning-decision agents.

In the process of appraising and implementing resource development projects, both physical and social sciences have necessary contributions to make. Data from the physical sciences are requisite to benefit-cost analyses. These data are the foundation without which adequate analyses cannot be made. The concept of marginality contained in traditional economic theory provides the framework for specifying projects, purposes, and practices which will maximize net benefits from resource use. Welfare economic theory supplies the criteria for resolving dissociation problems which may inhibit the achievement of an optimum use of resources from the group or community perspective. And finally, many disciplines must be called upon to ascertain the role of institutions and adjustments necessary to facilitate this achievement.

Achieving optimum resource development involves difficult problems of identification, measurement, and aggregation. But in the interest of enhancing public welfare through the reorganization of resource uses, these problems provide challenges and opportunities. Through inquiries leading to solutions, the physical and social scientist will find comfort and support in each other's contributions.

Welfare Economics and Resource Development

J. W. MILLIMAN

At the suggestion of the conference committee, I shall present a few of the conclusions and highlights of a recent water-supply study of which I am a co-author, along with Jack Hirshleifer and James C. DeHaven.[1]

Before turning to the book, however, let me make two general points. First, it seems to me that the major problems of natural-resource use and development are to be found not in the realm of theoretical niceties—granted that economic theory and social-welfare analysis are pretty crude tools—but rather in the operational or applied field. I suspect that our gross mistakes and blunders stem from our inability and unwillingness to apply more of the elementary principle of economic analysis to natural-resource decisions, particularly at the public level. There is nothing mystical about natural-resource capital. It should be subject to the same rules and analysis that apply to all economic goods.

Second, despite the abuse of benefit-cost analysis in public water projects, it is clear that the level and stringency of analysis—crude as it is—greatly exceeds that accorded to many other types of public investment. Conservation of *urban* resources and lands will probably be one of the major problem areas to be faced in the next century. Indeed, the amount of urban investment to be made in the next two decades will undoubtedly dwarf the total amounts spent on water resources in the last hundred years. But I have yet to see an urban-

---

[1] Jack Hirshleifer, James C. DeHaven, and Jerome W. Milliman, *Water Supply: Economics, Technology, and Policy* (University of Chicago Press, 1960). A RAND Corporation study. Many of the comments here are taken from ch. XII, "Some Controversial Conclusions and Their Implications."

J. W. Milliman is associate professor of business administration at Indiana University. At intervals during his academic career, he has served as research assistant or consultant to public agencies and private research and planning organizations on questions of public finance and public policy on water-resource development. The present paper presents some of the conclusions of a study for the RAND Corporation, which has kindly consented to this use of the materials.

renewal project which has been subject to a critical and searching benefit-cost analysis. In other words, there are presently no clear-cut standards for judging the proper amount, kind, scope, and direction of public investment in the urban sphere. It is my belief that the benefit-cost framework can be modified and reworked so that it may be used with other kinds of public investment. And public urban facilities and city planning are certainly logical candidates for the rigors of such analysis. What we need is a "Green Book" for city planning.[2]

ALLOCATION AND PRICING POLICIES IN WATER USE

The analysis in the water supply book was divided into two major phases: (1) an examination of the allocation of *existing* supplies; and (2) a study of the alternatives for developing *new* supplies. For each phase we first set forth the basic economic criteria and then examined current practices to see how these actual practices measured up to our theoretical standards. In this connection, we undertook two major case studies: the New York City "water crisis" and the proposals for carrying water to southern California.

Perhaps our most surprising finding was that water supplies are often grossly misallocated among uses and between uses. Discriminating and subsidized pricing patterns and defective systems of water rights are responsible for this waste. It is these misallocations and other defects of administration, rather than lack of water, which lead to the frequent claims of "shortage" and eventual rebuilding of water supplies.

In Los Angeles, as in many other cities, large users are charged prices less than the marginal cost of processing and delivering extra water to them. As a consequence, industries which are large water-users have no incentive to install recirculating devices which would permit a large reduction in the amount of water used. This is wasteful because more highly valued resources are used to supply the extra water used at these low prices than would be needed to build water-conserving devices.

Contrary to popular opinion, industry does not have a fixed "requirement" for water. Economic demands must consider costs and prices. The degree of substitution of other inputs for water will reflect changing economic feasibility. Time and time again we studied projections for the future use of water based purely upon crude extrap-

---

[2]*Proposed Practices for Economic Analysis of River Basin Projects,* Report to the Interagency Committee on Water Resources, by Subcommittee on Evaluation Standards (Government Printing Office, May 1958, revised ed.). This report is commonly called the "Green Book."

olations of present consumption patterns, with no consideration of economic substitutibility. In economic jargon, this amounts to the false assumption that the demand for water is perfectly inelastic.

A current example is to be seen in a recent report of the U. S. Senate Select Committee on National Water Resources, a report now being widely quoted as *the* authoritative study on the prospective demand for and supply of water in the United States in 1980 and 2000. Although the report was prepared by an economist, these projections of demand and supply were developed without reference to such basic factors as prices, costs, alternative uses of water, interregional shifts, and most of the factors affecting the elasticities of demand and supply.[3]

In contrast, we found that the demand for water has a good deal of price elasticity, particularly in such major areas of water use as irrigation and industrial cooling. I am certain that increases in water prices over the next 25 years will greatly increase the demand elasticity in all uses.

New York City presents another example of the way in which an improper pricing policy encourages wasteful use of water. In that city only about 25 per cent of water users are metered. By and large, only the larger commercial and industrial users are metered. Hence, 75 per cent of the water users pay a flat rate, and the cost to them of using extra water is zero. This means that they have no incentive to economize on its use, to fix leaks, or even to turn off faucets. The result is that New York has a high per capita domestic water use. The city is completing construction of the costly new Cannonsville project to increase its supplies, despite the fact shown by competent studies that the repair of serious leaks in the city mains and extension of metering could add as much to the city's water supply as the Cannonsville project at a small fraction of its cost.

In arid regions, irrigation agriculture typically pays very low prices for water and uses large quantities. In the state of California 90 per cent of total water use is for irrigation. The irrigator in Imperial Valley pays $2 per acre-foot for Colorado River water, while Los Angeles and other cities are paying over $25 per acre-foot, wholesale, to the Metropolitan Water District for imported Colorado River

---

[3]Nathaniel Wollman, *A Preliminary Report on the Supply of and Demand for Water in the the United States as Estimated for 1980 and 2000*, U. S. Senate Select Committee on National Water Resources, Committee Print No. 32 (Government Printing Office, 1960), pp. v, 2. These limitations are explicitly recognized by Wollman (pp. 31-34, 76) but not by most persons citing the study.

water. Retail prices go upward from $80 an acre-foot after distribution costs are added.

In presenting the advantages of *voluntary* transfers of water among uses and users and even between regions, we have been accused of wishing to dry up irrigation agriculture in the West. This is a completely unwarranted accusation. In California's Imperial Valley, for example, irrigators are using their two-dollar water to grow large amounts of low-valued crops. Suppose that only 25 per cent of their water rights—or about 1 million acre-feet—were purchased for transfer to urban use in Southern California. The irrigators would almost certainly remain in business. They could reduce the application to the initial crops, shift to crops demanding less moisture, or cut back the irrigation of low-valued crops (alfalfa, pasture, hay and grains, and field crops). Alternatively, they could eliminate some of the waste from seepage and evaporation, which often reaches 50 per cent of the amount delivered. It is our strong belief that the irrigators could make more profits from selling their valuable water rights than from growing low-valued crops.[4] The 25 per cent amount, furthermore, is a large amount by urban standards; the 1 million acre-feet involved is equal to about two-thirds of all the urban water used in the south central area of California!

OVER-INVESTMENT IN WATER SUPPLY

Undoubtedly, the most controversial substantive conclusion of the book, justified by a great variety of evidence from our survey of federal and municipal experience in water-supply decisions, is that in the United States *major water investments are typically undertaken prematurely and on an over-ambitious scale.* Consequently, at any one time there is over-investment in water supply.

Over-investment for any particular area is indicated when facilities stand idle or else are put to makeshift uses, either to avoid the appearance of idleness or to minimize the losses due to past mistakes. Uneconomic over-investment may be also indicated by relatively low return earned on capital invested in water supply. Here the water is actually being put to use, but the price charged is so low that the revenue to the water enterprise is small in relation to cost. There is over-investment because the same capital investment could have

---

[4]At $10 per acre-foot, the sale of 1 million acre-feet per year would bring $10 million net. In the latest year for which data are available (1954), the market value of *all* crops in Imperial County was $109 million, a gross figure from which all the costs of production must be subtracted. See Hirshleifer, DeHaven, and Milliman, *op. cit.*, p. 331.

been put to work producing goods and commodities valued more highly on the margin by consumers; consumers' marginal values in use for water are low in comparison with what could have been obtained if the dollars had been spent elsewhere. Specifically, our two major area studies revealed the highly premature nature of the decision to build the Cannonsville Project in the one case and the proposal for construction of the Feather River Project in the other. Or, looking at return to capital, we found that, for the public water-supply systems in general, this is of the order of 2 per cent—an astonishingly low figure.

The reasons for the prevalence of over-investment in water supply are complex and interrelated. To a great extent they are outside the sphere of economic analysis, and so we only speculate about them. One possible explanation is that those responsible for the construction of "engineering wonders" become romantic figures, heroes not only to their own age but to later generations—and heroes whether their great projects were wise or unwise, timely or premature. In contrast, individuals credited only with sound stewardship of the resources of society are scarcely known in their own day and certainly never appear in history books. "The gravy train runs in the same direction as the glory trail." Political scientists have pointed out the attractiveness to bureaucrats and politicians of the power inherent in being able to influence the award of contracts valued in the millions or hundreds of millions of dollars, the enhancement of real estate values on nearby lands, the creation of an enormous variety of business opportunities, and so on.

Perhaps the most important of these reasons for over-investment might be simple oversight; that, when the total of water use begins to approach system capacity, administrators simply do not think of attempting to make better use of existing supplies as an alternative to initiating new construction. The possibility of adjusting prices does not often occur to those responsible, even though studies have shown that demand is responsive to prices and the wide divergence of price levels and price structures in American cities suggests that a schedule currently in effect in a particular city is not necessarily the only one possible, or even the best available one in the circumstances. Peak-load pricing should be used to a much greater extent in water-supply systems. Introduction of a *peak-season* price (in the summer normally) will not require any special metering and seems clearly indicated as an alternative to expensive new construction when it is only the peak-season loads that press on system capacity.

Bias of Project Analysis

Another major class of error leading to over-investment in water supply is the systematic bias toward excessive construction inherent in conventional techniques of project analysis. An obvious error consists of excessive counting of secondary benefits. Also interesting is the history of over-optimism in estimate of project benefits and costs. Most important of all is the failure to evaluate the future benefits and costs at realistic rates of discount. Commonly, interest rates used for discounting purposes are based upon the borrowing rate of the agency concerned. Consequently, little or no allowance is made for the risks involved in the *particular* project in question.

We have argued that the risks involved in public water projects are about as large as those faced by publicly regulated utility companies. These companies usually require an 8 to 10 per cent rate of return before taxes in order to allow for risk of failure. Consequently, if one wishes to maintain neutrality on the margin between public and private enterprises, public agencies should restrict themselves to a comparable yield.

The adoption of such a strict standard would make uneconomic a large part of the investment programs of the major federal agencies in the field. It should be stressed, however, that the same conclusion can be arrived at *without* use of an 8 to 10 per cent discount rate. If cost and benefit estimates are correctly estimated, making *full* allowance for risk and for over-optimism, we would advocate use of a long-term riskless rate of 4 per cent. I wish to emphasize that none of this denies the existence or possibility of social benefits accruing to the community and nation from a proposed project. Certainly social benefits should be counted in making efficiency calculations. But there is no necessary reason for benefits, just because they are social, to be discounted at an artificially low rate of interest. Social benefits should be subject to the same rate of discount that applies to other benefits and to other comparable projects.

The most sophisticated of the arguments for the adoption of inefficient water projects is the claim that the subsidy to water users involved is justified by a region's need for "development," or "balanced development." Water is conceived as possessing special properties for stimulating growth. But such a subsidy may cause the development to occur in a manner ill-suited to the natural advantages of the region. In particular, in an arid region where water is costly to provide, making water artificially cheap to users will encourage them to be wasteful. A likely and unfortunate result is the development of water-using industries poorly adapted to the region. If the taxes to support the project are borne within the region, economic activities that are justified will, of necessity, be required to support the subsidized users. Of course. if the subsidy is borne from outside the region, the area will be benefited. Even here the benefit will not be as great as if more productive projects were chosen.

The sheer irony of water subsidies, designed to help out poor and small water users, is that they often fail to do what they are intended to do. Time and time again, the real value of subsidized water is quickly capitalized in higher land values. This means that users gain only insofar as they are large landowners. "Cheap water" is counterbalanced by expensive land. The gainers are those who own land at the time the subsidy is approved. Land prices soon jump upward. This is a type of windfall gain. All later comers face high land prices.[5]

Defects in Law

Much of the present misuse of water can be traced to imperfections in water law and its administration. Although the establishment of clear property rights to water does pose difficulties, we believe that the law of prior appropriation as developed in some western states has most of the elements required to make a workable system. This type of water law needs to be strengthened primarily in its provisions for the transfer of rights. Under the system we propose, the courts would function as they do for other real property, to adjudicate disputes as to the ownership and extent of the property right and to hear pleas relating to breach of contract in transfers or from parties who consider themselves injured by the actions of the owners of the water rights. The judicial system would be freed of its present inappropriate administrative-economic function of issuing and revising rights to use water based upon such fuzzy criteria as "reasonable" or "beneficial" use.

Even the humid regions have begun to recognize the inadequacy of their doctrines of water law. We believe, however, that they are taking the wrong direction in modifying present laws, to judge from the drafts of "model" state water codes and from recent state water laws. The tendency is to set up machinery so that the allocation of

---

[5] I have analyzed this matter in greater detail elsewhere. See J. W. Milliman, "Land Values as Measures of Primary Irrigation Benefits," *Journal of Farm Economics*, LXI (May 1959), 234-243, and "Land Values—A Further Comment," *Journal of Farm Economics*, LXII (February 1960), 178-179. Excellent work by Edward F. Renshaw is cited in both papers.

water between uses and users can take place only through grants or permits issued by central administrative commissions or by cumbersome court procedures. In these circumstances, the fabric of water rights is weakened by becoming dependent upon the changing wills of the commission or courts. We believe that this line of development will lead to serious misallocation of water between alternative uses, and it will tend to reduce local, regional, and private initiative in the development of water resources.

INVESTMENT IN WATER IN RELATION TO OTHER PUBLIC PROJECTS

In closing, I wish to stress that our study attempted to show that increased application of economic principles will produce greater efficiency in water supply *in relation to, and in competition with, all the other desires of the community as based upon values established by the community.*

Many of the conclusions we reach are at variance with the present practices governing both the use of existing water supplies and the development of new supplies. Also, they indicate that certain "reforms" now taking place may make matters worse. In other words, our study constitutes a plea for a major change in the current thought and practice on water-supply problems.

Welfare Economics and Resource Development

MORRIS E. GARNSEY

In recent years the increased requirements for water, the sharper competition for available funds from alternative public and private investments, and the rising competence of economists have brought about a substantial improvement in the quantity and quality of economic analysis devoted to problems of water-resource development projects. In the public sector, the self-examination of economists and their desire to improve their technical efficiency led to the publication of the so-called "Green Book" with all of the attendant reports and articles which preceded and followed its appearance.[1]

In the private sector the year 1958 marks a significant landmark in this field of theoretical and applied economic analysis. For in 1958 three books dealing with the economics of water resources were published by prominent and respected economists. These three books are: Otto Eckstein's *Water-Resource Development*, John Krutilla and Otto Eckstein's *Multiple Purpose River Development* and Roland McKean's *Efficiency in Government Through Systems Analysis, with particular reference to water resource development.*[2]

These books had several common characteristics. First, they were highly critical of economic analysis in the field of water-resource development. Second, many of their criticisms of analytical methods or

---

[1] Federal Inter-Agency River Basin Committee, Subcommittee on Benefits and Costs, *Proposed Practices for Economic Analysis of River Basin Projects* (May 1950).

[2] Otto Eckstein, *Water-Resource Development* (Harvard, 1958); John V. Krutilla and Otto Eckstein, *Multiple Purpose River Development* (Johns Hopkins, 1958); Roland N. McKean, *Efficiency in Government Through Systems Analysis* (Wiley, 1958).

Morris E. Garnsey is professor of economics at the University of Colorado. His special interest in resource development and regional economic analysis has led to consultant service for federal, state, and private agencies. As consultant to the state of Colorado, he has directed studies on which the state might base an integrated policy for conserving and developing its natural resources.

of administrative policies and practices were pertinent, valid, and very hard to ignore or even to refute. Third, these three books had a common theoretical foundation: they all depended explicitly upon the concepts of welfare economics and its criterion of economic efficiency.

The appearance of these books was a rude shock to me, as it must have been to many others. Long before 1958 I had acquired a certain familiarity with welfare economics, though very little confidence is its usefulness. Now I was forced to go back and read or reread the major books in the field and numerous articles as well.

As you no doubt know, the range of literature in welfare economics is very extensive. Nearly every economist who has some pretension to status in the field of theory has written at least one article on welfare economics, from Samuelson right on down. So, while I was struggling in the state of shock induced by these books, but gradually regaining confidence in the usefulness of benefit-cost analysis and other techniques of applied economics used to determine the economic feasibility of water-resources development projects, in 1960 along came my fellow panelist, Mr. Milliman, and his two colleagues with an even ruder book—a book much more controversial in nature but, if he will forgive me for saying so, a book in which the theory is much more simple, much more implicit, and much more vulnerable to attack than the theory in the other books.[3]

CONCEPT OF ECONOMIC EFFICIENCY

I shall confine my remarks to the crucial aspect of the problem and deal only with the theoretical background of the three 1958 volumes. To do this I shall begin by defining the concept of economic efficiency. I quote from Krutilla.

> Economic efficiency is defined as a situation in which productive resources are so allocated among alternative uses that any reshuffling from the pattern cannot improve any individual's position and still leave all other individuals as well off as before.[4]

This is, of course, fundamentally nothing more than a statement of the marginalist definition of equilibrium or optimum resource allocation. What is different about it is the use of the term "efficiency" rather than the older, more familiar "optimum."

The use of this word puzzles me. To employ it undermines the very foundation upon which the authors claim to have erected their

---

[3]Jack Hirshleifer, James C. DeHaven, and Jerome W. Milliman, *Water Supply: Economics, Technology, and Policy.* (University of Chicago Press, 1960).
[4]*Op. cit.,* p. 16.

theoretical structure. In their view, their criterion is not normative but strictly "scientific" and "objective." However, I doubt if there is a word more loaded with normative connotations than "efficiency." Efficiency is a "good" word. Everyone likes to be efficient, and no one likes to be inefficient. It may not bother some of the engineers in the Corps or in the Bureau to be told that they have designed a project in such a way as to not achieve the optimum allocation of a scarce resource, but I suspect it does bother them to be told that they have designed an inefficient project. Engineers, if anything, are efficient and to be told by any economist that they are inefficient is certainly calculated to be something of a shock.

I have no doubt that Eckstein and Krutilla used this word deliberately in order to bring home the sharpness of their criticism of federal practices of project evaluation. However, I am puzzled to know whether they borrowed it from other welfare economists or themselves appropriated it from the dictionary. The term "economic efficiency" is not to be found in the basic literature of welfare economics. Hla Myint, for example, does not use it in his comprehensive survey *Theories of Welfare Economics*. Little in his *Critique of Welfare Economics* does not use it. Graaf in his book *Theoretical Welfare Economics* uses it only in a special sense. Scitovsky in his review, "The State of Welfare Economics," does not use the term. Boulding does not use it in his "Welfare Economics." Samuelson does not use it in Chapter VIII of *Foundations*.[5] Krutilla uses it and Eckstein uses it! I wish that they had been satisfied to retain the accepted phrase "optimum allocation of resources." In my opinion the use of the term "efficiency" confuses more than it clarifies.

Redistribution Effects

However, my objections to the application of the efficiency criterion are not semantic but substantive. First, there is a technical reason why the efficiency criterion of welfare economics cannot be used to analyze the economics of water-resource development projects. The reason is this: one of the necessary conditions for the validity of the criterion is the absence of redistribution effects of a shift in the allocation of resources from a given point to a "more efficient" point.

[5]Hla Myint, *Theories of Welfare Economics* (Harvard, 1948); I. M. D. Little, *A Critique of Welfare Economics* (Oxford, 1950); J. de V. Graaf, *Theoretical Welfare Economics* (Cambridge, 1957); Tibor Scitovsky, "The State of Welfare Economics," *American Economic Review*, XLI (June, 1951), 303-315; Kenneth Boulding, "Welfare Economics" in *Survey of Contemporary Economic Theory*, American Economics Association Reading Series, vol. II (Irwin, 1952); Paul A. Samuelson, *Foundations of Economic Analysis* (Harvard, 1947).

Every author who has written about welfare economics recognizes this. Indeed, a large part of the literature is devoted to a search for ways to avoid this difficulty. This is the purpose of the compensation principle, to cite but one example.

Now the authors of our three books are fully aware of the importance of this problem. They are, unfortunately, unable to find a satisfactory theoretical basis for solving it. They fall back, therefore, on a proposal to ignore the redistributive effects of a reallocation. Thus Krutilla says:

> In a purely analytical sense, however, the issue of the distribution of income may arise to plague us unless it is clarified. Our efficiency criteria were derived analytically by taking as given the prevailing distribution of income. Changes in the distribution of income will affect the efficiency of a given allocation of resources. Since the decision to invest or not to invest—or a decision to employ untraditional approaches to water-resources development—may result in a redistribution of income, it is necessary to contend with both the distribution existing before the event and that reflecting its consequences. It is conceivable that what would be an efficient solution in terms of the prevailing income distribution may be less efficient following a reshuffling of costs and gains among the members of the community. While this is a valid theoretical objection to carrying out studies of comparative efficiency, its practical significance will be negligible for the problems encountered in this study. The income redistribution would affect our efficiency criteria only through the influence on the constellation of relative prices. This structure of prices arises out of the distibution of total income among individuals of differing preferences. (We take technology and resource endowment as given for this purpose.) The effect on the distribution of income of the magnitudes we will be treating, however, can be inferred from a numerical illustration. Assume a proposed river basin development program would involve a total investment of a billion dollars over a twenty-year period. The income redistributive consequences of alternative means of undertaking the development may approximate half the total. If we assume an average annual national income of $500 billion, this will aggregate to ten trillion dollars over the time span considered. A redistribution of income amounting to as much as half the total investment funds committed to the program would represent only five-thousandths of one per cent of total national income. As a practical consideration, the effects which this could have on the constellation of prices (and imputed prices) employed for evaluating comparative efficiency of alternatives can be ignored.[6]

Krutilla's example of the negligible effect of redistribution is acceptable as far as it goes; but unfortunately it does not take us nearly far enough in the direction of the effective economic analysis of re-

---

[6]*Op. cit.*, pp. 50-51.

sources projects. Such analysis rests upon the calculation of benefits and costs; and benefits and costs are not instantaneously diffused throughout the economy. Rather they accrue, not to the economy, but to individuals such as landowners and taxpayers; to selected groups such as contractors, cement manufacturers, and common carriers; and to specific geographic areas where projects are located or where electric turbines or farm implements are manufactured. Costs and benefits are not diffused so widely among individuals in the course of time that the redistribution effects can be disregarded.

Perhaps we should concede that Krutilla is half right. Some costs of development, such as relocation, can be traced directly to the ultimate bearer. But to the extent that water projects are financed by taxes, the burden is widely diffused.[7] Benefits, on the other hand, are much more easily located—at least to a very large extent. McKean's contention that one barber's loss is another barber's gain is correct in a narrow and strict sense. But if each one of a hundred barbers loses one customer and one barber in Page, Arizona, gains a hundred customers, the losses do not really cancel out the gains—certainly not in terms of real costs or in terms of the impact upon the national economy.

Or to take a more extreme example: If each of 100 million persons deprives himself in the course of a year of a 10-cent bottle of soda, and gives (transfers) the 10 cents to the March of Dimes, and the resulting $10 million is invested in laboratories and man-hours of research which ultimately produce the Salk vaccine, these authors would have us believe that nothing has been gained for the economy. The additions to the wealth of the society in knowledge and physical capital are offset by the losses of individual satisfactions represented by 100 million × 10 cents. This view is absurd. Even if one succeeds in completely ignoring the humanitarian values in the virtual elimination of the scourge of polio, the fact remains that the economic impact on society of the spending of $10 million in one place or for one

---

[7] In Chapter IV, Krutilla and Eckstein, the latter presents a statistical analysis of income and federal tax burdens by income groups in an attempt to determine the social cost of capital raised by federal taxation. I am told that this exercise has been described as "highly ingenious" by some of Professor Eckstein's senior colleagues at Harvard. It is ingenious, just as a clever crossword puzzle or a difficult problem in chess is ingenious. All three are about equally relevant to determining the correct interest rate to be used in calculating the cost of a water-development project. See Robert Dorfman, "Interest Rates for Public Investments," a paper presented at the December 1960 joint session of the Econometric Society and the Regional Science Association in St. Louis, Missouri.

purpose is more productive than the results of spending it in 100 million diffused places.

Moreover, if as the second example implies, benefits also become diffused through society in time, these ultimate beneficiaries are not necessarily the same persons as those who bore the costs. Redistribution effects, therefore, are large and significant. They cannot be ignored; and a tool of analysis which requires that there be no redistribution effects from the reallocation is a very limited tool, indeed.

"Competition" in the Private Sector

I turn now to a more basic criticism of the attempts of these three authors to evaluate methods of water-resource economic analysis in terms of the theory of welfare economics. I am somewhat hesitant to do this because effective criticism has already been directed against the welfare premises of these books by competent scholars.

In March 1959 Margolis published a review article of the three books in the *American Economic Review*, which raised some fundamental doubts about their approach.[8] Kneese also has pointed out the shortcomings of the efficiency criterion.[9] Krutilla himself, in a paper read at St. Louis in December, 1959, seems to have all but abandoned his confidence in welfare theory as a useful tool of analysis.[10] Indeed, Professor Milliman, in discussing the Krutilla paper on the same program, goes so far as to say:

> I find that it [the paper] very neatly states the conditions that must prevail if benefit-cost analysis is to be used to increase welfare in a theoretically conclusive sense. Much of the paper, then, is devoted to an exposition of the welfare conditions and a brief survey of welfare literature. Simultaneously, however, Krutilla directs a carefully organized, but reluctant, retreat from each of the theoretical welfare conditions. In several spots it appears that the retreat has become a rout, and at the conclusion of the paper it seems clear that he is willing to declare that any attempt to arrange a marriage between modern welfare theory and operational benefit-cost analysis is extremely premature.[11]

Nevertheless, I will venture one criticism which applies not only to the "troika" but also to Dr. Milliman's water-supply study. The

[8]Julius Margolis, "The Economic Evaluation of Federal Water Resource Development," *American Economic Review*, XLIX (March 1959), 96-111.

[9]Allen V. Kneese, *Water Resources. Development and Use* (Federal Reserve Bank of Kansas City, 1959).

[10]John V. Krutilla, "Welfare Aspects of Benefit-Cost Analysis," a paper presented at the December 1960 joint session of the Econometric Society and the Regional Science Association in St. Louis, Missouri.

[11]J. W. Milliman, *Decision Making for Public Investment: Discussion* (The Rand Corporation, 1961), p. 2.

fundamental error of all four books is that each one of them attempts to find a rationale for evaluating water-resource expenditures in the public sector of the economy by the application of the criteria of the private sector. Worse still, the "private sector" which they rely upon bears almost no resemblance to the behavior of the private economy of mid-century United States. Instead they have fallen back upon a simple, almost purely competitive model in which resources exist in small, homogeneous, transferrable units free of "lumpiness" and innocent of external economies. If you find this hard to believe, let me quote Margolis to convince you.

> Eckstein explicitly and the others implicitly assume that the allocation of resources and the structure of prices which rule in the economy are approximately close to those which would result if the economy were perfectly competitive, so that all welfare implications associated with a perfectly competitive economy would also apply to the actual economy.[12]

This assumption, Margolis says, "has a dubious basis."

This is a very mild way of putting it, indeed. The assumptions of the authors of these four books about the efficiency of the private sector achieved through free competition are so removed from reality that I fail completely to understand why they and their editors were led to advance, seriously, criticisms of water-resource development policy built upon such a flimsy foundation. But this is what they have done.

It may be useful, consequently, if I remind this audience, and Dr. Milliman, of a few items of evidence to the contrary. I shall not, of course, attempt a lengthy and detailed proof of the obvious. First of all, prices in the private sector are not, by and large, competitive prices. According to Gardiner Means, at least 60 per cent of prices are administered prices.[13] Prices have a high degree of administrative control in the following industries: steel, machinery, fabricated steel, rubber, plastics, pulp and paper, and tobacco. Administered prices are significant in furniture, chemicals, fuels, and power. Control extends from extraction to ultimate consumer goods. The agricultural sector remains almost the only area of competitive prices, and even here end-process prices to consumers show strong evidences of being administered also.

But this is by no means the whole story. The private sector of our economy is shot through with collusive monopolistic practices of

---

[12]*Op. cit.*, p. 100.
[13]Gardiner C. Means, *Administrative Inflation and Public Policy* (Anderson Kramer, 1959).

all kinds, many of which are overt rather than tacit. If we have any doubt about this, the recent revelations in the electrical equipment anti-trust cases would seem to be rather conclusive. This story has been reported in Fortune Magazine in two articles entitled "The Incredible Electrical Conspiracy."[14] One significant aspect of this conspiracy is that many of the defendants who were found guilty and, contrary to past practice in Sherman Anti-trust Act prosecutions, actually received jail sentences, looked upon themselves as the "fall guys" of U. S. business. They protested that they should no more be held to blame than many another American businessman, for conspiracy is just as much a way of life in the other fields as it is in the electrical equipment industry. "Why pick on us?" was their attitude. "Look at some of those other fellows."

Now, of course, this is not conclusive evidence of a generalized type, and Mr. Milliman might well object to it on that ground. Let me, therefore, offer additional evidence. The July-August issue of the Harvard Business Review carries a rather detailed report of a study by the Reverend Raymond C. Baumhart, S.J., of the ethics of the business community.[15] According to this survey, 80 per cent of the executives interviewed after selection by scientific sampling process affirmed "the presence in their industry of practices which are generally accepted but are also unethical." These executives then listed "the one practice I would most like to see eliminated."

It is most unfortunate that the six authors of these four books we are discussing did not have this knowledge at their disposal before they so blithely assumed the competitiveness of our society. According to Father Baumhart's survey the largest number, or 23 per cent, of the executives would most like to see eliminated the business practices of "gifts, gratuities, bribes, and 'call girls'." But the next largest number, 18 per cent, listed "price discrimination and unfair pricing"; 10 per cent listed other "unfair competitive practices," and 8 per cent listed "price collusion by competitors." 18 plus 10 plus 8 equals 36 per cent, thus showing more executives concerned with noncompetitive practices than with immoral behavior.

"Efficiency" in the Private Sector

Moreover, as these authors might well have realized, this noncompetitive private sector is not conspicuously efficient—certainly not

---

[14]Richard Austin Smith, "The Incredible Electrical Conspiracy," Fortune Magazine (April and May, 1961).
[15]The Reverend Raymond C. Baumhart, S.J., "How Ethical Are Businessmen?" Harvard Business Review (July-August, 1961).

efficient enough to be used as a standard for the public sector. Let me quote again the language of *Fortune*, which is clear, explicit, and colorful.

> What prompted this conspiracy? Chronic overcapacity, for one thing, overcapacity that put a constant pressure on prices. Soon after he went to Washington as defense mobilization chief in 1950, Electric Charlie Wilson announced that the nation's electric-power capacity needed to be increased 30 per cent over the next three years. The equipment industry jumped to match that figure, and added a little more as well. Thus an executive, who ebulliently increased capacity one year, a few years later might join a price conspiracy to escape the consequences of that increase. "This is a feast or famine business," summed up Clarence Burke. "At one time everybody was loaded with orders, and ever since they wanted to stay that way. When utilities decide they need more generating capacity, they start buying, and we have three years of good business—and then three years of bad. The decision to build capacity was delegated down to the managers (under decentralization).[16]
>
> ° ° °
>
> The consent decrees now being hammered out by the Justice Department are partial insurance that bid-rigging and price-fixing won't happen again. Yet consent decrees are only deterrents, not cures. The fact is that the causes which underlay the electrical conspiracies are still as strong as they ever were. Chronic overcapacity continues to exert a strong downward pressure on prices. The industry's price problem—outgrowth of an inability to shift the buyer's attention from price to other selling points like higher quality, better service, improved design—could hardly be worse: many items of electrical equipment are currently selling for less than in the ruinous days of the "white sale." Corporate pressure is stronger than ever on executives, who must struggle to fulfill the conflicting demands of bigger gross sales on the one hand and more profit per dollar of net sales on the other. These are matters that require careful handling if conspiracy is not to take root again in the electrical equipment industry.[17]

In *Water Supply*, Mr. Milliman and his co-authors have this to say:

> Perhaps the most controversial substantive conclusion in this book, justified by a wide variety of evidence from our separate case studies and from our survey of federal and local experience in water-supply decisions, is that in this country major water investments are typically undertaken prematurely and on an over-ambitious scale. Consequently, at any given time there exists an over-investment in water supply.[18]

[16]Smith, *op. cit.*, (April) p. 170.
[17]*Ibid.*, (May), p. 222.
[18]*Op. cit.*, p. 359.

The authors of *Water Supply* present considerable empirical evidence to support this conclusion and offer some plausible explanations for the existence of chronic overcapacity in water-supply facilities. Underlying all this, however, is the basic assumption that the private sector is by contrast efficient because competitive. In the face of the evidence cited above, I suggest that the authors of *Water Supply* ought to take another look at this problem. If over-investment is chronic in *both* the private and public sectors, perhaps there is a more fundamental explanation to be found in forces common to both sectors which they have overlooked. Alternatively, perhaps their definition or concept of "over-investment" is erroneous. Certainly over-investment cannot be defined solely in terms of a simple and unreal competitive model of the private sector of the economy.

ADEQUATE CRITERIA FOR WATER-RESOURCE PROJECTS

Four years ago my hopes were raised by the publication of three separate books dealing with the problem of effective economic analysis of water-resource development projects. I turned to them only to be disappointed. Those of us who followed these authors through their analysis have been led up a blind alley from which we and they can only retreat. Welfare economics is not the answer to water-resource analysis problems.

Where then should we look for a better answer? It seems to me that economists are capable, now, of giving fairly complete quantitative estimates of four important aspects of investment in water-resource projects. These are:

1. The economic justification of the project in terms of output and input.
2. The effects of the project on employment.
3. Its effect on growth over time.
4. The repercussions of the project on the distribution or redistribution of income.

The first aspect or criterion for determining whether or not to make a proposed investment falls in the sphere of cost-benefit analysis and such analysis is, of course, already supplied to the Congress. However, the other three criteria are almost entirely ignored, so I would like to say a few words about them in order to conclude this paper on a positive, even optimistic note.

Employment

The welfare economics-general equilibrium model applies only to conditions of full employment. Krutilla and Eckstein recognize this explicitly as far as unemployment is concerned. When cyclical unemployment exists, Eckstein points out (pp. 34-35), appropriate recalculations of both benefits and costs should be made in order to make it clear that the social costs of undertaking projects are low under such circumstances.

Here again, I feel that the analysis is less than complete. Until the publication of *The General Theory*, neo-classical economists were prone to make much of the "make-work" fallacy. Keynes created the first break with the neo-classical position against "make-work" proposals by showing that even "useless" work, such as digging up buried bank notes, is socially desirable and theoretically justified when unemployment exists. This view has long since become accepted doctrine and is so regarded by our authors.

There are other reasons, however, why the creation of employment is not merely making work. The validity of the neo-classical position depends upon the realization of (1) perfect competition, (2) perfect divisibility and independence of the factors, (3) perfect mobility of factors, and (4) a static equilibrium situation which involves an agreement among all persons supplying or hoping to supply factors that the optimum position of factor employment has been achieved. If any one of the conditions is not present, the possibility exists that an increase of output will follow a rearrangement of employments. In particular, water-resource development projects may provide men and materials with more productive (i.e., higher-paying) employment not only during the construction phase, but also later on in skilled and semi-skilled operations and maintenance jobs, and in new induced industries.

In short, the economic analysis of water projects should not ignore the fact that most people, their elected representatives, and their civil servants are keenly interested in the employment effects of water-resource development projects. Economic analysis, therefore, should attempt to deal extensively with such effects. These include not only short-run re-employment of the unemployed, but also the reduction of under-employment, the up-grading of employment, and the long-term expansion of employment opportunities—all of which potentially offer contributions to the income and output of the economy.

Economic Growth

The employment effects just listed extend beyond the ordinary concept of economic stability as a cyclical phenomenon into the area of economic growth. Here, as in so many cases, growth and stability are linked as parts of one broad economic problem.

Unfortunately, current agency practice tends to obscure the contribution of a project to economic expansion over time. Such effects are projected according to agency practice in terms of trends in acres irrigated or kilowatt hours generated, etc., year by year as a project is completed and operates in a society assumed to be one of growing population and rising GNP. However, these growth effects are then concealed by the practice of summarizing the total costs and benefits of the project over its projected life span in terms of *annual average* benefits and costs.

It is correct, of course, that the future is uncertain and projections of benefits over long periods are subject to wide margins of error. Nevertheless, this does not seem to be a sufficient reason for deciding that growth is a "higher criterion" above the reach of the lowly economic analyst. The economist should not be satisfied with the negative view that benefits due to growth over time almost certainly are overestimated because they are uncertain.[19] Rather, he should be concerned with the problems of projecting growth factors within defined limits of uncertainty, and also with methods of dealing with uncertainty, once its presence has been established. I see no reason why a list of projects cannot be compared with each other in terms of their potential contribution to regional and national growth as measured in terms of income and employment. Certainly, this important criterion for investment should not be ignored merely because it is difficult to measure precisely.

Distribution

Water is a scarce resource. At mid-century the demands of the United States for water in its numerous uses are such that increasing effort, greater technological ingenuity, and heavier capital investment must be expended in order to satisfy consumers and producers alike. It is easily understandable, therefore, that economists, engineers, and administrators should try to find more efficient factor combinations, techniques of physical control, and organizational devices to employ in the development of water resources.

It should be equally clear that, in a society where individual enterprise and the pursuit of self-interest are dominant economic institutions, individuals and groups are going to attempt to manipulate the conditions of water supply to their individual advantage. Indeed, there are situations in which the latter motivation appears paramount. I have read hundreds of pages of hearings and debates on water projects—state, local, and federal documents, pamphlets and "analyses" of local groups—and I sometimes think that the uses of water are

[19]See Eckstein, *op. cit.*, pp. 245-248.

only incidental to the distribution of the advantages of the program among contractors, suppliers, bond salesmen, grocers, real estate speculators, etc., etc.

The laissez-faire concept of government as an impartial umpire, or remote non-participant, may still prevail in the courts and perhaps in some of the regulatory agencies. In most areas, however, government is regarded either as a benevolent uncle generous with his assistance or as a potential ally in the life-and-death struggles of that economic jungle—the market place.

It follows, I believe, that economists should analyze the effects of a proposed water-resource project on the distribution of income as accurately as possible, and that the results of the analysis be published as widely as possible so that the acceptability of the results can be debated as fully as possible by all who are concerned. We ought to know *who* benefits from a water resource and *how* this comes about. Such discovery and debate should do much to help Congress arrive at the final decision.

Regional Development

This last statement gives me an opportunity to speak briefly of a problem in which I have a primary interest as a regional economist— that of the geographic distribution of the costs and benefits of a water project. I object to the non-spatial character of general-equilibrium analysis which assumes, in effect, a single-point, non-dimensional economic process. Actually, water-resource projects are located in different spatial areas within an economy, and the economic impact of development is felt strongly at the location of the project. Even if we assumed that there were no existing regional concentrations of activity or regional patterns, the expenditure of funds in a particular spatial area would of itself create regions—i.e., foci of economic activity—where none existed before. Thereafter, the economy would no longer be non-dimensional or homogeneous over space. It would have become an area within which sub-areas of concentration of economic activity exist, separated from each other by less active, less concentrated expanses of economic activity.

Of course, patterns in space exist before a current project is undertaken, and expenditures for water-resource development will modify these existing patterns. Therefore it becomes necessary to take these spatial factors into account and to determine which are relevant for the analysis of the economic effects of a given project or program. Fortunately new techniques of regional analysis have been developing rapidly through the work of Isard, Wollman, and many others.[20] Economists are now in a position to give a reasonably accurate evaluation of the regional impact of costs and benefits of public expenditures. This need not be left solely to the intuitive judgments of the Congressional log-rolling processes.

In my opinion, it is possible also for the professional economist to provide objective, quantitative, and reasonably accurate measures of the effect of investment in water resources on employment, on growth, and on income distribution in addition to cost-benefit analysis. Moreover, it is high time that we did so. Policy-makers, from voters to Congressmen, could then have at their disposal a much wider range of quantitative information than at present. They need such information keenly, as we face a quarter-century of almost explosive expansion in private and public investment in water-resource development.

[20]See, for example, Walter Isard, *Methods of Regional Science* (Wiley, 1960); and Nathaniel Wollman, *The Value of Water in Alternative Uses* (University of New Mexico Press, 1962).

INDEX